THE NAZI, THE PAINTER AND THE FORGOTTEN STORY OF THE SS ROAD

D1614772

THE NAZI, THE PAINTER AND THE FORGOTTEN STORY OF THE SS ROAD

G. H. Bennett

REAKTION BOOKS

Dedicated to the Memory of Roland Levinsky –
Researcher, Educator and Leader

Published by Reaktion Books Ltd
33 Great Sutton Street
London EC1V 0DX, UK
www.reaktionbooks.co.uk

First published 2012

Copyright © G. H. Bennett 2012

Printed and bound in Great Britain by
TJ International, Padstow, Cornwall

British Library Cataloguing in Publication Data
Bennett, G. H. (George Henry), 1967–
The Nazi, the painter, and the forgotten story of the SS road.
1. Daghani, Arnold, 1909–1985.
2. Jewish artists – Romania – Social conditions – 20th century.
3. Jews, Romanian – Ukraine – History – 20th century.
4. Ukraine – History – German occupation, 1941–1944.
5. World War, 1939–1945 – Conscript labor – Ukraine.
6. Forced labor – Ukraine – History – 20th century.
7. Holocaust, Jewish (1939–1945) – Personal narratives, Romanian.
8. Roads – Ukraine – Design and construction – History – 20th century.
I. Title
940.5 318134 092–dc23

ISBN : 978 1 86189 909 5

CONTENTS

The Road to the East.

A PUZZLING REEL OF FILM

SERIOUS academic enquiry is often rather dry. It usually begins with a historian identifying a gap in our understanding on a particular event or historical theme and carefully reading around the subject in the secondary sources before proceeding to archives. There he or she will locate the documents and other evidence to write the journal article or monograph which will address the area of concern. This book arises from a rather different process – a mystery, a puzzle, an enigmatic piece of film lasting less than ten minutes. It reverses the normal working method of the historian in working backwards from the broad landscape of history into the evidential minutiae of archives. The book also departs from historical convention in the way that it makes the process of historical research an explicit part of the narrative. My purpose is both to engage the reader and to make visible some of the problems and dilemmas which face all historians in pursuing their craft, particularly in sensitive and disturbing areas like the history of the Holocaust. Despite the differences in approach the scholarly underpinning of this book is nonetheless fully rooted in archival research in the repositories of four nations and the very extensive secondary literature on the Third Reich. Writing the book has been a journey: a journey into the corners of every frame of an old film; a journey into a forgotten and dark episode of history; a journey across continents; across the past and into Europe's present.

The story begins with a medium with which we are familiar if not fully conversant. During the last 50 years we have grown accustomed to seeing images captured by an army of amateur cameramen wielding ever more sophisticated, inexpensive and easily operated video cameras or even mobile telephones which incorporate a video recording capability. In the early and middle years of the twentieth century amateur cameramen were already at work recording people, places and events on cine film. Admittedly, those enthusiasts were few in number. Cine cameras, cine film, film processing and film projectors all involved significant expense, while the cameraman needed to develop a steady hand and acquire an understanding of arcane technical matters such as shutter speed, aperture, focal length, exposure, zoom, close-up and panning. It was, therefore, a hobby which tended to attract prosperous businessmen or well-paid professionals whose fascination with moving images of the world around them was matched by technical curiosity, adequate leisure time and a well-filled wallet.

The productions of these pioneering enthusiasts usually aroused a transient interest among people who were thrilled by the novelty of seeing 'on the silver screen' moving images of themselves, their friends and places they knew well. In time, however, the reels of film were left to languish in their tin boxes, often gathering dust and cobwebs in attics, garages and garden sheds. The films inevitably deteriorated, because much of the early film stock was inherently unstable. Many eventually ended their days on bonfires or refuse tips.

Fortunately, in the last 30 years historians, archivists and librarians have begun to appreciate the value of these old amateur films in providing a visual record of the commonplace details of a bygone way of life. In consequence, a number of special film archives have been established to act as depositories for such films so that they may be preserved, catalogued and made available to scholars and a wider audience.

The South West Film and Television Archive (SWFTA) in Plymouth was established in 1993. In 2005 the archive was presented with a typical collection of old films that had been discovered in a cupboard at the Baptist church in Cullompton, Devon. Some of the collection proved to be commercially produced 'shorts' in black and white, but other films, many of them in colour, had been shot in the 1950s and '60s by a keen amateur cameraman living in the small Devon market town. They were the work of Reg Whitton, who was the proprietor of a successful road haulage company, a business which he combined

Opening titles of the Cullompton film.

with active involvement in charity work, being a pillar of the local community and serving as an Elder of the Baptist Church. Before his death he had been held in high regard by his fellow townsmen, although some would say that they found him difficult to get to know really well because 'he was a very private man'.

As well as being shown to family and friends, Reg Whitton's home-made movies had occasionally been given a public showing to entertain the members of Cullompton Baptist Church and other local people. Most of the 16mm films were about ten minutes long. They dealt with such themes as his trucking business, aspects of life in Devon, the Cullompton carnival and family holidays in places like Ireland.

One of the films in the Whitton collection was quite different in character from all the others. It was black and white. It did not feature the Devon countryside or the good people of Cullompton. Instead it showed fields of sunflowers, some unusual buildings, expansive panoramas of open farmland, men dressed in uniforms of various kinds, and what appeared to be an enormous river. This 'mystery film' had no title or explanatory captions. It bore no labels establishing its provenance. Before the archivists could catalogue it, they needed to answer some questions. When and where was it filmed? Who filmed it? Why did they film it? Who were the people featured in the film? What were they doing? What was Reg Whitton's relationship to the film?

A close examination of the film revealed important clues to answer some (but by no means all) of those questions. The eagle and swastika insignia of Nazi Germany could be discerned in some of the close-up shots of men in uniform, and where the cameraman had focused on road signs, all the place names were in Ukraine. Clearly, Reg Whitton had not been responsible for shooting this particular reel of film, and its location was a far cry from Cullompton.

Graeme Spink, a member of the archive staff, was sufficiently familiar with Nazi propaganda films to realize that this film was something out of the ordinary. It was too informal, too personal, too slow-moving to compare easily with the slick propaganda films produced in large numbers by the German newsreels. Having a keen interest in the Third Reich, Graeme could identify enough of the images to appreciate that interest in the film would be considerable and that it would be of more than historic and academic interest to some agencies. It would require sensitive handling.

Elayne Hoskin of SWFTA asked various experts, including the Imperial War Museum in London, to take a look at the film. Considerable interest was aroused but very few hard facts emerged. A provisional date of late summer 1942 was suggested for the actual filming, and there was some speculation about the mix of German military units depicted in the film. That interest and puzzlement was maintained when the film was picked up by the BBC and screened on national television. From there it went around the world, finding its way onto the Internet via YouTube and the BBC news website. Despite this national and international exposure, authoritative answers to the key questions were not forthcoming. Inevitably, as with any news story, interest soon dwindled, threatening to leave SWFTA with a piece of film that was no more than an interesting historical curiosity.

In an effort to discover more, SWFTA arranged a film show in Cullompton Baptist Church. Reg Whitton's 'mystery film' was exhibited alongside some of the other films from his collection. The church was filled to capacity. Local people were intrigued at the chance to see again some of the short local films Whitton might have shown them many years before, but they were also keen to watch the film that had attracted international media attention. No one had any information to offer about it, however. So far as anyone could remember, the 'mystery film' had never featured in any of Reg Whitton's amateur film evenings.

I was in the audience at the Cullompton film show that evening. Elayne had asked me to look at the film to see whether I could suggest any answers. Historians, like journalists, know a good story when they smell one, and a Devon 'Nazi film', about which there were plenty of questions but few answers, seemed promising, to say the least. The images on the screen in the church added to my interest. This was no ordinary piece of wartime propaganda. As an action film it left a lot to be desired. The opening couple of minutes were marked by fascination with the rural environment in which it had been shot. Images of healthy and happy peasants at harvest time belied the reality of German rule in occupied Russia after 1941. The person behind the camera had an eye for beauty, whether in the form of a peasant girl's face or the flowers growing on the graves of German soldiers who had fallen for the Fatherland during the invasion of Russia in 1941. The opening two minutes were followed by images of German officers demonstrating their importance by inspecting things and instructing subordinates. One man in particular stood out from the crowd. Without any other name to go by, I later came to think of him as 'The Fat Man'.

Like the character with the same nickname played by Sydney Greenstreet in the 1941 film *The Maltese Falcon*, The Fat Man seemed to be a strange amalgam of the sinister and the charming. He seemed to be at the very heart of the film – or at least he was the figure most often seen in it. Like a good cabaret artist, he went through several changes of outfit during the film. Both his rather drab and worn

The Bald Man and The Fat Man.

The Bald Man and The Fat Man at tea.

field jacket and his immaculate white summer uniform were a little tight around the waist. I sympathized with his problem. We were of a similar age – both in our early forties – and both of us were grappling with the onset of 'middle-age spread'. Here was a man who liked the good life, and from what one could infer from the film, life was good for a German officer in occupied Russia. At several points The Fat Man was seen drinking coffee in the presence of ladies. He was relaxed, self-confident – an image of authority.

The film was silent, but The Fat Man's body language spoke volumes. It said 'I'm in charge' – 'I love my job' – 'I'm a hands-on manager getting the job done no matter what the problem.' The body language and facial expressions of the people around The Fat Man suggested their deference, unease and occasionally respectful familiarity. I was both intrigued and repulsed by this central character's manner, his determination to play to the camera and those occasional slips and foibles, such as shooting a glance at the camera for disturbing him while eating, that underlined his fragility and human weakness. I instantly wanted to understand him.

Other characters in the film were also intriguing. One of the scenes in which The Fat Man featured took the form of a pleasant afternoon tea party on the veranda with a strikingly tall, thin and balding German officer wearing shorts. This man liked his cigarettes; he was chain-smoking in every scene. He seemed a little nervous, with an air of resentment and anger in his occasional and very self-conscious glances into the camera lens. I figured 'Bald Guy' was a better label for him than 'Smoking Man'. During the course of the film my pseu-donymous cast list would extend to include Old Man, Laughing Woman, Rat Face, Lemon Head and a host of other minor characters. My cast list read like the nicknames of characters from an American gangster film.

As I watched their flickering images on the screen, questions soon began to form in my mind. Who were these people? What had been their precise roles in Ukraine? What had become of them? Could I find the answers?

ONE

MARCHING EASTWARDS

B Y a non-aggression pact signed on 23 August 1939 Nazi Germany and Soviet Russia officially ended almost two decades of mutual antipathy. The pact secretly shared out agreed territorial spheres of influence in Eastern Europe, and it left Hitler free to pursue his territorial ambitions elsewhere. For the time being it removed the strategic risk of Germany having to fight a war on two major fronts simultaneously; and Russian oil and wheat could help Germany circumvent any Anglo-French naval blockade.

Only 22 months later Hitler suddenly abrogated the pact. On 22 June 1941 he launched more than 140 German army divisions totalling three million men, supported by Finnish, Hungarian and Romanian troops, in a massive invasion of the Soviet Union. With Britain still determined to fight on in the west, the invasion opened up an Eastern Front extending, even measured as a straight line, for over 2,500 kilometres from the Barents Sea to the Black Sea.

Hitler's calculation that his forces would very quickly achieve a knockout victory proved to be over-optimistic, but their well-tried blitzkrieg tactics soon overran huge areas of Russia in Europe. In the first six months, before they ground to a halt in the Russian mud and snow, German advanced units penetrated over 750 kilometres into Russian territory. They raced to the very gates of Leningrad and Moscow, and further south to Rostov at the mouth of the river Don. In further advances during the summer of 1942 German troops who reached the Volga at Stalingrad and Mosdok in the northern Caucasus had penetrated more than 1,250 kilometres into Soviet territory.

German cameramen captured every aspect of these enormously costly campaigns. There is no shortage, therefore, of still pictures and cine film of German troops on Russian soil. In countless dramatic images we can see them advancing through the dust clouds of the Russian steppes, skirmishing through burning towns, heaving vehicles out of clinging mud, rounding up hordes of Russian prisoners, building pontoon bridges, driving horse-drawn wagons, shivering in the snow, throwing grenades or hanging Russian partisans. Every aspect of German military operations was visually recorded but, except for a limited number of well-known senior officers and officials, virtually all of the men who stare out at us from these photographs and films are unidentified. The images record for posterity just a few fleeting seconds of their anonymous lives (and deaths).

Realistically, that almost universal anonymity seemed certain to be the fate of the Germans featured on the puzzling reel of film that had turned up so mysteriously in Cullompton among the Reg Whitton collection of home movies. Perhaps its SWFTA catalogue entry would have to be no more informative than 'German servicemen, Ukraine (South Russia), probably 1942–3'. The film did not show scenes of actual fighting, and the men featured most prominently were not wearing ordinary German army uniforms. Close inspection of the film, frame by frame, identified various badges and other insignia that showed they belonged to the *Schutzstaffel* (SS) or the police.

Almost everyone has heard of the SS, yet few appreciate the full complexity of the organization built up in Nazi Germany by Heinrich Himmler. Its activities ranged from industrial plants to battle units; its personnel from convicted criminals to scientists, archaeologists and ethnographers. Originally formed as Hitler's personal protection force, under the control of Heinrich Himmler the SS grew quickly in the 1930s. Turning the SS into a personal power base in the anarchic interplay of organizational rivalries within the Nazi state, Himmler ultimately wanted to make the SS independent of both the National Socialist German Workers' Party (NSDAP or Nazi party) and the State. This meant that the SS began to replicate some of the structures of the state and extend its influence into areas such as the economy in order to secure the financial independence of the organization. As the ultimate safeguard, and to challenge the monopoly of armed force in the hands of Germany's Wehrmacht, the SS would have its own military force, the Waffen SS, who eventually fought as elite soldiers on both the Western and Eastern Fronts. Almost invariably, they enjoyed preferential treatment in the allocation of the most modern weapons and supplies. Fanatical in combat, some of them were involved in atrocities against Allied troops and innocent civilians, and some were brought to trial by the Allies after the Second World War.

The SS as a whole was condemned as a criminal organization by the International Military Tribunal at Nuremberg: the regular German forces escaped such labelling. The SS was a large and easily misunderstood organization. As Robert Koehl has succinctly put it: 'The SS was anything but a monolith.'[1] Its guilt was certainly not unique, despite the label of criminality which was attached to it by the Allied powers in 1945.

The German police, perhaps contrary to what one might expect, were to be feared almost as much as the SS between 1933 and 1945. As Germany had erupted into revolution in 1918, the police force had proved quite incapable of restoring or keeping order.[2] This failure provided an impetus for reform, especially since the 1919 Treaty of Versailles limited the German army to just 100,000 men, a figure considered the bare minimum to keep order and avert the danger of communist revolution. The police service required reform in order to guard against that danger more effectively. It was thought that turning the police force into a paramilitary organization could also be a way of circumventing the military clauses of the Treaty of Versailles, since policemen could easily be converted into soldiers in any national emergency. A more heavily armed and authoritarian police force was also seen as a necessary response to the killing of policemen by communists and other violent groups. Over 400 policemen were killed in the line of duty between 1919 and 1933.[3]

The shift towards paramilitarism became even more marked after the Nazis took power in January 1933. Many policemen, especially in cities such as Berlin and Hamburg, were happy to be given more licence to deal with 'undesirables' such as communists. The separate constabularies that had operated under the network of German states were swept away in a process of *Gleichschaltung* (co-ordination and assimilation) and the new service was thoroughly infused with National Socialist ideals. Ideological education was provided as part of the training of German policemen from 1935 onwards. Over time, older policemen were replaced by younger, more radicalized members of the Nazi party. Heavily armed, and a key part of the Nazi terror apparatus, the German police dealt with threats to the state, whether from ordinary criminals or left-wing agitators. As Christopher Browning has written:

> After 1936 when Himmler was appointed Chief of the German Police, in addition to his position as Reichsführer-ss, he felt the need to integrate more firmly the component parts of his empire. On the organizational level, these efforts proved largely futile owing to the intense rivalry between the different agencies within his apparatus. The office of . . . [Higher ss and Police Führer], designed to link ss and police functions, in fact increased the degree of decentralization by creating 'little Himmlers' bound into the existing structure by their personal allegiance to the Reichsführer rather than by bureaucratic ties. On the ideological level, however, the self-image of a *Staatsschutzkorps* (state defence corps) – a diversified security agency that would defend the Reich against inner enemies just as the Wehrmacht provided protection against external foes – began to take root among the officers of the ss and police even before the war.[4]

In 1936 the police went through a major reorganization. The Geheimstaatspolizei or Gestapo would act as Himmler's political police force. They would seek out and nullify the opponents of the National Socialist German Workers' Party, whether from the left or the right politically. The Kripo or Criminal Investigative Police would deal with ordinary matters of criminality. The Sicherheitsdienst (SD) was the intelligence service of the ss and from 1938 the German state. The Orpo or Ordnungspolizei (Order Police) was divided between the rural gendarmarie and the metropolitan Schupo or Schutzpolizei (protection police).

To underline the paramilitary nature of the formations, separate companies of police would be housed in barracks. These could be deployed to back up police at the local level, or to deal with any particular threat that might be identified. In March 1938, during the German takeover (*Anschluss*) of Austria, 20,000 members of the

Ordnungspolizei were sent into Austria. They were also used in the German takeover of the ethnically German Sudetenland from Czechoslovakia in the first week of October 1938.

On the outbreak of war in 1939 the companies became police regiments, with seventeen of them taking part in the destruction of the Polish state. By September 1940 the number of police battalions had grown to 101. Yet despite the expansion of the force in the early months of the year, the police force retained its reputation as one of the most Nazified elements of the German state. In February 1942 Kurt Daluege, the syphilitic, 'insensitive, hard-boiled', hard-drinking head of the Orpo, could reassure Himmler that 76 per cent of the officer corps were members of the Nazi party.[5] Of these, 30 per cent were also members of the ss.[6] Within the lower, and predominantly younger, ranks of the Orpo, Nazi party members constituted an even higher proportion.

A 1945 report into the German police drawn up by the intelligence section of Supreme Headquarters, Allied Expeditionary Force, concluded: 'The German Police force is probably the most powerful organization of its kind in the world. It is also the most ruthless.'[7] In the occupied territories during the Second World War the German police established a reputation for ferocity as they dealt with partisans, saboteurs, resisters and other groups classed as social undesirables. To cope with new and heavily armed enemies, police units received the requisite equipment, including tanks.

While the Allied powers classed the ss as a criminal organization at Nuremberg in 1945, they avoided giving the police the same label. That decision was arbitrary, to say the least. All this background information is important because the German officer who featured most prominently in the film which had aroused my curiosity, the man I had nicknamed The Fat Man, carried the insignia of the German police on the sleeve of his tunic – a large German eagle, with wings stretching beyond the confines of a wreath of oak leaves. His mannerisms showed a man used to giving orders and seeing them obeyed. Undoubtedly, he had all the hallmarks of one of the 'little Himmlers' mentioned by Christopher Browning. The shoulder flashes on his uniform, and those of Bald Man, Old Man, Rat Face and others, showed that they were not just ordinary policemen; they were

The Fat Man and friends.

officers of high rank. It was impossible to guess what they were up to in Ukraine, but it seemed reasonable to assume that it was unlikely to have been conducive to the overall welfare of the local inhabitants. There would have been victims of their activity and the outcomes would almost certainly have been murderous.

TWO

THE ARYAN IMPERIAL DREAM

DESPITE the impressive advances made by the German armies in their 1941 and 1942 offensives, the complete victory Hitler had expected to achieve in a mere four months never materialized, for the Russians showed great resilience in stabilizing the front and launching counter offensives. While the German army exercised control over zones of active military operations, Himmler's SS organization was made responsible for supervising the rear areas in the Baltic States, White Russia and Ukraine. The SS provided the administrators, translators and police officers needed to cope with the difficult but essential tasks of ensuring public order in these occupied territories and keeping open the over-extended lines of communication along which vast quantities of ammunition, weapons and all manner of other war materials must pass to sustain the front-line units.

If it could have been achieved, complete military victory would have secured important strategic advantages for Germany: the collapse of the Communist ideology, removal of a possible Russian air threat to Berlin and the Romanian oilfields, unchallenged control of the Baltic, and safeguarding the eastern frontiers while Germany attempted an invasion of the British Isles. It would also have eliminated a fear voiced in the diary of Josef Goebbels, Hitler's Propaganda Minister, that Russia might 'keep out of the war until Europe is exhausted and bled white. Then Stalin will move to Bolshevise Europe and impose his own rule.'[1]

Military victory was not, however, the sole objective of the German invasion of the Soviet Union. At a meeting held at Hitler's headquarters in East Prussia on 16 July 1941, the Führer told Göring, Keitel and other leading Nazis that, in occupied Russian territory, 'we now have to face the task of cutting up the cake according to our

needs in order to be able: first, to dominate it; second, to administer it; third, to exploit it.'[2] That exploitation would be vital to the
German war economy if hostilities continued with Britain and, in
due course, the United States. The great wheatfields of Ukraine, the
oilfields of the Caucasus and the coalfields of the Donetz basin would
go some way to enabling Germany to escape the constraints on trade
and supplies of raw materials imposed by the overwhelming sea power
of Britain and the USA.

A rebellious, uncooperative local population in the occupied areas
of Russia would seriously hamper Germany's ambitious plans for
economic exploitation. Administering and exploiting the occupied
areas would have been infinitely less troublesome if the willing
cooperation of the local people could have been guaranteed. There
was every prospect that imaginative and sensitive policies would have
been able to win the cooperation of large groups who had no great
love of Russian Communist rule: nationalists from various non-
Russian minorities such as Ukrainians, devout believers of the
Orthodox Church, rank and file soldiers resentful of compulsory
military service, army officers fearful of more purges of the officer
corps, farmers opposed to collectivization. Some German officials
were prepared to advocate policies aimed at winning the 'hearts and
minds' of such groups, but the leading Nazis from Hitler and Himmler
down had determined on harsh, oppressive policies even before the
campaign in Russia began. They were determined to employ a reign
of terror in ruling and exploiting the occupied areas, even if that
meant deliberately slaughtering hundreds of thousands of civilians,
and leaving hundreds of thousands more to die from hunger, exhaustion and disease.

Knowing that the mysterious and long-forgotten reel of film that
I had watched with such interest in Cullompton Baptist Church
featured German SS and police officers 'somewhere in Russia', I
thought it highly probable that their activities were concerned, in
some way, with the responsibilities of the SS for controlling occupied
areas. The film opened a window on a dark corner of history long
since forgotten or deliberately ignored. Who was The Fat Man? What
did he and his colleagues get up to? Were they involved solely with
ordinary policing; were they employed on economic exploitation;

or were they mass murderers of civilian men, women and children? What ultimately became of them as the tide of war first turned against and then overwhelmed Nazi Germany? In their individual cases, was justice ultimately done?

Perhaps just as importantly, could the film provide a way into understanding the far-reaching ambitions and harsh realities of German policies in the occupied areas on the Eastern Front? The posturing of the characters, the nature of what was filmed and how it was filmed might all offer clues about the inner thoughts and values of the people associated with the film. Was it just a harmless 'home movie' to serve as a wartime souvenir for some important ss officer; was it no more than an interesting footnote to history; or did it illustrate the terrible mainstream of life in Heinrich Himmler's ss-controlled empire in Russia?

The Fat Man, in particular, seemed to exhibit a love of power and a brutish desire to control human life. As a subject for historical enquiry he repelled me and attracted me in equal measure. I decided that I would do my best to find out about him and try to understand his brief appearance before the film camera. He would be my quest – my challenge as a professional historian. Confronting his evil would be my task. It may sound more than a little naive but The Fat Man aroused within me the hunter's instinct. I would track down this nameless officer, representative of an evil regime. Of course, more than 60 years after the end of the Second World War, time and events would undoubtedly have combined to leave only a slim chance of actually tracking him down physically. He might well have died during the fighting on the Eastern Front that cost so many German families their loved ones, or he might have died of natural causes subsequently. Despite the probabilities, my upbringing was sufficiently old-fashioned enough to dictate that I had to try and see justice done, if only in the writing of history.

The film itself provided my only lead into the world of The Fat Man. There was no paperwork with it, and the film canister yielded no useful details. Every frame would need to be explored with great care. The dark corners of each image might hide tiny clues about the location, identities and purpose of the men in the film. There might also be clues about the film-maker, and something might even

The Fat Man.

explain the film's strange journey to a cupboard in Cullompton Baptist Church. Hundreds of hours would be spent looking for clues by going backwards and forwards, frame by frame, through the film. Every image, every picture of a sign, every medal, badge, piece of insignia, horizon, car number plate, landscape, uniform and facial expression had to be carefully assessed.

Some of those enigmatic individual clues might be capable of being interpreted in three or four different ways. The investigation would call for establishing a series of hypotheses to make sense of the clues, testing those hypotheses by research and revising them until a 'best fit' for all the clues could be arrived at. The task would be infinitely more complex than doing a two-dimensional jigsaw puzzle in which each piece could only be fitted in one place. It would be much more akin to cracking a lock in which six separate levers had to be dealt with individually and collectively to open it and allow entry into the silent film's story.

The first break in the investigation was the realization that at least two of the locations in the film could be identified by signs on buildings. In one scene The Fat Man could be seen leaving a police station at Novi Bug, a town in southern Ukraine. In another he could be seen chatting to an SS officer outside an SS post at Kerch, the most easterly port in Crimea. Those scenes established the precise geographical context of the film – modern Ukraine, at that time one of the Union of Soviet Socialist Republics. A third location – a small village – was clearly identified by name but, frustratingly, no modern source could identify any village in Ukraine or Russia spelled as it was in the film. Name changes represented a considerable problem. Wartime sources identified places in Ukraine by both their German and Slavic names, but there might be Ukrainian or Romanian spellings as well. Some of those places had changed their names in the post-war period, and some had had different names before the Bolshevik revolution.

In addition to place names, views of the landscape also offered useful clues. Images of farm land, in which the harvest was being gathered in and sunflowers were in full bloom, suggested that the film had been shot in the late summer – July to August perhaps, in 1942 or 1943. The tranquillity of the images ruled out the same period in 1941, when the German invasion of the Soviet Union had been in full swing, or 1944, when the Germans had been in full retreat and had lost most of Ukraine. Some of the general views, showing a great river and a considerable body of water, further suggested Ukraine, Crimea and the Black Sea. The port of Kerch is on the Black Sea and

An unidentified headquarters in the Cullompton film.

the low-lying landscapes in the film also suggested a coastal area of Ukraine. Even if these clues were rather inconclusive, the wartime history of Ukraine looked like a promising place to search for further evidence about the world of The Fat Man.

The techniques employed in the film might also offer certain insights into the conscious and unconscious minds of those who made it, those who appeared in it and those who were intended to watch it. The spoken and unspoken dreams, fears, attitudes and philosophies of all three groups are intimately bound up with the process of recording and ordering visual information. What film-makers choose to shoot, how they shoot it and how it relates to the wider narrative are influenced by an intimate process that is rarely explored consciously or fully by the people involved. In trying to find ways into interpreting the film and the lost world which it depicted, it might be helpful to understand something of the mindset of those who had been behind the camera, appeared on screen and provided an audience. Uncomfortable though that process would be, I needed to understand the most influential core beliefs and principles of Hitler's Nazi movement, for Himmler and his ss organization saw themselves as the *corps d'élite* and spiritual guardians of the true Nazi 'faith'. Did the film touch upon this in some way?

As well as securing the strategic lines of communication to the battlefront and extracting the greatest possible quantities of essential raw materials, the ss in Ukraine (and certain other key areas in Russia) saw themselves as preparing the foundations for an even more ambitious project – nothing less than ensuring Germany's political, economic and military domination, in perpetuity, of the whole region as far as the Ural mountains far to the east.

This grandiose German vision of an extensive imperial domain pre-dated the Nazi era. In the late nineteenth century ideas had emerged within Germany which stressed the need for extra living space (*Lebensraum*) for the German nation. These ideas were partly a response to rapid industrialization and urbanization. The countryside, and with it the peasant way of life, appeared to be under severe pressure. Friedrich Ratzel, a German geographer, was the first to coin the term *Lebensraum*. In 1897 he published *Politische Geographie*, in which the term *Lebensraum* first appeared, and in 1901 he wrote an essay specifically titled '*Lebensraum*'. Building upon Charles Darwin's ideas about the origin of species, Ratzel argued that species evolved in relation to their environment, with migration playing a vital role, particularly in the evolution of man. Successful adaptation to one's environment made it more likely that the species would be able to spread and conquer new areas. Migration and the enlarged living space of a particular species were the surest signs of the health of that species. Colonization of fresh areas represented an important element in the process of natural evolution. For convinced German nationalists the word 'species' in Ratzel's thesis could very easily be replaced by the word 'race'.

This then opened up a further argument. The evolution of the nation state and the emergence of fixed borders interfered with the essential process of evolution, since they formed protective barriers that shielded weaker branches of the human race and exerted a powerful restriction on the territorial expansion of the healthiest. If such barriers were allowed to remain, then the most vigorous races would inevitably wither, constrained within artificial borders. Ambitious Germans were determined that such barriers should not be allowed to stand in the way of the growth and evolution of the German nation.

Where would the necessary extra living space be obtained? Great Britain, the pre-eminent nation in the late nineteenth century, had found an outlet for the vigour of the British race by conquering lands in the Americas, Africa and Asia. The emergence of the white overseas dominions of the British crown – Australia, New Zealand, Canada and South Africa – was seen as proof in some circles that great nations had to expand and that the process of migration and conquest was part of the inevitable order of human affairs. By the late nineteenth century, however, as a newly united Germany began to yearn for imperial possessions, there were comparatively few parts of the world that had not been claimed already by one European empire or another.

Any German overseas possessions, even if they could be obtained, would always be under threat from British sea power in time of war. They might be snatched from Germany within days of the start of hostilities. This threat was a powerful reminder that Germany was a continental nation and that, if an empire were to be won, it would be best if it took the form of an extension of Germany's land borders. The powerful German army could guarantee the security of these lands, just as the Royal Navy guaranteed the British Empire.

The industrialization of Germany produced impressive economic strength, but it was not welcomed unanimously by German artists and thinkers. Some feared that a nation which could not feed itself would be vulnerable to blockade; others lauded the simple, country life. This contrasted strangely with the growth of great industrial cities in north and west Germany. Within the cities lay crime and vice; within the countryside lay traditional German strength and respectability. Expansion of the territory, if it could be achieved, could offer self-sufficiency and a way back towards the supposed rural virtues of the Fatherland.

The acquisition of territory in Ukraine became one of Germany's war aims during the First World War. Significant transfers of territory from Russia to Germany was the price of peace under the Treaty of Brest-Litovsk, signed in 1918. The terms of the treaty were dictated by the Germans and gratefully accepted by the Bolshevik government which had seized power in St Petersburg in October 1917. At the stroke of a pen, *Lebensraum* moved from being a romantic dream to tangible territorial expansion.

Germany had only a brief interlude in which to develop her new lands in the east, however. Defeat on the Western Front in November 1918 brought an abrupt end to German expansion; the coveted *Lebensraum* was snatched away and restored to Russian or Polish control. What were perceived as the injustices of the Treaty of Versailles helped the growth of right-wing political parties in Germany. Leading figures within those parties very quickly began to articulate the grievances of the German people against the territorial settlement under the treaty. They also began to return to familiar nineteenth-century themes justifying territorial expansion in the east, with the crushing of Bolshevik Russia as an inevitable and very desirable pre-requisite. This was a goal which inspired Adolf Hitler: 'The German people are imprisoned within an impossible territorial area.'[3] 'When we speak of new territory in Europe to-day we must principally think of Russia.'[4] 'This colossal Empire in the East is ripe for dissolution.'[5]

Within the rambling incoherence of Hitler's *Mein Kampf*, a number of very consistent themes of this kind can be identified. Dictated in 1924, while Hitler was incarcerated in the Fortress of Landsberg am Lech following his failed 1923 putsch in Munich, *Mein Kampf* became a bestseller and a rallying call for the German right. Hitler dedicated the first volume of *Mein Kampf* to the sixteen members of the National Socialist German Workers' Party who had been killed during the attempted revolution. *Mein Kampf* sets out both an analysis of the course of recent German history and a manifesto for the future of the National Socialist movement.

Reading *Mein Kampf* disturbed me in a number of ways. The text translated into English was challenging enough, but securing a copy of Hitler's testament from a second-hand bookseller was, in itself, not an easy process. To ask for such a text, in anything other than the most hushed tones, seemed to invite suspicions about one's own (possibly extremist) political beliefs on the part of the book-seller or other customers who were in the shop at the time. The copy I eventually secured, a 1939 English translation, presented further embarrassments, with the Nazi eagle displayed prominently on the front cover and a large photograph of Hitler immediately inside.

When *Mein Kampf* first appeared it should have left no doubt as to the attitude of Hitler and the Nazis towards Russia. Hitler argued that Germany's borders of 1918 had to be restored, but that she also required additional land commensurate with her status as a reborn Great Power. That land was needed to ensure that Germany could feed herself in the future, but it also had another purpose. Hitler regarded the peasantry as the foundation of the German nation and the basis from which the nation could be reborn. Hitler and Himmler both firmly believed in the importance of the peasant to the life and well-being of the whole nation:

> Too much importance cannot be placed on the necessity for adopting a policy which will make it possible to maintain a healthy peasant class as the basis of the national community. Many of our present evils have their origin exclusively in the disproportion between the urban and rural portions of the population. A solid

stock of small and medium farmers has at all times been the best protection which a nation could have against the social diseases which are prevalent to-day. Moreover, this is the only solution which guarantees the daily bread of a nation within the framework of its domestic national economy. With this condition once guaranteed, industry and commerce would retire from the unhealthy position of foremost importance which they hold to-day and would take their due place within the general scheme of national economy, adjusting the balance between supply and demand.[6]

Picking up on the themes of the nineteenth-century German Romantics, Nazi artists would later offer powerful images of the virtues of rural life and agricultural labour in nurturing healthy, happy and expanding families.

Hitler's conception of the importance of the peasant was part of a wider set of ideas about the nature of society under the control of the Nazis. Physical fitness, the virtues of discipline and beauty, a sense of community and martial spirit were all highly prized. One French writer in the 1930s likened National Socialism to 'the spirit of Sparta':

> [Hitler] urged the organization of a new society founded on strong national solidarity, on the rude, coarse virtues of the peasant, the artisan, and the soldier, and on the practice of strict discipline and voluntary sacrifice by the individual for the community – in a word a society founded on the civic, robust and virile qualities which, in antiquity, made for the glory of Sparta. Hitler began to believe in the necessity for a Spartan training of the new generations very early in his life and in his *Mein Kampf* he presented a detailed program of the kind of education which he considered necessary.[7]

Hitler's new Sparta would produce a new generation of warriors to conquer the land needed to secure the long-term future of the German *Volk*. The processes of training for conquest and its execution would in themselves be valuable tempering of the steel of the German people.

Land was both an end in itself and a means to the end of breeding a vigorous population.

The lands to the east were the most obvious targets for the Nazis in respect of the additional territory which Germany needed to conquer if her racial and geopolitical destiny was to be fulfilled. Poland would have to be broken up in order for Germany to receive back the lands taken from her under the Treaty of Versailles. It made sense to incorporate Polish lands into the Reich. In 1940 one American political scientist was ready to argue that the quest for *Lebensraum* had been the driving and guiding force behind Germany's pre-war foreign policy:

> A review of the foreign policies of National Socialist Germany during the past years discloses many colorful events, complex interactions, different behavior patterns, and tensions – an unsatiated state, discontented, ambitious, restless, and bent upon modifying the status quo to her advantage, in order to aquire the coveted Lebensraum.[8]

Hitler's ambitions also extended, however, well into Russia, where there were even larger and more tempting opportunities for the seizure of territory. In addition, Hitler's animus against Russia was fed by his detestation of the Bolshevik regime. Hitler regarded Communism and National Socialism as being locked in a clash of ideologies which would inevitably result in the destruction of one or the other.

Whatever the precise nature of their wartime duties, The Fat Man and the other ss officers who featured so tantalizingly in the film were playing some part in the gargantuan task of translating the German national dream of *Lebensraum* into an impressive, prosperous and secure reality for centuries to come. That reality would assure an unchallengeable, pre-eminent position for the German people, a pre-eminence which their incomparable courage would have won, a pre-eminence to which they were entitled by their outstanding national characteristics, and a pre-eminence which it was their quasi-sacred duty to take up. These ideas featured prominently in Nazi doctrine; they were the kind of ideas that had inspired many patriotic Germans to join the SS; and they were ideas which the SS had sworn to uphold.

Convinced Nazis found justification for those expansionist ideas in politico-scientific theories that had originated in the nineteenth century. In essence, they sought to explain differences between human groups by applying lessons from the selective breeding of animals and Charles Darwin's work on the evolution of species. The publication in 1859 of Darwin's *The Origin of Species by Means of Natural Selection* had called into question a substantial part of what, up to then, had been uncritically accepted as fact about humanity and its development. A key question resulting from the maelstrom of opinions and discoveries centred around the issue of national identity. Did some branches of humanity represent evolutionary dead ends or sub-species? Did the process of industrialization threaten the process of evolution by divorcing humanity from the natural environment?

The issue of national identity focused attention on conceptions of prehistory. The Nazis followed in a long tradition of dictatorial regimes by projecting forward a utopian view based on an interpretation of the past and human progress.[9] The very framework of prehistory, with neat divisions between periods distinguished by dominant technologies, seemed to confirm that the broad outline of Darwin's ideas could be applied to human development. The people of the Stone Age inevitably had to give way to the people of the Bronze Age who, in turn, were superseded by the Iron Age. The historians' labels and divisions seemed to stress discontinuity and minimize adaptation. The settlement of particular areas could be talked about in terms of successive waves of invaders – the new, superior peoples ruthlessly sweeping away the inferior people who had gone before. Conquest, subjugation and annihilation were accepted as part of the natural order of evolution in a warped pseudo-Darwinian interpretation. The dominance of one race over another was not only acceptable; it was necessary and natural. Embracing the need for eternal struggle between different elements of mankind was the only means of safeguarding the future development and improvement of the human race.

In support of these theories, some European ethnologists, noting language links between Indian and European languages, argued that the European peoples came from an ancient people known as the Aryans. Originating from the inner Asian steppes (India, Persia, Afghanistan), their use of the horse and chariot, cultural and linguistic sophistication, and personal qualities had allowed them to dominate and supplant other races. In time they had migrated to Europe, providing the impetus for the evolution of Greek civilization.

Writers such as the French aristocrat Arthur de Gobineau, in his *Essay on the Inequality of the Human Races* (1853–5), were ready to conclude that the Aryans were an innately superior race. In Germany the noted archaeologist Gustav Kossinna, in his 1896 lecture on the 'Pre-historical Origins of the Teutons in Germany', gave an added twist to the story of an Aryan super-culture diffusing its gifts across Asia and Europe. The location for the emergence of the super race was shifted from central Asia to Germany and Scandinavia. With this narrative of human history, the people of Germany were the genetic heirs to the racially supreme Aryans. They were quite separate from Jews and Africans, who could not trace their origins back to the Aryans. Kossinna used arguments about pre-history to proclaim that the racially superior German people had a historic right to occupy the territory which had once belonged to Germanic tribes such as the Goths, the Huns and the Vandals.

The narrative also warned of a fall from grace. Interbreeding with lesser strains of humanity had diluted the Aryan genius, the German essence being polluted and defiled as a consequence. On this theme, Hitler later wrote:

> As soon as the subjected people began to raise themselves up and approach the level of their conqueror, a phase of which probably was the use of his language, the barriers between master and servant broke down . . . The Aryan gave up the purity of his blood and, therefore, lost his sojourn in the paradise which he had gradually made for himself. He became submerged in a racial mixture and gradually lost his cultural creativeness.[10]

In Hitler's eyes, miscegenation had weakened the German race, and the political divisions of the German nation before 1870 had been a symptom of this. For the adherents of the myth of an all-conquering Aryan race, Germany's rise to the political dominance of Central Europe by 1870 directed attention to the long-term future. If German dominance was to continue, then one aspect of the future had to be the racial security and purity of the German (Aryan) people.

The First World War had proved a vital catalyst in the process by which the German nation ultimately embarked on the pursuit of the Aryan myth. Outstanding German success on the battlefield seemed to confirm theories about the high racial quality of the German nation until, assailed by a powerful coalition of enemy powers and 'stabbed in the back' by communists, socialists and Jews in Berlin, the German military had been forced to concede defeat in 1918. The Treaty of Versailles raised questions about the nation's future. Germany had lost territory, had to pay financial reparations and had strict limits set on her military forces. 'Robbed' of her few overseas colonies and forced to cede territory to 'inferior nations' such as the Poles and Czechs, Germany looked to be in decline. Was all the brave talk about Aryan superiority no more than a myth? The perception of decline was particularly acute in Austria, another Germanic country with Aryan roots. Shorn of a great empire in southeastern Europe, where she had once lorded it over 'lesser races', Austria was a state with a questionable economic future. The possibility of unification with their fellow Aryans in Germany had been outlawed by the Allied powers which imposed the peace treaties. By 1920 the German nation was once again splintered and enfeebled: the Rhineland was under enemy occupation, and in parts of Poland and Czechoslovakia important German minorities were subject to the whims and antagonisms of 'inferior' Slav majorities.

Once he had risen to power in Germany, Hitler needed only six short years to reunite the various fragments of the German race and create a more extensive Aryan power base. Bit by bit, the slogan '*Ein Reich, Ein Volk, Ein Führer*' (one people, one nation, one leader) took solid and menacing shape. Winning the Saar plebiscite of 1935, reoccupation of the demilitarized Rhineland in 1936, the *Anschluss* with Austria in 1938, occupation of the Sudetenland and Memel in 1938 and the seizure of Danzig and the German areas of the Polish 'corridor' in 1939 can all be seen as a systematic reunification of the Aryan race, while the conquest of Norway, Denmark, Holland, Flanders, Alsace and Lorraine in 1940 added other peoples who could also be said to exhibit important Aryan characteristics.

The attack on Russia in 1941, whatever the immediate military and political motives, was eventually intended to acquire for the whole Aryan race the impressive legacy of ample *Lebensraum* which their outstanding qualities required and deserved.

The interest of some senior Nazis in Ukraine was heightened by racial considerations. Southern Ukraine, in particular, had been settled by German tribes in antiquity and ethnic Germans still formed an important minority in the region. Archaeologists working for the ss would later toil without result to find evidence of early Aryan genius in places like Kerch, while Himmler insisted that Kiev was an old German city named Kiroffo.[11] Both Himmler and Hitler were eager to forge links with the ethnic Germans (*Volksdeutsche*) of Ukraine and other parts of Russia. They envisaged a situation, after victory over Bolshevik Russia, where the *Volksdeutsche* would provide the basis for a new Aryan civilization in the east. To their number would be added the pure Aryan stock of the ss, where Himmler insisted that all eighteen-year-old recruits must have acceptable Aryan ancestry stretching as far back as 1750. Like Roman legionaries, ss men would be rewarded for their loyalty and service in war with large estates in the east. In time specially selected new settlers would arrive from Germany and other Aryan parts of the German empire, such as Norway or the Netherlands. With plentiful resources and living space at their disposal, these Aryan settlers would make Ukraine into a Nazi vision of utopia. As the German population grew, the Ukrainian Slav population would wither. Extermination, forced labour and sterilization programmes for Slavs, Jews and other non-Aryans would ensure that, in time, the population in Germany's eastern realms would become pure Aryan. They would raise increasingly pure generations of sturdy farmer soldiers who, if need be, would hold the eastern lands as a bulwark between European civilization and Asiatic savagery.

Understanding the aspirations, prejudices and visions for the future of the Nazi philosophy helps to clarify speeches and writings

The Fat Man at his desk.

by Hitler and others: the allusions to 'shared ideas' and a 'common project' becoming instantly recognizable. In just a few words Hitler could evoke a range of themes from Aryanism, *Lebensraum* and the right to territory, while at the same time outlining the distant future and touching on the past and the present:

> The German colonist ought to live on handsome spacious farms. The German services will be lodged in marvellous buildings, the governors in palaces . . . What India was for England the territories of Russia will be for us. If only I could make the German people understand what this space means for our future! Colonies are a precarious possession, but this ground is safely ours.[12]

These shared aspirations for the future, based on a common understanding of the past, would animate German policy in Ukraine.

I could already identify traces of these attitudes in the film. Images of ss officers sitting on a veranda and sipping coffee on a hot day seemed strikingly similar to images from the British Raj. The confidence and assurance of the rulers in their new land suggested a sense of racial superiority, of assured entitlement to *Lebensraum* and a cast-iron historic claim to the lands of Ukraine. To make further progress in interpreting the film – and, if possible, in identifying the roles and names of The Fat Man and other people – it would be necessary to examine Nazi occupation policies in Ukraine and the steps by which attempts were made to put the Aryan dream into effect.

THREE

THE MASTER RACE
IN CONTROL

MANY Germans who were not enthusiastic believers in Nazi
ideology or the Aryan interpretation of human history still
participated enthusiastically in the invasion of the Soviet Union. Catholic
aristocrat Philipp von Boeselager was certainly no supporter of Nazism
(and played a minor role in the attempt by German army officers to
assassinate Hitler on 20 July 1944) but his hatred of communism was
absolute. He regarded the Soviet Union as a deadly threat not only
to Germany, but to the whole of civilized Christendom:

> When the fighting on the Eastern Front began, German officers
> felt that they represented civilization in a battle against a barbarous
> nation. What is barbarism? First of all, it is a complete disrespect
> for the rights of individuals, brutality in human relationships,
> savagery in the actions of everyday life, and finally indifference
> to all the achievements in culture and comfort, to everything that
> centuries of labour and the progress of the human spirit have
> produced that is beautiful. These communists whose agents shot
> down without hesitation soldiers who had retreated, these officers
> without conscience who, in order to exhaust German munitions,
> sent ragtag groups of women, old men and children, gathered
> together in haste, towards us to be mown down by our machine
> guns; these enemies who systematically killed the wounded, put
> out the eyes of their prisoners, and didn't deign to bury their own
> dead – they all seemed barbarians to us.[1]

Nazi policies in the east would soon show that communism did not
hold a monopoly on barbarism.

The German advance into Russia in 1941 was rapid and relatively problem free. Tanks and aircraft operated together to wage blitzkrieg. Hundreds of thousands of Russian troops were captured in a series of wide enveloping movements. Armoured spearheads, supported by aircraft, would push deep into Soviet territory before linking up and encircling whole armies of Russian troops. The German Army Group South encountered little effective resistance as it penetrated Ukraine. In Anthony Beevor's assessment: 'The advance into the Ukraine across the open, rolling prairie with sunflowers, soya beans and unharvested corn, seemed unstoppable. The greatest concentration of Soviet forces, however, lay round the Ukrainian capital of Kiev.'[2] German cameramen were on hand to capture vivid images of German tanks rolling through the cornfields of Ukraine. Filmed going in the opposite direction were long lines of prisoners heading towards oblivion in German transit (Dulag) and prisoner-of-war (Stalag) camps.

In early August 1941 the Germans took the route centre of Uman, along with 100,000 prisoners. The key port of Nikolayev was captured on 16/17 August. At this point Hitler faced a difficult decision. German troops could push on to take Leningrad in the north, Moscow in the centre or Ukraine in the south. To attempt to take all three of these tempting objectives would involve such a dissipation of strength – spread across an ever-widening front – as to invite failure. The leading German generals were in no doubt about their choice of principal objective. General Heinz Guderian, father of the blitzkrieg and the armoured tactics which had served Germany so well since 1939, later explained:

I had already given orders for an attack on Moscow for 15 August with my panzer army. Instead . . . [Hitler] decided, after weeks of thought, to conquer the Ukraine first. Thus, on 25 August, I had to back in a southwesterly direction towards Kiev, instead of being allowed to start my drive toward Moscow. Well, at least the capture of Kiev resulted in the isolation and surrender of an army group. But it set us back 4 weeks in our advance toward Moscow. It got us into the muddy season, where the mud made traffic on ordinary roads impossible, and retarded it very much even on hard surfaced roads . . . You mustn't underestimate

Moscow's importance . . . Whoever controlled Moscow also controlled the political affairs, a powerful armament industry, and a traffic and communications centre of that nation, and could split Russia into two parts.[3]

The fall of Kiev in the middle of September 1941, with hundreds of thousands of Russian soldiers surrendering, marked an effective end to the battle for Ukraine. For the next two years Ukraine would be under the control of the Nazis, as well as being the vital hinterland behind the front line further to the east.

The victorious Germans treated the Soviet prisoners of war captured during the course of these military operations very callously. German troops were ordered not to look on Soviet prisoners as fellow soldiers. They were to remember that, since the prisoners remained communists and constituted a continuing threat to the German nation, they were to be dealt with in the harshest manner. 'Notes on the Guarding of Soviet Prisoners of War' were issued on 8 September 1941:

Bolshevism is the deadly enemy of Nazi Germany. For the first time in this war, the German soldier is encountering not only a military opponent, but one, at the same time, politically educated, who sees in communism his ideal and in National-Socialism, his most provocative enemy. In the fight against National-Socialism, every method is, to him, legal: sniping, guerrilla warfare, sabotage, incendiarism, seditious propaganda, murder. Even a Soviet soldier in captivity, however harmless he may appear on the surface, will snatch any opportunity to show his hatred of everything German. It is quite possible that the PWs received corresponding instructions on how to act in captivity. It is essential, therefore, to treat them with the utmost vigilance, the greatest caution and complete mistrust.[4]

The harsh treatment of Soviet prisoners of war extended to the network of Stalags and Dulags. A deliberate policy of neglect was pursued. Soviet prisoners died in massive numbers as a result of disease, cold and inadequate rations. By December 1941 Army Group South was drawing the attention of the Army High Command (OKH) to the high mortality rate in the camps, and to the consequent loss of a pool of cheap labour which could usefully be put to work for their captors: 'The mass dying of undernourished prisoners of war in the transit camps increasingly attracts unwelcome attention among the civilian population. The bulk of the prisoners of war . . . [are] unable to work owing to exhaustion.'[5] In December 1941 the camps in the rear area of Army Group South held 52,000 prisoners of war, with death rates running at between 10 and 50 deaths per day.[6] The policy of neglect was both a crime and a wanton waste of the labour resources needed to build the Nazi empire in the east.

The heartless disregard for the lives of prisoners of war also extended to the lives of civilians. On 2 May 1941, even before the attack on Russia was launched, the experts of Economic Staff Oldenburg, responsible for planning the subsequent economic exploitation of occupied areas, warned: 'There is no doubt that many millions of people will starve to death in Russia if we take out of the country the things necessary for us.'[7] The true extent of Nazi readiness to apply ruthless policies in dealing with what they saw as the inherently inferior peoples of the Soviet Union went far beyond calmly accepting deaths running to six figures as a kind of grisly but inevitable by-product of military operations or economic exploitation. Their preliminary planning included setting up arrangements for initiating mass slaughter, a process whose implementation in the occupied areas was to be overseen by the Higher ss and Police Leaders, who reported directly to Himmler.

The Fat Man watches as Red Army prisoners march past.

The first step involved the elimination of the ideological enemies of the German state and all potential sources of opposition to German rule. The leadership of the Communist Party was to be targeted in the first instance, and an operational order specifically called for the execution of any captured political commissars attached to Russian military units. Elements of the Soviet intelligentsia, who might also provide leadership to the conquered masses, were also subject to arrest and summary execution. From the local population, saboteurs, resistance fighters, gypsies and Jews were also scheduled for the same fate.

Hatred and contempt for Jews was by no means confined to Germany. Elements of anti-Semitism could be found in many countries, including Britain, but it featured with exceptional virulence in the philosophy, policy and propaganda of Hitler and other leading members of the Nazi party. Jews were regarded as racial enemies of the German state. That attitude had three main origins. First, Jewish expertise and success in financial dealings were condemned as a cunning international conspiracy to 'feather their own nest' and enhance the influence of co-religionists without regard to the loyalty they owed to host communities within national boundaries. Second, on the political level, Hitler regarded the links between Judaism and communism as being so evident as to be inescapable, since many of the leading Bolsheviks during the Russian Revolution had been Jews, as were many of the communists plotting to bring about revolutions in Germany and other countries. Third, Aryan racial theories saw the Jews as a genetically inferior 'race' whose physical, mental and moral 'inadequacies' were harmful because, by interbreeding and their example, they 'polluted' the 'superior' Aryan blood line and prevented the Aryan race from achieving its full potential. For men who held such beliefs, the whole history of human evolution seemed to call for the 'superior' race to eliminate the 'inferior' and 'polluting' blood line.

Very quickly, German policy in occupied areas moved on from removing the potential leaders of any insurgency and cowing the local population by making examples of a few troublemakers to the wholesale slaughter of Jewish communities in Ukraine and other parts of the Soviet Union. As the troops advanced across Ukraine, small-scale atrocities against Jewish communities grew into an ever larger and better-planned programme of mass murder. The extent to which this evolution had been planned long before Operation Barbarossa, with the necessary orders issued verbally by Heinrich Himmler, is the subject of ongoing debate among historians.

Much of the killing in Ukraine was carried out by special police units called Einsatzgruppen, specifically recuited in readiness for the actual attack on Russia. The formation and operation of these units involved a certain amount of deception and self-delusion. The precise tasks envisaged for the new formations were deliberately hidden from the men who were recruited into them. The full horror of their work would emerge only slowly. Men were drawn from the ranks of the Gestapo, Criminal Police, Order Police and SD, but there was little enthusiasm for service in these units. Nevertheless, by May 1941 some 3,000 men had been gathered together for service in the four Einsatzgruppen (designated simply as A, B, C and D), which were to follow in the wake of the advancing army. Each Einsatzgruppe was supposed to have an establishment of 700 to 800 men, divided into headquarters staff and subordinate formations called Sonderkommandos and Einsatzkommandos. From time to time, for special assignments they might be reinforced by other attached units.

Ukraine was the field of operations for Einsatzgruppen C and D.[8] Einsatzgruppe C comprised Sonderkommandos 4A and 4B, and Einsatzkommandos 5 and 6. They were commanded until October 1941 by SS Gruppenführer Dr Otto Rasch. Ensatzgruppe D (under strength with only 500 men) comprised Sonderkommandos 10a and 10b and Einsatzkommandos 11A, 11B and 12. They were commanded by SS Gruppenführer Professor Otto Ohlendorf. Neither commander was an obvious choice for leadership of a mobile killing squad: Rasch held two PhDs and Ohlendorf was an economist and academic. Rasch would die while awaiting trial for war crimes on 1 November 1948 and Ohlendorf would be executed for war crimes on 7 June 1951. At the Nuremberg Trial Otto Ohlendorf insisted that his appointment had been a punishment for a series of disagreements with Himmler: 'It was against my will that I was ordered to an Einsatzgruppe in Russia.'[9]

The German army in the field badly needed the Einsatzgruppen as a counter-insurgency force. Russia was too vast and the advance in 1941 too rapid for the military commanders to be wholly satisfied with the security of their lines of communication (or possible line of retreat if things went wrong). The Einsatzgruppen would secure the rear areas and deal with partisan activity, spies and potential civil unrest. In addition to these roles, the German High Command knew that the Einsatzgruppen were to pursue some ill-defined tasks of a political nature, but many officers preferred not to enquire too closely about what these other tasks might entail.

In rural areas killing of civilians was often ad hoc and not prosecuted particularly systematically. Convenience at every stage, from rounding up Jews through to the disposal of bodies, was one of the features of the killing arrangements. The large rivers running down to the Black Sea offered a particularly convenient means of disposing of communist activists and murdered Jews. Evgeniya Mazhbitz's grandparents were disposed of in this way:

All the prisoners, including my grandparents, were brought to the Southern Bug, near the Bratslav brewery. The prisoners had to cut the holes in the ice themselves; then the Germans and the police ordered everyone to strip naked. My grandparents were killed first because they asked to be killed with one bullet. Then they were thrown into the ice holes.[10]

In larger cities the process of execution would usually involve summoning all the Jews to assemble in a given area before transporting them to a mass grave site out of the city. As the Jews assembled and were marched off, many Ukrainians suspected the fate that awaited them. Father Sviridovskii, an Orthodox priest, witnessed the assembly of Jews in the port city of Nikolayev on 14 September 1941:

[The] streets that led to the cemetery were crowded with Jews. In tears the population bade farewell to them . . . I personally saw this procession of the condemned . . . The cemetery was packed with 10,000 Jews of all ages. For three days, the Gestapo, the police, and the gendarmerie drove Jews on trucks from the cemetery to the ravine, where they shot them.[11]

These mass shootings were the initial means by which the Nazis set about destroying their ideological and racial enemies among the local population of the occupied areas of the Soviet Union. Some convenient feature in the landscape – a ravine, shell holes, anti-tank ditches – would be pressed into service as a mass grave. The Einsatzgruppen, and their subordinate commands, reported their tally of 'kills' back to Himmler's office in Berlin via radio. Much of this radio traffic was picked up and decoded by the British, despite German confidence that their Enigma encoding device made such eavesdropping impossible. Nevertheless, Himmler seems to have sensed that greater prudence ought to be exercised. On 13 September 1941 the three Higher ss and Police Leaders commanding huge areas of occupied Russia were advised of the potential danger of their messages being intercepted and decoded. They were instructed to stop sending details of executions by wireless.[12]

As early as October 1941 planning was underway for Heinrich Himmler to pay a personal visit to Ukraine. In addition to some of the major cities, such as Kiev and Krivoi-Rog, the ss Leader hoped to examine some of the settlements of the *Volksdeutsche* – local communities with an Aryan ancestry – on whom he pinned high hopes for creating an Aryan-dominated empire in southern Russia. Himmler's tour would involve meeting the officers of the ss, police and Einsatzgruppen to encourage them in their duties, to identify particular problems and to gauge morale within the ranks. From personal experience of the killing of civilians in Poland, Himmler understood that participating in mass executions could have profound effects on the men who pulled the trigger.[13] One of Himmler's right-hand men, Erich von dem Bach Zalewski (Higher ss and Police Leader for Russland Mitte) was later profoundly affected by his own involvement in mass killings.

To deal with the trauma of men being required to take part in these killings, leaders of the Einsatzgruppen employed a variety of techniques. Ohlendorf, for example, ensured that the work of Einsatzgruppe D was carried out in the most soldierly manner possible, while Rasch insisted that every member of Einsatzgruppe C must participate in the killings to create a brotherhood of murder and shared guilt. Alcohol flowed freely, and euphemisms were used as a mental insulation against the criminal realities of the work at hand. A German historian has explained:

> In the murderer's vocabulary the word murder did not appear; instead he used a picturesque selection of ostensibly innocent code words – 'special actions', 'special treatment', 'elimination', 'execution activity', 'cleansing', 're-settlement'. An unending stream of propaganda, even more intense in Russia than elsewhere, aimed to eradicate any feeling among the executioners that the Jew was a human being; he was presented as a pest or vermin.[14]

Within German legal definitions, the language also helped to insulate men coldly and dispassionately carrying out military orders from the perception that they might be carrying out such a crime as 'murder' when they were officially engaged in 'liquidating' or 'cleansing' *Aktions*.

Despite Himmler's hopes and expectations, the ethnic Ukrainian population in most areas proved remarkably reluctant to join in attacks against the Jews. A report on the activities of the Einsatzgruppen for October 1941 noted:

> The population on their own part refrains from any action against Jews. It is true that the population reports collectively of the terror of the Jews to which they were exposed during the time of the Soviet regime, or they complain about new encroachments of the Jews, but nevertheless, they are not prepared to take part in any pogroms.[15]

To try to counter the reluctance of most Ukrainians to take part in the extermination campaign, and the willingness of some of them to hide fugitive Jews, German propaganda in the occupied territories tried to fan the flames of anti-Semitism. The pro-German newspaper *Ridna Zemlya*, published in Lvov, urged:

> Don't let a Jew enter your house, for that Jew is your worst enemy!

All a Jew desires is to cheat you and secure himself an easy life at the expense of your toil. Beware of the Jews, because they spread disease with their own dirt.[16]

In spite of such crude propaganda efforts, as early as 1941 the Einsatzgruppen had to cope with the first stirrings of a partisan movement in Ukraine. As revealed in their regular reports, the Germans reacted forcefully to any threat, or perceived threat, of resistance:

> A commando of the Security Police and the SD succeeded in a fight with partisans in shooting the Secretary of the Communist Party for the administration district for Nikolayev-Cherson-Crimea.

> The leader of a partisan group of five was captured after an exchange of shots near Odessa. He has the task of spotting artillery positions and of reporting them to a Soviet command post.

> An action against partisans near Kostromka resulted in the arrest of 16 persons . . .

> The Jew Herschko Salomon, who had belonged to a parachute defense-assault battalion, was located at the city hospital at Nikolayev . . .

> In Belabanowka the former president of the village soviet, who had attempted to form a partisan group of his own, was arrested.[17]

Only two obstacles delayed the progress of the Germans in cementing their hold on Ukraine. In eastern Crimea 40,000 Russian troops were landed by sea in December 1941. They were able to recapture the Kerch peninsula and hold it until a German offensive launched on 8 May 1942 forced a Soviet withdrawal by 20 May. In desperation, soldiers of the Red Army and a substantial number of the city's Jews attempted to swim the Kerch Strait to escape from the advancing German units.[18] Most drowned in the attempt, their bodies being washed northwards into the Sea of Azov.

The other obstacle encountered by the Germans was the protracted Russian defence of the great Crimean naval base at Sebastopol.
For nine months the city endured a siege by German forces. To
complete the conquest of Crimea, the German army had to bring up
its heaviest artillery, and after very heavy and prolonged bombard-
ment the city surrendered on 3 July 1942.

The development of the Nazi empire in the east faced a number
of significant administrative and logistical difficulties. Considerable
efforts had to be made to develop the command and control infrastructure of Ukraine. A new forward command post for the Führer
was established near Vinnitsa. It was a virtual copy of Hitler's headquarters in East Prussia (the Wolf's Lair). It had its own water and
power facilities, barracks accommodation, gym, summer swimming
pool, bomb shelters and a log cabin to accommodate the Führer
himself. Much of the complex, possibly as many as seven floors, was
underground. In the villages around Vinnitsa the different branches
of the German war machine set up their own headquarters which
would allow them to report directly to the Führer. Two squadrons
of fighter aircraft were based at Kalinovka to provide air cover.
Strenuous efforts were made to rid the Vinnitsa area of Jews and
others who, in the eyes of the German authorities, might pose a
security threat. Utilizing prisoners of war, Ukrainian civilians, Jews
and other groups as slave labour, the headquarters was constructed
between December 1941 and June 1942. Many of the labourers ended
up in mass graves at Strizavka and Kolo-Mihajlivka. The headquarters was connected to the road network via a spur off strategic
highway (*Durchgangstrasse* or DG) IV. In addition, the headquarters
was served by air and rail links to Berlin. Hundreds of trees were
planted to camouflage the site.

As in other parts of Russia, Ukraine was divided into military
and civil occupation zones. The civil zone was under the control
of Reichskommissariat Ukraine, based at Rivne, and further divided
into six districts headed by a general commissar: Volhynia-Podolia,
Zhitomyr [Zhitomir], Kiev, Nikolayev, Dnjeperpetrovsk [Dnepro-
petrovsk] and Crimea. In overall charge of Reichskommissariat
Ukraine was Erich Koch.[19] From 1941 onwards Koch pursued policies which brought him into conflict with his immediate superior in

Berlin, Alfred Rosenberg, Commissioner for the Central Control of Questions Connected with the East-European Region, a lengthy title which meant that he was virtually the Minister for Occupied Russia.[20] Rosenberg, a former journalist, had been with Hitler since the earliest days of the Nazi movement and had taken part in the Munich putsch. Although he was an enthusiastic believer in Aryan superiority, he realized that, with the right policies, the Ukrainians could become valuable allies in the fight against the Soviet Union. Rosenberg's evident desire to initiate policies aimed at winning over the Ukrainians earned him a sharp rebuke from his own superiors. In July 1942 Martin Bormann, wrote to remind him of Hitler's views on the east:

> The Slavs are to work for us. In so far as we don't need them, they may die. Therefore compulsory vaccination and German health services are superfluous. The fertility of the Slavs is undesirable. They may use contraceptives or practise abortion – the more the better. Education is dangerous. It is enough if they can count up to 100 . . . Every educated person is a future enemy. Religion we leave to them as a means of diversion. As for food they won't get any more than is absolutely necessary. We are the masters. We come first.[21]

Erich Koch needed no such reminders. He was a firm advocate of adopting the harshest policies in Ukraine. His view was encapsulated in a speech at Kiev on 5 March 1943:

> We are the Master Race and must govern hard but just . . . I will draw the very last out of this country. I did not come here to spread bliss . . . The population must work, work and work again . . . We definitely did not come here to give out manna. We have come here to create the basis for victory. We are a master race, which must remember that the lowliest German worker is racially and biologically a thousand times more valuable than the population here.[22]

At almost every level German policies and the German armed forces antagonized the local population:

The German district and ward commandants shocked the Ukrainians by their coarseness, their gluttony and weakness for the bottle. German soldiers resting in the rear villages spent their entire time hunting for food, gorging themselves, swilling liquor and playing cards. Judging by the statements of war prisoners and the letters found on the dead soldiers, it was obvious that the Germans in the Ukraine considered themselves representatives of a superior race living among rustic barbarians. They felt that their cultured habits could be discarded in these savage eastern regions. And hence they walked about naked in the presence of the village women, made obscene noises when the old folk sat down to supper, and gorged themselves until they vomited. And the neat intelligent, fastidious Ukrainian peasants looked with disgust and scorn at the fascist 'conquerors'.[23]

Initially, many Ukrainians had been inclined to welcome the Germans for liberating them from Bolshevik rule, but the brutality of the new rulers quickly made them realize that, far from being liberated, Ukraine had merely exchanged one reign of terror for another. There were honourable exceptions, however. For example, Alfred Frauenfeld, German Gauleiter of Crimea, tried to apply the kind of moderate, conciliatory policies that Rosenberg favoured and Hitler and Koch despised. Frauenfeld was very successful in playing off the different competing German agencies in Ukraine, and his administration of Crimea verged on the autonomous, to the great anger of Koch, his nominal superior.

The biggest miscalculation in German policy was their failure to appreciate that Stalin's collectivization of agriculture in the early 1930s, which had resulted in mass famine in Ukraine, offered a potential opportunity for winning local support. Instead of embarking on a process of land reform and returning the land to the peasantry, the Germans declared that former Soviet land was now the property of the German state. The Germans would remain the landlords and the tax collectors, and the demands would not cease there. Manpower would also be demanded by the occupying authority. In March 1942 Koch ordered the supply of 380,000 farm workers and

247,000 industrial workers for service in the Reich. Further demands for more labourers would follow.

Manpower policy was not the only area in which the local population within Reichskommissariat Ukraine was antagonized. The one per cent of Ukrainians who were ethnically German (*Volksdeutsche*) were accorded generous special treatment. Lands owned before the revolution were returned to them. They were free to travel to Germany and, within Ukraine, to settle in specially reserved zones in cities such as Dnepropetrovsk. They could easily find employment in the German armed forces or within the administrative organs of the occupied territories. The *Volksdeutsche* also enjoyed their own publication, the journal *Deutsche Ukrainezeitung*.

Only on the religious front was there some effort to conciliate Ukrainian opinion. In January 1942 the Germans took limited steps to recognize the Ukrainian Orthodox Church. Religious liberty was proclaimed in Ukraine by a decree of the German authorities. Such limited freedoms could not prevent the growth of tensions within the peoples of Ukraine and within the Germans' own network of competing hierarchies – civilian, military, party and SS – that met in Ukraine.

On 1 April 1942 the formation of Arbeitsbereich Osten der NSDAP (a Nazi party organization for the Eastern Territories) triggered a growing power struggle in Ukraine between Rosenberg, who headed the ministry in Berlin, Koch in Ukraine and Himmler. The Nazi attempt to set up an alternative administrative system in Ukraine threatened both the authority of Rosenberg's ministry and the local control of the SS in the east. It also did not help that many of the senior figures in the Reichskommissariat belonged to the Sturm Abteilung (SA) and had longstanding grievances against the SS. The SA had come into existence before the Nazi Party and in 1934 the SS had played a leading role in the murder of leading SA men in the 'Night of the Long Knives'. The killings had brought the SA more firmly under Hitler's personal control, but the feud between the brownshirts of the SA and the blackshirts of the SS smouldered on at lower levels.

The initiative for the creation of the Arbeitsbereich Osten der NSDAP seems to have come from party loyalist Martin Bormann. The power struggle between Koch and Rosenberg continued throughout

1942 and into 1943. On 30 September 1942 Rosenberg's ministry issued an inter-departmental report attacking the recruitment and treatment of Ukrainians for work in Germany. Food and clothes rations for eastern labourers were condemned as 'insufficient' and wages as 'insufficient or unjust'.[24] In December 1942 the Reich Ministry for the Occupied Eastern Territories completed a secret report which underlined the failures of Koch's policies.

> The greatest mistake of our entire Eastern policy is to be found in [our approach to the Slavs] . . . First of all we have to win the war. Having won it, we can shape the area as we see fit. Every proclamation of an aim that repulses those who are of the most use for us in the Eastern area today, which makes them resent the German leadership, is, from a soldier's point of view, a mistake which has to be rectified by the commitment of German blood.[25]

Winning the war and constructing the Nazi utopia in Ukraine would depend heavily on the region's agricultural productivity. Goebbels recorded in his diary on 20 March 1942:

> I described to him [Hitler] in detail how difficult it will be in the next few days to make people understand why food rations must be reduced, and how hard it will be to put these reductions into effect. The Führer has done everything possible to avoid them. He will still make every effort to ensure greater supplies of food, especially from the Ukraine. For the moment, however, this is utterly impossible in view of the exceptionally strained transport situation . . . I don't share the Führer's optimism that we shall succeed within a reasonable time in getting worthwhile supplies out of the Ukraine. We lack the manpower, the organization, and especially the transport to do this.[26]

The scorched earth policy of the retreating Soviet troops greatly reduced Ukraine's economic (including agricultural) productivity after 1941. The fact that the Soviets had evacuated a large number of city-dwellers partly offset the decline in agricultural productivity by reducing the number of mouths to be fed. By late 1941, however, the Germans still faced a situation which meant that their hopes of securing a large agricultural surplus to feed the German army in Russia and supplement civilian rations in the Reich were going to be thwarted. The population of the cities of Ukraine, rendered largely unproductive by Soviet evacuation or destruction of machinery and industrial infrastructure, could not be fed; and the transport infrastructure was inadequate for transporting surplus agricultural produce to where it was needed. Little was to change in this respect during the German occupation. By December 1942 a special train carrying butter from Ukraine to Berlin was hailed as a fulfilment of Germany's hopes, but Goebbels saw that the train was greater in propaganda value than in practical terms.[27]

Hitler considered that targeting the extra food from Ukraine at particular groups in German society might bring rich dividends:

> The Führer holds the opinion that additional food-rations are a pre-requisite for special drives for the production of weapons of decisive importance. Over and above all measures taken so far, the workers should be fed so well that their performance would not be lowered when they have to work longer hours. The Führer proposes to ask Gauleiter Koch that leave-parcels should be made available for about 300–400 men and distributed amongst the men from time to time in the Führer's name. Furthermore, from reserves at the Führer's disposal special Christmas-parcels are to be provided for workers who have to work over Christmas.[28]

Despite the agricultural bounty, which was seen as crucial for sustaining the German war effort, the zeal with which German security units in Ukraine and Crimea went about the business of killing requires some analysis. Removing potential enemies from the rear areas made military sense. Removing large parts of the population not engaged in food or war production increased the possibility of an agricultural surplus which could potentially be exported to Germany or used to feed German forces engaged along the front line to the east.[29] Removing sections of the population considered to have no part in the future of the reborn Aryan race made sense in terms of the Nazis' long-term plans for the area.

Putting Nazi racial theory into practice meant that the native inhabitants of the east would be treated according to their perceived racial worth. Hitler considered that the climate of southern Ukraine, and Crimea in particular, meant that it ought to be established as an invincible stronghold of the Aryan race. With its warm climate Crimea would provide fine wines, citrus fruits and perhaps even rubber to help the Reich become self-sufficient. Those elements of the local population considered to be ethnic German were to be allowed to prosper. Ukrainians were to be retained as long as they were useful as slave labour. Jews and others considered racially undesirable were to be murdered. This is a significant and contentious point. Many Holocaust scholars would take serious issue with the idea that the elimination of the Jews was actually a secondary consequence to Hitler's primary goal of seizing *Lebensraum* in the east. However, it was sufficiently clear in *Mein Kampf* for one Oxford academic to note in 1939: 'For Herr Hitler's *Weltanschauung*, as a whole, much more important than his religion of Jewish repression is his religion of German expansion.'[30]

Elated by the breathtaking initial victories gained by the German forces in Russia, the Führer felt that the moment had arrived when he could confidently turn his attention to the development of the Nazi empire in the east. The first steps in a long-term transformation were in hand. The Einsatzgruppen were spearheading the development of German racial policy in Ukraine by ethnically cleansing the land. Ukrainian *Volksdeutsche*, considered a potential seedbed for the growth of the German race in Ukraine, enjoyed the protection and favour of German forces. He must have felt that his dream of 'a million square miles of Slavic helots, ruled by a handful of *Herrenvolk*' was within realization.[31] The Aryan race would enjoy a new golden age, with the German nation freed from the shackles of Germany's old borders.

Plans were put in hand to create the infrastructure which would be needed to support a Germanized Ukraine. To facilitate both the continuing military operations and the full economic development of the occupied lands there was to be heavy investment in the road and rail links running across Ukraine. Many of the existing roads were merely dirt tracks. Two main highways (DGIV from Lvov to

Stalino and DGV from Hrubiesow to Kharkov) would form the key highways in a new road system. DGIV would be the more important, and a network of connecting roads – spurs off DGIV – would connect key cities to the highway system.[32] German road signage would be introduced throughout the network and rules of the road standardized between the Reichskommissariat Ukraine and the greater German Reich.[33]

There would be similar development of the rail network. The Soviet railway gauge would not support German rolling stock. Hitler envisaged a post-war world in which 'Sebastopol shall be developed as a German town in every respect, becoming the most important Black Sea naval port.'[34] On 24 November 1941 Hitler appointed Albert Speer, a professional architect who was Head of Military Production, to oversee the construction of new towns in the conquered lands of the Soviet Union. This was to be the second phase in the Germanization of Ukraine and Crimea.[35] Later in 1942, while at Vinnitsa, Hitler talked about his dreams to Albert Speer:

> The Reich peasant is to live in outstandingly beautiful settlements. The German agencies and authorities are to have wonderful buildings, the governors' palaces. Around the agencies, they will cultivate whatever serves the maintenance of life. And around the city, a ring of lovely villages will be placed to within 30 or 40 kilometers . . . That is why we are now building the large traffic arteries on the southern tip of the Crimea, out to the Caucasus mountains. Around these traffic strands, the German cities will be placed, as though pearls on a string, and around the cities, the German settlements will lie. For we will not open up Lebensraum for ourselves by entering the old godforsaken Russian holes. In terms of settlements, the Germans must stand on a higher level.[36]

Hitler's visits to Ukraine in 1942 confirmed his prejudices and dreams for the future of a Germanized Ukraine. He was impressed by the number of peasants with blond hair and blue eyes. He commented to Albert Speer:

Aren't there still enormous German splinters [in Ukraine]?
Where else could the blond, blue-eyed children come from? . . .
Where did the remnants of the ancient Goths wind up anyway?
Languages can be lost, but the blood must remain somewhere.[37]

Speer was not left alone to develop his plans for model new towns
connected by modern road and rail links. Himmler, with an eye to
expanding the economic influence and power of the ss, was determined that he would play a leading role in the development of the new
German settlements in the east. In mid-July 1942 Hitler approved
plans that Himmler had put forward. The plans involved the development of new settlements, industrial areas and forest regions linked
by a series of autobahns. Himmler's mood was so euphoric that it
registered on his personal physician. The doctor could barely examine Himmler, so excited and determined was the ss Leader to talk
about the project:

Everything I have been considering and planning on a small scale
can how be realized. I shall set to at once on a large scale – and
with all the vigour I can muster . . . The Germans were once
a farming people and must essentially become one again. The
East will help to strengthen the agricultural side of the German
nation – it will become the fountain of youth for the life blood of
Germany, from which it will be constantly renewed. Villages
inhabited by an armed peasantry will form the basis of the settlement of the East – and will simultaneously be its defense: they
will be the kernel of Europe's great defensive wall.[38]

Himmler had been preparing for this moment for some time, even
going so far as to have model ss farmhouses built at Mehrow, north
of Berlin. While the fulfilment of the masterplan would have to wait
until the end of the war, of course, he was ready to launch immediate plans for a model German colony at Hegewald in Ukraine.

Somehow, these tremendous events and ideas – the invasion of
Russia, Bolshevism, Nazism, the ss, *Lebensraum*, Aryan theories,
anti-Semitism, Einsatzgruppen, economic exploitation of Ukraine,
forced labour – contained the clues to understanding the people

depicted in the short silent film which had so intrigued me as I watched it in Devon. At the time the film was shot, all of the people shown, from senior German officers to forced labourers, were living in a social and psychological 'climate' created by those wider events and ideas. As they gave their orders, took their ease, rolled logs or dug ditches in front of the camera, unfolding events and underlying ideas were at work determining their life chances, their hopes and fears, opportunities and limitations, daydreams and nightmares, aspirations or despair, gluttony or malnutrition, job satisfaction or drudgery, life or death. Was it possible to find out more about them? Would it ever be possible to elevate them from anonymous stereo-types, typical of the period, to reliably identified individuals? The chances might be slim, but I felt impelled to make the attempt.

FOUR

PUTTING NAMES TO FACES

S TUDYING the history of the German occupation of the Soviet Union between 1941 and 1943, I steadily built up a list of the names of German officers who had held key administrative and military posts in the police, SS and army. In their different roles they might have had occasion to become involved with the film in one way or another. One of them might have ordered the film to be made; aspects of life under their command might be featured in the film in some way; most tantalizingly, they might even have made a brief personal appearance in the film itself. Wherever possible, to the list of names I added photographs which could be compared with the images in the film.

Another line of enquiry was to prepare selected 'stills' of key characters in the film and send them by email to various experts on the period to ask whether they could identify any of the officers featured. Even enquiries which eventually led down blind alleys could be interesting and useful, if only for purposes of elimination. They all contributed to an understanding of the total background into which any interpretation of the film needed to be fitted.

For example, the Higher SS and Police Leader (HSSPF) for South Russia from late 1941 onwards was Hans-Adolf Prützmann. He was an intriguing and unpleasant figure. Born in East Prussia, Prützmann had played a key role in the development of Nazism and the SS in the Hamburg area. In April 1941 he was appointed Lieutenant-General of the police. With the German invasion of Russia in June 1941 he was appointed Higher SS and Police Leader for North Russia, but towards the end of the year he was transferred to the southern zone, including Ukraine. For the next three years he played an influential role in the exercise of German rule and the cruelties which that involved. In 1944 Himmler gave him the job of organizing the German resistance movement which was planned to operate after an Allied victory. As leader of the putative 'werewolves', Prützmann was of considerable interest to the Allies. Captured along with Himmler in 1945, Prützmann suffered a lingering death after taking poison. His distinctively wide mouth, evident in every photograph, proved beyond doubt that he was not one of the officers who appeared in the film.

Likewise, I could find no trace in the film of the rather studious features of Erich von dem Bach-Zalewski, the Higher ss and Police Leader for the central zone in Russia (Russland Mitte). Possibly embarrassed by his Germano-Polish origins, ss personnel lists usually referred to him simply as Erich von dem Bach.[1] He may have carried out his duties under the impression that he had something to prove to his masters in Berlin. Spilling substantial quantities of Jewish blood would be his way of demonstrating that he was a good Nazi. Philipp von Boeselager, who served in Russia as a cavalry officer in the Wehrmacht, has left a particularly insightful description of the HSSPF for Russland Mitte:

Erich von dem Bach-Zalewski was not a harmless person. People trembled at the mere mention of this name. He was in his forties, a massive, rather ordinary-looking man. He was very experienced in military affairs and no one could accuse him of incompetence in that domain. But his service record did not inspire respect. Having entered the army when he was very young, during the last years of the Great War, in 1918–19 he had allowed himself to be drawn into the activities of the *Freikorps*. There he had lost his values and even the slightest sense of humanity. Since June 1941 he had been high commandant of the ss and the police . . . in the central Russia sector. He reigned like a satrap over a sinister empire that included Minsk and Mogilev. Ruthless, coldly calculating, he was truly a creature of the Devil. Among the officers, Bach Zalewski had a scandalous reputation as an unscrupulous careerist who was full of bitterness against the military men who had expelled him from the army fifteen years earlier.[2]

The photographic trawl was useful in allowing me to establish that certain figures were not in the film, but the process could also be disturbing. Accounts of the inhumanity of men like Bach-Zalewski made far from easy reading. They were a powerful reminder of the probable temperament and activities of the men pictured in the film, whatever their names might have been. Moreover, some of the publications bought in my search for photographs revealed, at the very least, a kind of emotional involvement of their authors with their subject-matter. The heroism of Waffen-ss men, outnumbered five to one by attacking Russian troops, seemed to evoke in certain – mainly American-based – authors some kind of romantic admiration and affection for men who had faithfully fought for a doomed cause. This attitude seems to have developed after the defeat of Germany in 1945. In post-war interrogations senior German officers had cultivated an image of the German army on the Eastern Front which emphasized its blamelessness for the Holocaust and the heroism of its troops when faced with overwhelming odds.[3] The Cold War soon led to a new relationship between Germany and America, and it became politically convenient to accept the Eastern Front myth put forward by German officers in 1945. In the later years of the twentieth century the myth has been nurtured by authors to whom Smelser and Davies refer as 'The Gurus': 'authors [who] combine a careful attention to detail and authenticity when it comes to battles, dates, uniforms, and decorations, with either a slanted or revisionist historical context – or none at all – embedded in an heroic ethos'.[4] The work of these 'Gurus' is usually rich in original photographs, often as a result of good relations between the authors and former members of the ss. Trying to put names to faces was making me strangely and uncomfortably reliant on some rather unfortunate sources.

Less influenced by disturbing overtones of neo-Nazism were the many websites which serve as information interchanges between experts and other people who are keenly interested in various aspects of the history of the Third Reich. Posting still photographs from the film on these websites led to the first real breakthrough in identifying the men in the film. A short-statured ss Brigadeführer who featured in the final scene, and whom I suspected was also pictured in another scene socializing with the The Fat Man, was identified as

Hans Döring. Born in Hannover on 31 August 1901, he had joined the Nazi party in 1928, the ss in 1929 and the police in 1935.[5] During 1941 and 1942 he served as an officer in the Leibstandarte Division of the Waffen ss during the attack on Russia. On 20 April 1942, having already taken up a post as head of the ss and police in Stalino, he was promoted to the rank of ss-Brigadeführer and Generalmajor of the Polizei. Renamed Donetsk after the war, Stalino was in the heart of Ukraine's industrial belt, and it was a vital jumping-off point for the German offensive towards Stalingrad in the summer of 1942. Döring survived the war. He died in Nuremberg on 2 July 1970. The identification of this officer was consistent with both the probable date of the film and the date of his posting to Stalino. That city also fitted nicely with other locations identifiable in the film.

A second identification also came, via the Internet, from the ever helpful experts on the history of the Third Reich. Three people suggested that a very distinctive ss officer, to whom I had given the pseudonym Bald Man, was Ludolf von Alvensleben. Tall, thin, balding and chain-smoking, the available images of this officer, when compared to the man in the film, left no doubt that the identification was correct. This was encouraging – and Alvensleben was not just another German officer. Regarded as a 'brutish nazi who claimed that he could not enjoy his breakfast unless he had first killed twenty Poles', Alvensleben was a convicted war criminal who managed to escape to Argentina after the war.[6] The potential importance of the film had clearly moved up a couple of notches with this discovery.

Alvensleben, the son of a distinguished German family, had been born on 17 March 1901 at Halle.[7] Descended from the nobility, his father had been a major-general in the Prussian army, and as a child Ludolf had served in the Prussian cadet corps between 1911 and 1918. He then joined the army, entering the 10th Hussar Regiment in 1918. After the First World War he had served in paramilitary veterans' organizations: the Freikorps (1920) and Stahlhelm (1923–9). Other than this, Alvensleben had worked on his estates. Marrying in 1924, he and his wife had four children. On 1 August 1929 he joined the Nazi party, being appointed Ortsgruppenleiter for Eisleben. For the next three years he played an important part in the growth of the party in and around Eisleben. Following Hitler's appointment as

Chancellor, Alvensleben held a variety of administrative posts, such as Acting District Administrator of Eisleben and Member of the Provincial Parliament of Saxony.

In 1934 Alvensleben joined the ss, rising steadily in the organization until, with the rank of Brigadeführer, he became Hitler's adjutant for a time in 1941. After the attack on Russia Alvensleben moved to new duties as ss and Police Leader for Simferopol in Crimea. On 7 January 1942 he received further promotion to the rank of Generalmajor of the Police. In October 1943, with the rank of ss-Gruppenführer and Generalleutnant of the Police, he became Higher ss and Police Leader for the Black Sea, but soon afterwards, as a result of health problems, he was invalided back to Berlin.[8] The ill-health turned out to be fortuitous. Alvensleben was safely in Berlin by the time the Red Army's 1943 offensive cut off the German forces in Crimea. During 1944 he occupied administrative posts in Germany, before being appointed ss and Area Police Commander for the Adriatic in October 1944. With his headquarters at Udine, in Italy, Alvensleben was well away from the worst of the fighting at the war's end, and he was handily positioned to avoid having to surrender to the Red Army, which would have been the equivalent of a death sentence for him. He again displayed immaculate timing when he escaped from a British prisoner-of-war camp at Neuengamme in 1945. The escape had been well prepared. Collecting his family, he disappeared from Europe, heading for South America.

Alvensleben was a wanted man. He had been implicated in some of the worst excesses of German rule in Russia, especially as Simferopol was the location for the headquarters of Einsatzgruppe D in 1941–2. The regular reports from Einsatzgruppe D provide a detailed insight into their murderous activities and the professional world which Alvensleben inhabited. For example, in March 1942 Einsatzgruppe D reported:

> During the period under report, the areas north of Simferopol in the Crimea were searched again. The western part as far as the Yevpatoria Ak-Sheih line, the eastern part as far as the railway line Simferopol-Dzankoy, as well as the rural area in the north as far as Dzankoy heights, have now been thoroughly worked over.

The Teilkommando that has been posted in the central region is greatly handicapped by the bad conditions of the roads . . . In the period under report, further success was achieved concerning the arrest and the disposal of unreliable elements thanks to the extended network of secret informants . . . From February 16 to 28 June, 1942, 1,515 people were shot, 729 of them Jews, 271 Communists, 74 partisans, 421 Gypsies and asocial elements and saboteurs.[9]

As early as 1943 a Soviet court in Kharkov heard evidence from Colonel George Heinisch, the former German commissar for Melitopol, which tied Alvensleben to the use of mobile gas vans for the murder of Jews.[10] In 1946 a Polish court convicted Alvensleben *in absentia* for having been involved in the murder of 4,247 Poles. The murders were part of a series of reprisals against Polish communities which, in the immediate aftermath of the outbreak of war in 1939, had conducted pogroms against ethnic Germans in Poland. In 1947 Alvensleben was further implicated in war crimes during the trial of two ss men before a West German court. They were accused of involvement in the murder of a group of Polish intellectuals as reprisal for an act of arson in occupied Poland. Ludolf von Alvensleben was identified as the senior officer who gave the order for the reprisal to take place. The chairman of the court, noting that German public opinion had turned increasingly against putting men on trial for such crimes, remarked that it was a pity that 'the "wire pullers" behind the scenes were either dead or had evaded justice by flight'.[11]

By that time, Alvensleben was safe and secure in Argentina. On 27 November 1952, under the name of Carlos Lucke, he was given Argentine citizenship. He lived in Buenos Aires until 1956 when, sensing that attempts might be made to bring him to justice, he left for more remote parts of Argentina, where he was able to evade the West German government's attempts to secure his extradition in 1963. He continued to enjoy the protection of the right-wing Peronist government of Argentina for the rest of his life. Indeed, the government even gave him a civil service post as a fish-farming inspector. The West German government received no response to its request for extradition, and Alvensleben lived openly at the Villa Belgrano, Sierra

Calamuchita, until his death from lung cancer in 1970. His ultimate fate may have been portended by the fact that, in the film made more than 25 years earlier, he can be seen puffing away with all the carefree abandon of a confirmed chain-smoker.

Alvensleben's posting to Crimea in 1941 tied in nicely with the locations already identified in the film. Yet what was he actually engaged in when the film was shot? Whatever may be thought about the standards of post-war Polish justice in 1946, he was certainly a convicted war criminal who had escaped justice. The positive identification of one of the officers in the film as a war criminal meant that some of the scenes that appeared on the screen took on an even more sinister complexion, increasingly pointing towards some connection with the Holocaust. Was Alvensleben the only war criminal in the film? Intriguingly, in the film he appeared nervous in the presence of The Fat Man. Occasionally his eyes would shoot towards the camera lens. The expression on his face was a mixture of nervousness and resentment. He looked as though he did not like being filmed, but lacked the authority to stop the filming. He seemed to have doubts about whether or not he was striking the right image before the camera. Alvensleben was an unpleasant character whose career in the Party and ss had been marked with violence. His position as ss and Police Leader for Simferopol put him at the heart of the German effort to eradicate the Jewish population and other selected groups in Crimea, an ethnic cleansing considered necessary to turn the region into the cradle for a reborn greater Germanic *Volk*. Yet here was a man nervous before the camera. What kind of man was The Fat Man to inspire such apparent nervousness in a man like Alvensleben? Might it be possible to discover the identity of The Fat Man by tracing the known associates of Alvensleben and Döring.

Working through the wartime history of Ukraine, I encountered one name again and again. Obergruppenführer Friedrich Jeckeln is one of those monsters whose personal culpability has not been adequately recognized by history; his mass murders are merely subsumed into the horrific whole which is the Holocaust; his guilt is transmuted into a general impression of the 'evils of Nazism'. Little has been written about him, but his life, career and crimes most certainly excite passions in those who know of him. One writer has commented:

Never a professional military officer, he was an example of the pre-1933 SS street fighters of the Allgemeine-SS . . . A radical and brutal supporter of Himmler's policies in Russia, his actions were among the most destructive in terms of human life. [Jeckeln was] crude, short-tempered and cruel.[12]

The son of a factory worker, Jeckeln was born in 1895 at Hornberg, in the Black Forest. He studied engineering for a semester at the Polytechnic at Köthen. In 1914 he joined the army, rising to the rank of Leutnant in 1915.[13] Awarded the Iron Cross (2nd Class) and the wound badge in black, Jeckeln had distinguished himself in Field-Artillery Regiment 76 and then in a rifle regiment. In March 1915 he was appointed adjutant to the 40th Rifle Regiment. By the end of the war he had begun training to be a pilot. After the war he served as farm manager on an estate owned by Paul Hirsch near Danzig. A member of the Freikorps and the Young Teutonic Order until 1924, Jeckeln, like many other former soldiers, was disenchanted with Weimar Germany. He married Hirsch's daughter Charlotte. Remarkably, Jeckeln does not seem to have been aware that Hirsch and his daughter were Jews. Realization of this fact, probably combined with alcohol problems, seems to have played a key role in the breakdown of the marriage. By then the couple had three children. Jeckeln turned his back on his family and refused to pay the maintenance ordered by a German court.

By the late 1920s Jeckeln had begun to rebuild his life. In 1929 he remarried, and his new wife had a substantial income to support them both. Jeckeln joined the Nazi party on 1 October 1929, becoming a member of the SS in December 1930. In Brunswick he played a very full part in the street battles against communists and socialists. Within the ranks of the SS he prospered, being promoted to the rank of Sturmbannführer in March 1931. Before the end of the year he had risen to Standartenführer in command of the 17th SS Standarte. Taking part in a Nazi 'reign of terror' in the early 1930s, he made an influential contribution to the Nazis' rise to power in Brunswick and the subsequent Nazification of the state. In 1931 the city played host to a rally of 70,000 Nazis who were carried in 38 special trains from across the Reich. The following year Brunswick made a small but critical boost to Adolf Hitler's rise to power. As an Austrian, the Nazi leader was not entitled to German citizenship and all that went with it in terms of voting and eligibility for election to important offices. However, he could qualify for citizenship if he could secure appointment to an official post in one of the German states. With the Nazis having won a controlling interest in Brunswick, Hitler was appointed to the Brunswick commercial legation in Berlin in 1932.[14]

During 1932 Jeckeln was elected as a member of the Reichstag and promoted to the rank of SS Brigade Commander with the rank of Oberführer. His personal rise within the SS was as dramatic as the rise of the Nazi Party in the years when Weimar Germany was suffering the economic consequences of the great recession. The Nazis' success in Brunswick can be seen as the launching pad from which they went on to take control of the whole country. Localities like Brunswick and second-tier men like Jeckeln were the bedrock on which that success was built. He could not claim to be a national figure but his regional significance could not be doubted. After Hitler's appointment as Chancellor of Germany in January 1933, Jeckeln was put in command of SS Group South with the rank of SS Gruppenführer, a role he combined with serving as a political police commissioner.

It was in this latter capacity that he was implicated in the Rieseberg murders of 1933. Jeckeln had shown his willingness to commit murder the previous year, when he had been involved in a series of bomb attacks on political opponents of the Nazis in Brunswick. On 4 July 1933 members of the SS murdered eleven men, mostly communists and socialists, near the town of Rieseberg, 30 miles from Brunswick. Jeckeln used his position in the police to ensure that the murders were never properly investigated. Indeed, investigations in the 1950s suggested that, while Jeckeln did not participate personally in the murders, it was probably on his orders that they were carried out.

The Rieseberg murders were part of the process of cementing the Nazi hold on power in Brunswick in 1933, when the city began to vie with Munich for the title of 'most German city' in the New Reich. Socialists and communists were not the only groups to suffer. The local Nazi party forcefully and brutally also brought into line the Nationalists, the Stahlhelm and other right-wing groups. In the case of the Stahlhelm, that meant summary dissolution.[15] *The Times* commented in April 1933: 'In this State there are now to all appearances only Nazis.'[16]

Jeckeln's contribution was recognized by promotion to the rank of Obergruppenführer in 1936. At the same time he was appointed ss and Police Leader of Western Germany. Only one thing cast a shadow over his rapid rise within the ss. In February 1932 Charlotte Hirsch, his first wife, wrote to Adolf Hitler asking the leader of the Nazi party to ensure that his loyal ss man paid the child maintenance that he owed.[17] History does not record whether Hitler actually favoured her with a reply, but Jeckeln became concerned that he might be perceived in the eyes of the party hierarchy as an inexplicable phenomenon – a Nazi who had married a Jew. His personal anti-Semitism had been fuelled by the circumstances surrounding the breakdown of his marriage to Charlotte Hirsch and by increasingly acrimonious relations with his father-in-law afterwards. Jeckeln's anti-Semitism would have been intensified by feeling that he might be regarded by the Nazi hierarchy as having something to prove on that score.

Jeckeln complicated the situation further by being, in Nazi terms, something of a liberal in his attitudes towards Aryanism. In a Nazi party meeting in Brunswick on 18 June 1937 he attacked the obsession of some party members with the importance of blond hair and blue eyes as evidence of the racial make-up of individuals. Bluntly describing their obsession as 'this blond nonsense', he went on to argue that fit and healthy bodies, evidenced in the case of women by the award of the Reich Sports Badge, were far more important than blond hair and blue eyes. His speech attracted the attention of the foreign press.[18] His more liberal approach to this key aspect of Nazi philosophy would later lead him into direct conflict with Hitler and Himmler.

While his outspoken attitude toward definitions of Aryan worth brought him into conflict with senior Nazis, there could be no doubt of his anti-Semitism. From 1933 onwards the Jews of Brunswick found their businesses boycotted and their families targeted on the street by ss men. Later Jeckeln played a very prominent role in organizing the Kristallnacht pogroms of November 1938 in Brunswick and

Hannover. Paul Szustak, a party member since 1928 and a friend of Jeckeln during the 1930s, provided post-war investigators with a detailed account of events in November 1938. Ensuring close liaison between the police and ss, Jeckeln had shown efficiency, cruelty and a willingness to exceed his orders in carrying through the pogroms. Synagogues and businesses were targeted, and hundreds of Jews were assaulted and arrested across Lower Saxony.

With the outbreak of the Second World War Jeckeln was sent to join the ranks of the Waffen ss, the armed formations that had been set up by the Nazis as a check on the power of the German army. His unit, the 2nd Regiment of the Totenkopf Division, was at the spearhead of the German assault on the Low Countries in May to June 1940. They established a fearsome reputation during the campaign, and they were involved in the murder of at least one group of British soldiers who had surrendered.

Jeckeln's time with the Totenkopf ended early in 1941. With planning well under way for the attack on the Soviet Union during the summer, Himmler asked him to serve as Higher ss and Police Leader for South Russia. The promotion, which carried the rank General of the Police, proves that he was regarded as one of Himmler's most trusted subordinates. As a Higher ss and Police Leader he would be responsible for ensuring that German policies were applied in the zone of occupation and for keeping a careful check on the loyalties of the ss and police under his command. Himmler wanted to ensure that within the Nazi movement there could never again be the kind of schism that had culminated in the 'Night of the Long Knives' in 1934. The Higher ss and Police Leaders would act as Himmler's check on the ambitions and loyalties of his own ss. In addition, they would be responsible for the control of the Einsatzgruppen (security troops), who would ultimately be responsible for the deaths of millions in the occupied areas of the Soviet Union.

Whether or not an order for the implementation of the 'final solution to the Jewish question' was given prior to the invasion of the Soviet Union is the subject of ongoing debate among historians. No written order has ever been found and the documentary record provides only the briefest glimpses into the Nazi planning process for what would follow Operation Barbarossa. At the end of the war hurriedly lit bonfires would consume many incriminating documents and Nazi intentions were often hidden from historians by the use of verbal orders and the employment of opaque euphemisms about what was to take place.

One thing is perfectly clear, however: a man like Jeckeln needed little prompting to make the fullest use of his authority in exploiting the wide latitude of orders requiring him to deal with security risks and 'social undesirables'. A forceful personality could not only cope with the overlapping and competing spheres of influence that characterized the Nazi state (a form of checks and balances designed to minimize any threat to the hierarchy); a particularly determined individual could exploit them to good effect. Indeed, he would have the opportunity to thrive. Thus Jeckeln's appointment as Higher SS and Police Leader for South Russia offered him considerable opportunities to build up his power base and demonstrate his loyalty to the cause. His conduct in the campaign against the Jews would lay to rest any lingering suspicions about his attitudes and judgement. Moreover, the frequency with which Jeckeln and Himmler met in 1941 and 1942 leaves no room for doubt about the latter's knowledge, encouragement and involvement.[19] Himmler was perfectly prepared to see Jeckeln cut a bloody swathe through Ukraine and to encourage other members of the SS to show the same levels of efficiency, dedication and ruthlessness in effecting the final solution of the 'Jewish problem'.

The Einsatzgruppen murdered their way through the communities of Ukraine and Crimea from August to December 1941. Jeckeln soon proved that he was ready to innovate in order to speed the process of killing Jews. The massacre of over 23,000 Jews at Kamenets-Podolsk from 27 to 28 August was a particularly significant moment in the development of the Holocaust. Kamenets-Podolsk was the location of the first massacre where the number of Jewish victims exceeded five figures. That was a key step on the path from sporadic mass killings to organized genocide on a grand scale. Holocaust historians have fully recognized the significance of the moment:

Like his counterparts further north, HSSPF Jeckeln played a key role in coordinating and expanding the murder of the Jews. In

Ukraine, Jewish women and children had already been killed by individual units since late July. For several weeks the number of killings remained relatively steady, but the threshold to genocide was crossed at the end of August. At that time, Jeckeln offered Wehrmacht commanders to relieve the crisis in Kamenets Podolsky, the destination of mass deportations by Romanian and Hungarian authorities, before the formal transfer of the city to the civil administration on September 1. As a result, about 23,600 Jews . . . were murdered in that city between August 27 and 30 by Jeckeln's *Stabskompanie* (staff company), a detachment of Einsatzgruppe C, and Police Battalion 320.[20]

Many of the victims at Kamenets-Podolsk were Jews from Hungary. In July 14,000 Jews resident in, but not citizens of, Hungary had been forced into German-controlled territory. They were eventually taken into the control of the ss and brought to Kolomija near Kamenets-Podolsk. On 25 August, at a meeting in the headquarters of the Wehrmacht logistics division at Vinnitsa, Jeckeln promised to dispose of the Hungarian Jews and a substantial number of the Jewish residents of Kamenets-Podolsk. The presence of so many Jews in poor conditions was a drain on the manpower and resources of German forces in the field, created the risk of an outbreak of disease, and was perceived as a security risk.

Murdering so many people created a further set of problems. Those charged with the task of killing would be outnumbered by the victims. How was it possible to ensure an orderly killing process in which victims would neither try to escape nor attack those about to kill them? Jeckeln devised a solution.[21] He was on hand at Kamenets-Podolsk to watch the process which he had devised. It involved using bomb craters as mass graves and managing a steady flow of victims to each site. Guards would line the route to the bomb craters and the victims would be kept on the move constantly; they would be given no chance to reflect on what was happening or what might lie ahead of them. If necessary, beatings would be administered to ensure that the flow of victims to the execution site remained constant. Compliance with the instructions of guards would ensure freedom from beatings. In this way victims would be pressured into compliance all the way to their deaths. Andrej Angrick has described the procedure:

> The victims were forced to run through a line of guards made up of regular police from police battalion 320, the so-called 'hosepipe', to the craters; there they had to throw their possessions to one side, and some were also ordered to disrobe. Finally they were compelled to climb down into the crater, lie on the bodies of those who had already been murdered, and were killed instantaneously by a shot to the base of the skull. 'Forbearance' was only shown for the riflemen: if any marksman was unable (or no longer able) to kill small children, he could ask to be relieved, drink some schnapps, take a break, and then return if possible to resume work at the pit. With the massacre at Kamenets-Podolsk, mass murder ordered by the state reached new heights . . . Jeckeln had now made mass murder an acceptable and recognized instrument of population policy for the civil and military authorities in the Ukraine by this massacre.[22]

Evidence from post-war trials indicates that methods of executing Jews varied greatly in the early stages of the invasion of Russia. Mass shootings were by far the most common, but they were carried out in a variety of different ways with varying levels of efficiency. Clearly, in the lead-up to the invasion, whatever instructions had been given about killing Jews, little thought had apparently been given to the logistics and operational problems of carrying out mass murder. Jeckeln put into operation a carefully conceived programme at Kamenets-Podolsk. It took into account the mindset of both killers and victims; it involved efficient management of people; and it worked with a high level of logistical efficiency from the arrival of victims through to their interment. The process was also cost effective at every stage, from the use of a single rifle bullet for each killing to the retrieval of valuables and clothing. Kamenets-Podolsk saw the perfection of Jeckeln's system for the mass murder of tens of thousands of Jews in a matter of hours. He was soon ready to employ the system on an even bigger concentration of Jews.

Between 29 and 30 September 1941, at the Babi Yar ravine, Jeckeln's forces organized the murder of the Jews of Kiev. Prompted by the Russian NKVD's demolition of part of the city centre, on 26 September Jeckeln met with Rasch, head of Einsatzgruppe C, Paul Blobel, commander of Sonderkommando 4a, and Major-General Eberhard, Army Commander-in-Chief at Kiev. After that meeting, signs appeared throughout the city ordering the Jews to congregrate in an area of parkland. The technique perfected at Kamenets-Podolsk to ensure a continuing stream of victims to the point of execution was again in evidence. One of the few survivors later testified:

> [People] took off their clothes, while the Germans mercilessly beat and unleashed dogs on them. Some people begged for mercy . . . others silently undressed and walked down to the ditch. Some went insane . . . [The] Germans ran them in a single file through an opening in the earthen wall, from where I heard the rattle of a machine gun.[23]

Some 33,771 people were rounded up and subsequently murdered in the two-day killing spree. Einsatzgruppe C's report before the massacre on 28 September expressed hopes for an even higher death toll. The report showed that the German army was fully in support of the operation and that Jeckeln was about to arrive to take personal charge: 'Execution of at least 50,000 Jews planned. German Army welcomes measures and demands drastic procedure. Garrison commander advocates public execution of 20 Jews . . . *Vorkommando* of the Higher SS and Police Leader arrived.'[24] The mass killing was later hailed as an act of 'liberation'.

By the end of 1941 many parts of southern Russia were substantially *'Juden frei'* (Jew-free), as the result of Jeckeln's efficient arrangements for eliminating Jewish communities, from initial round-up, transport, stripping and processing to final execution by firing squad and interment. He made a special contribution to the 'final solution' by solving the irksome problem of bodies falling untidily into the mass graves prepared for them. Shooting was the principal means employed, but the process could result in the formation of voids in the mass grave as it slowly filled with victims. Such voids were uneconomical.

They meant fewer bodies could be accommodated as bodies fell haphazardly upon other bodies contorted in agony. Jeckeln realized that the answer was to place those about to be executed into their final position before any triggers were pulled. The first tier of victims would be forced to lie on the floor of the newly opened grave in an arrangement that maximized space utilization. They would then be executed *in situ*. The second tier of victims would be forced to lie neatly on the first tier of bodies. They too would then be executed by firing squad. Jeckeln's system was called 'sardine packing', and had numerous advantages. Not only did it maximize the number of bodies in an execution pit, but it also made it less likely that any victim might fortuitously escape their intended fate. With the victim lying prone, a head shot from above was not likely to miss, whereas shooting victims at the edge of the pit produced a surprising number of survivors, who either feigned death by falling into the pit at the critical moment or were seriously, but not fatally, wounded. Jeckeln's system had the added advantage – for the executioners – that they did not have to look directly into the eyes of their victims as the trigger was pulled. Even hardened killers of the Einsatzgruppen could be psychologically affected by the mass murders they carried out.

Oral and archaeological evidence gathered more than 60 years later by Yahad In-Unum investigators at mass grave sites in Ukraine has suggested that, at least in some cases, Ukrainian children were forced to act as pressers for the 'sardine packing' method.[25] They were employed to spread earth over each layer of corpses and to trample over the new surface to compact and level it. The work was emotionally and physically draining. To process group after group of Jewish victims, the pressers had only a brief period in which to complete their work. Depending on the scale of the *Aktion*, the pressers might have to work continuously for ten or twelve hours.

Before the end of 1941 Jeckeln had left Ukraine to take up a new appointment as Higher SS and Police Leader for North Russia, with headquarters in Riga. His anti-Semitic zeal in Ukraine had impressed Himmler, who could make the new appointment with every confidence that Jeckeln would be just as zealous in dealing with the Jews of the Baltic States and those transported to the east from Germany itself. His career continued to prosper and in February 1945, promoted to the rank of General of the Waffen SS and Police, he was placed in command of the SS-Freiwilligen-Gebirgs-Korps. Two months later he was taken prisoner by the Russians.

After the war Russian war crimes investigators subjected Jeckeln to prolonged and rigorous interrogation.[26] He insisted that he had simply obeyed orders and carried out the official policy of the Nazi state. Despite the murderous record of his rule in the occupied lands of the Soviet Union, he was at great pains to emphasize that he personally had not killed any Jews, even though the Russians had collected evidence that, in the midst of a shooting, he had executed with a pistol an old man who tried to take his own life with a knife. Jeckeln was heard to shout: 'You have no right to kill yourself.'[27] He was questioned closely about topics ranging from the mistreatment of Soviet prisoners of war through to the development of gas as a method of killing Jews.[28]

The Russian interrogators wanted to ensure a good show trial in which the murderous intent of the fascists against all Soviet citizens would be established before the court and the Soviet people. At his trial, held at Riga on 3 February 1946, Jeckeln eventually admitted his guilt. That same day he met his end dangling from a noose in front of an audience of Soviet soldiers and civilians. He had been directly responsible for the deaths of certainly more than 100,000 Jews, and possibly as many as 250,000.

If Jeckeln had been such a dominant figure in the history of the occupied areas of the Soviet Union, could he have had some connection with the film in which I had become so interested? The opening shot of the film, showing a sign that made reference to the South Russia command that Jeckeln had once held, suggested that it was a possibility worth considering. Opening shots in silent films were often used to establish identities and locate the film for the benefit of the viewer. Might the building in the opening sequence have been Jeckeln's headquarters? Bearing in mind Jeckeln's transfer to the North Russia command in late 1941, it seemed unlikely that he could be one of the officers in the film, and yet, with uncertainty over the date of the film, could it be entirely ruled out?

Few photos of Jeckeln were available to compare with the images in the film. In the photographs that were found his weight fluctuated quite considerably and the images of him at his trial in 1946 illustrated the rigours of life in a Soviet prisoner-of-war camp. No two photographs seemed to be of the same man but, in at least some of them, he certainly bore a resemblance to The Fat Man. Hair, face shape, general build, eyes, ears and jaw were all scrutinized carefully and compared. The similarities were striking. Jeckeln in his more portly photographs just might have been The Fat Man, and his uniform insignia corroborated the possibility, at least in part. Certainly The Fat Man, like Jeckeln, had been awarded the Iron Cross and The Fat Man's epaulette insignia, as far could be made out on the grainy film, were appropriate for an ss officer with the rank of Gruppenführer. True, Jeckeln had reached the higher rank of Obergruppenführer before the war, but he had been required to drop a rank with his appointment to the Totenkopf Division in 1939. The situation was made more complicated by the fact that ss rank insignia were known to have changed in 1942. How long would it have taken for a change of insignia promulgated in Berlin to take effect in the field on the Eastern Front?

Likewise, there was room for uncertainty in the medals that could be identified. If The Fat Man in the film did not display all the medals and awards that Jeckeln was entitled to wear, would that have been altogether surprising? He was a 'hands-on' manager, seemingly eager to identify himself with the men in the field. Jeckeln was also experienced enough as a soldier to know that an overly ostentatious display of medals, awards and insignia of high rank was an imprudent way to attract the unwelcome attention of the Russian partisans.

Even if the film was unlikely to have been shot in 1941, when Jeckeln was known to have been serving in Ukraine, was it possible that he might have had some reason to pay a visit to his former command during 1942 or 1943? His involvement in anti-partisan warfare after 1941 suggested the possibility that he might have returned to Ukraine to inspect and advise on operations of that kind. The war against the partisans was one of the most pressing concerns of the German High Command in early 1942, and the Higher ss and Police Leaders in the occupied Soviet Union were playing a leading role in developing a counter-insurgency doctrine. In June 1942 Jeckeln was wounded in an anti-partisan action.[29] Might he have undertaken some kind of inspection tour in Ukraine and Crimea as part of his convalescence? Could he have been sent to spend some time in Crimea, undertaking a few light inspection duties along the way, during his convalescence? Parts of the film certainly pictured a tour of inspection of troops, potential targets for partisan attack and the kind of fixed defensive posts that were constructed along roads and railway lines for their protection. Identifying Jeckeln as The Fat Man made sense, and that identification would be consistent with a significant proportion of the film's subject-matter. Could Jeckeln have ordered the film to be made as a way of showing senior Nazi figures the exemplary efficiency of the Higher ss and Police Leader in laying the foundations for the new Aryan empire in the east? The evidence might not be conclusive, but in the absence of any other credible candidate Jeckeln's name had to be pencilled in as the principal suspect.

I would need to go to Washington to test that hypothesis against the material in the United States Archives. Could I establish Jeckeln's movements after 1941, either to link him definitely to the film and events in Ukraine or to exclude him with confidence? If The Fat Man were Jeckeln, then I would have done my duty to bear witness to the film, its contents and the evils it represented. The Jeckeln story was as powerful and compelling as it was horrific. A definite identification would be a satisfying achievement and would open the door for others to shed fresh light on some aspects of the Holocaust.

FIVE

THE FAT MAN IDENTIFIED

WASHINGTON, DC, is a place of dreams and frustrations. For the historian interested in the Second World War the United States National Archives II at College Park, in Maryland, contain vast amounts of material gathered during and after the war by the American government, the military and intelligence services. The quantity of captured German records is staggering. Of particular interest to me was the material relating to the SS, from personnel files through to Heinrich Himmler's papers.

A short train ride away on the Metro system, just off the Washington Mall, is the United States Holocaust Memorial Museum. One of the leading research centres, it has gathered documentary material from around the world, including some from the archives of the former Soviet Union. The staff and academics at the Holocaust Memorial Museum could not have been kinder or more helpful to a visitor from overseas bringing with him a historical curio in the shape of a silent film that had turned up inexplicably in the Baptist church in Cullompton, Devon. Professor Richard Breitman, one of the foremost scholars of the Holocaust and a biographer of Heinrich Himmler, offered the most remarkable hospitality, patience and good nature in helping a British scholar with his tale of a 'mystery film' and his suspicion that Friedrich Jeckeln was the officer who featured most prominently in it. Richard Breitman is one of the few academics to have written anything on Jeckeln. Crushingly, he was convinced that The Fat Man in the film was not Jeckeln. Nevertheless, I was reluctant to abandon the hypothesis: Jeckeln as The Fat Man made too much sense in terms of the film.

Day after day in Washington I spent my time going through file after file in the archives. Signal logs from German security units in the Ukraine were examined in the hope that one of them might refer to a visit from Jeckeln or a film crew, or both. Personnel files were consulted to determine Alvensleben's movements, and to establish when Jeckeln might have visited the Ukraine during 1942 and 1943. As the gaps in Jeckeln's wartime career were filled in, it became less and less likely that Jeckeln could have had any opportunity to escape his murderous duties in north Russia to appear even briefly in the Ukraine and Crimea. The prime suspect was slipping away; and yet The Fat Man still looked like him.

In a search for further leads, and in the hope of finding just one narrow window of opportunity when Jeckeln might have made his way south, the personnel files of men significant in the administration of the occupied Ukraine were checked. Most personnel files featured only the briefest information (name, party number and ss number, dates of promotion and letters of appointment). Certain awkward customers, such as Alvensleben and Jeckeln, had particularly fat personnel files, but for the most part they were rather bland, sparse and unilluminating records. Few contained photographs.

One of the files to be checked was that of Walter Gieseke. An Oberstleutnant (lieutenant-colonel) of the police and ss, his surname was familiar because it was one of the names listed on the signpost that was clearly shown in the opening sequence of the film. After many disappointments, my hopes began to rise. On the front cover of Gieseke's ss personnel file were two passport photographs. As soon as I saw them I knew that I had looked into this man's eyes a thousand times before. Behind them lay an arrogance and self-importance that typified the performance of The Fat Man in the film. The connection was instant and disturbingly deep. I had got to know The Fat Man, and those same eyes stared back at me from the front cover of Walter Gieseke's personnel file. Admittedly, the photograph had probably been taken before the war when he had a rather fuller head of hair than he carried in the early 1940s. Nevertheless, this was definitely the man for whom I had been searching.

Gratifying though it was, the revelation also brought a measure of disappointment. Jeckeln, my former prime suspect, had been one of

Walter Gieseke, from his personnel file.

the principal architects of the final solution to the Jewish problem, a monster and mass murderer, even if his crimes had largely been forgotten. Now it was certain that The Fat Man, only a rather obscure police lieutenant-colonel, could not be regarded as being in the same league; and yet, as I read his personnel file, Walter Gieseke proved to be every bit as interesting and complex a personality as Jeckeln. Whereas Jeckeln's guilt of serious crimes against humanity was beyond question, Gieseke was fascinating for his ordinariness and the ambiguous nature of his involvement in Nazi crimes in Ukraine.

Born on 26 November 1901 at Hohenhameln in Germany, Gieseke had joined the old German army on 15 April 1919. The signing of the Treaty of Versailles threatened to cut short his military career, since Germany was obliged to demobilize troops to bring the army below the ceiling of 100,000 men imposed by the Allied Supreme Council. He was, however, one of the fortunate few to be demobilized on 3 August and allowed to enlist in the new Reichswehr the following day. He served in the army for over a decade before leaving it to take up life as a civilian on 14 April 1931. After Hitler's appointment as Chancellor of Germany in January 1933 Gieseke shrewdly concluded that future career progression would depend on membership of the Nazi party. He joined the party on 1 May 1933 with party membership number 1,853,472.

In October 1933 Gieseke also joined the Sturm Abteilung (SA). However, that organization was set on a collision course with the hierarchy of the Nazi party. Internal rivalries within the party culminated in Hitler ordering the murder of many leading members of the SA in the 'Night of the Long Knives' on 30 June 1934. With the SA increasingly seen as an irrelevance after that, Gieseke left to become a member of the reorganized police force on 1 December 1934. He served with the police for five years until being recalled to the army in 1939. His career progress had been swift in comparison with less politically astute members of the police force. He made the rank of Oberleutnant on 11 April 1935, Hauptmann on 26 January 1937 and major on 1 October 1940.[1] Serving as a military policeman from 1939 until 1942, Gieseke had a solid if unspectacular war, being awarded the Eastern Front Winter War Medal for his service during the 1941–2 campaign in Russia.

On 26 March 1942 Gieseke received orders from the SS Personnel Office to take command of a new Einsatzstab (task force). The headquarters of Einsatzstab Gieseke would be at Dnepropetrovsk, a large industrial city that had been largely cleared of Jews by Jeckeln and Einsatzgruppe C. Organization Todt, Germany's very experienced and efficient construction experts, already had a presence in the city, having worked through the winter of 1941–2 to repair some of the damage inflicted during the fighting to eject the Red Army.

Dnepropetrovsk made sense as the location for the new task force, but why did the authorities select an otherwise undistinguished policeman for a new, and seemingly high-profile, appointment? Gieseke was not even a member of the SS at the time of his appointment. From the trail of correspondence on Gieseke's file emerged a darkly comic tale of mistaken identities.

Apparently, the SS Personnel Office had managed to confuse Walter with his brother, the far more experienced SS Obersturmbannführer

Otto Gieseke.[2] Both Giesekes had been born at Hohenhameln, but Otto was ten years older than Walter. Otto had become a soldier as early as 1910. After the First World War he joined the police in 1920, rising to the rank of major on 1 April 1935. He became a member of the ss on 1 June 1940 and rose to be an Obersturmbannführer in the Waffen-ss on 1 April 1942. He gained rapid promotion, and by 10 June 1944 he had risen to become ss-Brigadeführer and Generalmajor of the Polizei. He won the Iron Cross 1st and 2nd Class, not once but twice, together with the Baltic Cross (1st and 2nd Class), the Infantry Assault Badge in Silver, the German Cross in Gold and the Knights Cross. For much of 1944 he served at Police Headquarters, Reichs-kommissariat Ostland, at Riga – a post that meant working alongside Friedrich Jeckeln. Otto Gieseke survived the war and died at Hannover on 21 July 1958.

From 26 March 1942 the clerks in the ss Personnel Office duti-fully logged correspondence relating to Einsatzstab Gieseke on Walter Gieseke's file until, in August, one of the clerks queried whose file this material ought to be going on. That prompted uproar among the ss bureaucrats – there appeared to be some uncertainty over which Gieseke had been appointed. If they had appointed the wrong man, who was going to tell Heinrich Himmler? On 18 August the Personnel Office in Berlin asked Walter Gieseke to send photographs of himself urgently and to confirm immediately that he had received the request. The photographs sent in reply were those I found stapled to his personnel file.

The photographs also provided the ss Personnel Office with the alarming evidence that they had perhaps appointed the wrong man to lead a project in which the head of the ss was taking a personal interest. No one could have been eager to explain all of this to Himmler person-ally. Instead, it looks as though a cover-up had to be hurriedly cobbled together. At breakneck speed Walter was prepared for induction into the ss. His genealogy was researched as far back as 1750 and accepted as appropriately Aryan.[3] On 10 September 1942 he was accepted into the ss and given the rank of Sturmbannführer. In Himmler's voluminous and detailed desk diary I could find no evidence that he ever met Walter Gieseke. The evidence strongly suggested that, if there had been a mix-up of identities, it was never uncovered or admitted.

While his little drama was being enacted at ss headquarters in Berlin, Walter Gieseke had taken up the command of his Einsatzstab, a rather vague term which can best be translated as 'task force'. The name Einsatzstab Gieseke no doubt gave the new leader a justifiable measure of personal satisfaction, as visible proof that his qualities as a conscientious policeman were at last being recognized in high places, but it offered no clue for future historians as to the type of work on which the unit was engaged. In fact, Gieseke's task force had a role in the important, but rather unexciting, work of road construction.

At that point the research might have been brought to an end. Something had been achieved, much of it against the odds. The location and approximate date of the film had been established and previously unknown officers appearing in it had been identified by name as Hans Döring, Ludolf von Alvensleben and Walter Gieseke. Was any more worthwhile information likely to come to light, or was the whole film nothing more than a piece of self-indulgence showing aspects of the humdrum world of German officers battling against potholes, landslips, drainage ditches, collapsed bridges and minor acts of sabotage? If the activities shown on the screen were to be properly understood, the research had to go on. I needed to find out more about the tasks in which Gieseke and his men were engaged if I wanted to do justice to all the people whose lives were represented by no more than a few flickering images, and to those who had happened to be out of camera shot and were not even selected by chance for that brief moment of posterity. There was also a possibility that the names of other German officers in the film might yet come to light.

SIX

DURCHGANGSTRASSE IV:
HIGHWAY OF THE SS

To understand why an organization like the ss had become involved with road-building in Ukraine in 1942 one has to look again at the painful experience gained by the Germans during the advance into Russia in 1941. One German general remembered well:

Summer, the season in which Operation Barbarossa began, was the most favourable for operations in European Russia. Days were warm, nights cool and only in the southern regions was the heat intense. Moors and swamps dried up, and swampy lowlands that were otherwise impassable during the muddy season could be used by peasant carts and – to a limited degree – by wheeled and tracked vehicles. All roads were passable during the summer, and even driving in open terrain was possible, despite numerous fissures and cracks in the ground. Summer not only dried out roads but reduced the level of rivers and streams as well; rivers could be forded, and smaller streams represented only minor obstacles, even though swampy terrain remained a serious barrier. All arms, therefore, enjoyed optimum mobility. Even in summer, however, weather and terrain created severe challenges for the troops to overcome. Sudden thunderstorms could almost instantly change passable dirt roads and open terrain into mud traps. Once the rain ended and the sun returned, dirt roads dried out rapidly, provided that undisciplined, over-eager drivers had not plowed them up while the roads were still soft. During dry periods, on the other hand, dust wreaked havoc on our motor vehicles. Even our panzers sustained severe damage from the clouds of dust they stirred up while crossing vast sandy regions because many of them had no dust filters, and those so equipped soon became thoroughly clogged.[1]

The Germans were shocked at the poor quality of the Soviet Union's transport infrastructure. Roads disintegrated under the weight of traffic generated by armoured and motorized fighting formations and the logistics echelons essential to keeping them in the field. As early as 19 August 1941 *The Times* was reporting the activities of Organization Todt:

This organization since the campaign in the east began has followed up the German advance with hundreds of thousands of skilled road builders, reinforced by men and women volunteers from the former Baltic States, all equipped with the newest road-building drills, electric hammers, and steam-rollers. New hard roads have been laid.[2]

The task of improving the road system in the western Soviet Union was so enormous that their best efforts made little initial impact on the overall problem. Organization Todt acted as the construction arm of the Nazi state. It was named after Fritz Todt, an ss officer and distinguished civil engineer who had been inspector-general of the German road system since 1933. From 1940 Todt also served as Hitler's Minister of Munitions, until he was killed in an air accident in February 1942.

The onset of winter in the last months of 1941 turned what had been little more than dirt tracks into vast quagmires:

The season of rain and mud, the *rasputitsa*, set in before the middle of October. German ration lorries frequently could not get through, so single-horse farm carts, know as panje wagons (panje was Wehrmacht slang for a Polish or Russian peasant), were commandeered from agricultural communities for hundreds of miles around . . . A Landser would often lose a jackboot, sucked from his leg in the knee-deep mud. Motorcyclists could only advance in places by getting off to haul their vehicles through. Commanders, who never lacked for manpower to push their staff cars through a boggy patch, wondered how anyone could make war in such conditions.[3]

Even as they hurried forward in pursuit of the retreating Russians, some German combat units had to be withdrawn from front-line duty and employed in trying to keep the roads usable. Ukrainians, Jews and some of the vast number of Soviet prisoners of war taken in 1941 were also forced to work on road repairs alongside civilian contractors and experts working for Organization Todt. As the autumn rains and winter freeze set in, the Germans recognised that the state of the roads would impose serious limitations on their ability to prosecute the war in the east. In some places even the dead of the Red Army were tossed into quagmires to try to solidify them, at least temporarily. Other temporary expedients, such as felling trees and laying their trunks transversely across key stretches of road to create so-called 'corduroy roads', required a substantial investment of time and labour. In any case, the rough nature of the temporary road surface severely limited the number and type of vehicles that could use the route.

The German High Command decided that a number of strategic highways would have to be built from west to east across the conquered lands of the Soviet Union, in order to serve the battle front and the supply lines stretching right back to Germany. A similar investment programme would be required to bring the Russian rail system up to an acceptable standard.

One of the key road routes for upgrading was designated *Durchgangstrasse* (highway) IV, often abbreviated to DGIV. Originally established by Catherine the Great at the end of the eighteenth century, this route between Lvov and Stalino was 'unimproved', little more than a poor-quality track prone to dusting in summer and mud in autumn. The road ran through the heart of Ukraine, via Tarnopol, Letichev, Vinnitsa, Gaisin, Uman, Kirovograd, Krivoi-Rog, Dnepropetrovsk and Stalino, along Germany's main axis of advance on the southern sector of the Eastern Front. Ambitious German plans called for the road to be widened to eight metres and tarmacked. Drainage would need to be improved by digging channels.

Even as work was put in hand all along the road, Hitler had a premonition that this project, vital as it would be for the long-term

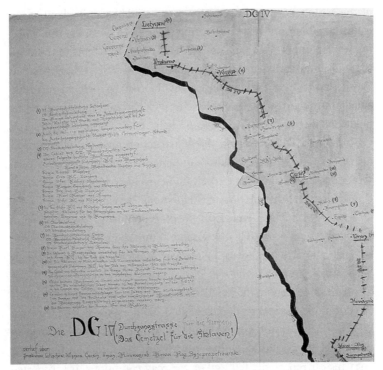

Daghani's map of DGIV.

future of any Nazi empire in the east, ought to focus initially on the immediate military requirements. On 19 February 1942 he told Albert Speer, his new Minister of Armaments and Production in succession to Todt, that any road should only be a temporary expedient, built 'in the most primitive way' with a surface to last '2–3 years'.[4] In practice that meant constructing a road surface from reasonably flat large stones or whatever other surfacing material was available locally. 'Around Krivoi Rog the complete absence of any sort of gravel or suitable stone . . . prevented even an attempt to lay down hard surfaced roads over the deep, soft clay of the region.'[5]

As early as September 1941 Organization Todt had begun establishing seven labour camps along the central section of the road between Vinnitsa and Gaisin.[6] In late 1941 groups of Russian prisoners of war were transferred to Vinnitsa. Work gangs would be sent out from there to smaller camps set up along the length of the road, one approximately every 15 kilometres or so. Under the supervision of the SS each morning forced labourers would be marched out of the camps to labour on the road: cutting stone from quarries; transporting it (sometimes with the use of a light railway system) to the work site; selecting and shaping the stones to form a suitable pavement; and then settling them into the bed of the road to form a reasonably smooth surface. Some would have to pick through the surrounding fields looking for small stones to help bed in the large pieces. Organization Todt managed the construction projects, which drew on the expertise and specialist equipment of major German construction firms such as Arbeitsgemeinschaft Dohrmann KG of Remscheid, Arbeitsgemeinschaft Horst and Jussen of Sinzig, Firma Teeras of Munich, Firma Eras KG of Nuremberg, Firma Ufer of Koblenz-Moselweiss, Firma Kasper-Emmerich of Miesenheim, Firma Fix of Bad Neuenahr, Firma Karl Kaiser of Hanau and Firma Stohr KG of Munich.

Heinrich Himmler, the Reichsführer-SS, had become directly interested in DGIV. He had gained some first-hand experience of the poor state of the roads in Ukraine. While he was making a tour of inspection of SS troops on the southern sector of the Front in December 1941 his car repeatedly fell foul of the road conditions. It is reported that on one occasion Himmler personally had to push the car through the mud. On reaching the headquarters of the SS Division Wiking he ordered them to do more to maintain the roads in their sector of operations.[7]

Perhaps more significantly, Himmler also had his eyes on the economic possibilities the road would eventually open up. He wanted the SS to get involved in commercial ventures to generate profits for use in financing the organization's activities, guarantee its supplies and enable it to act with a certain amount of independence. Thus, early in 1942 Himmler founded the SS-Wirtschafts-Verwaltungshauptamt or WVHA, under the leadership of Oswald Pohl, a 'soft-spoken' former naval officer who had joined the Nazi party in 1926.[8] His deputy was Dr Hans Kammler, one of the mercurial evil talents of the Third Reich. By 1945 Kammler would become one of the most important figures in the SS as the man entrusted with the V-2 rocket development programme. The WVHA acted as the economic and administrative arm of the SS. It was made up of five main groups:

Amtsgruppe A – Finance, Law and Administration
Amtsgruppe B – Supply, Administration and Equipment
Amtsgruppe C – Buildings and Works
Amtsgruppe D – Concentration Camps
Amtsgruppe W – Economics

Amtsgruppe C, of which Kammler was appointed head on 1 February 1942, would provide the overall management and supplies for the work on DGIV.[9] Construction of the road would make a profit for the ss and also help it towards the longer-term goal of controlling the German construction industry, including brick and stone supplies. Civilian firms would carry out the actual road-building, under the guidance and supervision of the ss, with the ss providing the necessary labour and quarried materials. For both labour and hardcore the contractors would have to pay fees to the ss. Most of the money paid for things like rations simply went into ss coffers.

On 7 February 1942 Himmler wrote to Hans Adolf Prützmann, the Higher ss and Police Leader for South Russia (a post he had taken over from Jeckeln in late 1941), ordering him to make arrangements for procuring the labour needed to complete the DGIV project. He was also given formal responsibility for the building of the road. Prützmann, in turn, ordered Oberstleutnant of the gendarmerie Paul Geibel, one of his staff officers, to oversee the work. Himmler formalized the appointment in a note circulated to all commands.[10] Himmler described the road as the *Schwarzmeerstrasse* (Black Sea road) and specified Taganrog, on the Sea of Azov, as its eastern terminus.

Geibel was both a police officer and a member of the ss. After serving in the navy in the First World War, he had joined the SA in December 1931, the police in April 1935 and the ss in July 1938. In 1939 he was promoted to the rank of Obersturmbannführer in the ss.

Himmler's appointment diary shows that a key meeting to discuss the work on DGIV took place in Berlin on the afternoon of 19 February 1942. Attending the meeting were Geibel, Prützmann, Dr Frank, Oberführer Hans Kammler and Arnold Adam for the Organization Todt.[11] Shortly after that meeting, however, Geibel was transferred to new duties. Eventually he rose to become ss and Police Leader in

Poland in March 1944, and he was involved in the heavy fighting which devastated Warsaw in that same year. Captured in Prague in 1945, he was tried by a Polish court and sentenced to life imprisonment in 1954. On 12 November 1966 he committed suicide while still serving his sentence.

Paul Geibel's sudden transfer before he had any opportunity to make his mark on the road construction project meant that the SS had to mount a hurried search for some suitable officer to replace him as overseer of the DGIV project. The replacement was Oberstleutnant of the Gendarmerie Walter Gieseke, the man whose image projected on the cine screen in a Devon church had led me to think of him as The Fat Man.

Whether he realised it or not, Walter Gieseke had been handed an enormous task. The road was planned to run for 1,300 kilometers. He did not have the luxury and personal satisfaction of supervising the whole enterprise from preliminary planning to triumphant completion. He was taking over responsibility for work already in progress at widely scattered points along the entire route of a road that was subjected to continuous heavy traffic. Working under his direction were four Senior Construction Offices (*Oberbauabschnittsleitungen*), headed by SS officers with the title of inspector. One of these was SS Brigadeführer Ludolf von Alvensleben, who was based at Vinnitsa. Others were at Kirovograd, Krivoi-Rog and Stalino. Below the Senior Construction Offices were a number of Subsidiary Construction Offices (*Bauabschnittsleitungen*) at Letichev, Gaisin, Uman, Novo-Ukrinka, Alexandriya, Sofiyevka, Gurovka, Dnepropetrovsk, Grishno, Pavlograd and Makieyevska. There were also several local offices (*Streckenbauleitung*) scattered along the route of the road. Alongside each of the main SS offices would be an Organization Todt office. They drew up the actual construction plans and then the various German private firms would be brought in to carry out the construction as required. The working relationship between the SS, Organization Todt and private contractors was occasionally less than completely harmonious. Some of the German civilians working on the project were not always in full agreement with the methods employed by the SS.

This great civil engineering undertaking would require vast quantities of labour. Between 110,000 and 140,000 men and women would be needed during 1942.[12] They were drawn from three main sources. Some 50,000 labourers came from the huge numbers of Soviet prisoners of war captured during the summer of 1941.[13] As the Soviet government had never signed the Geneva Convention the German military felt that they were under no obligation to ensure civilized treatment for Russian prisoners of war. About 85 per cent of all the Russian prisoners died in German hands as a result of poor treatment and disease. This was especially pronounced during the winter of 1941–2 when hundreds of thousands of Soviet soldiers taken prisoner during the opening stages of Operation Barbarossa starved or froze to death. This was not death by neglect in the strict sense of the term. German policy towards Soviet prisoners was deliberately brutal from the outset. An order to murder Commissars and NKVD secret police on capture had been given on 6 June 1941. As Karel Berkhoff has argued:

> The shootings of the Red Army commissars and other Soviet POW's, along with the subsequent starvation of millions more, constituted a single process that started in the middle of 1941 and lasted until at least the end of 1942. Moreover, we may call it a genocidal massacre.[14]

Before the end of 1941 the first Soviet prisoners of war had been put to work on the road. They were usually organized in units of 1000 men formed into four 250-man companies. The prisoners turned out to be unsuitable for three reasons: they were in no fit condition for heavy manual labour; they were susceptible to outbreaks of disease; and they had no incentive or desire to help the Germans. The death rate for Soviet prisoners of war working on DGIV was undoubtedly high. For example, of 1,052 prisoners allotted to the 45th Construction Troop at the end of 1941, 183 were dead and 174 were sick by the time Gieseke was put in charge of the project in March 1942.[15] Hitler himself later recognized that serious mistakes were being made in the treatment of prisoners required for labour details. In August 1942 Field Marshal Keitel 'promised to allocate immediately 6,000 Russian POWS organised in building battalions for the construction of the Mo-Fauske railway'. Hitler advised that increased food rations should be given for this job in order to ensure full work by POWs even in bad climatic conditions . . . for by appropriate feeding the amount of work done can be doubled and the number of labourers halved, thus facilitating housing, clothing and supplies in general. Clothing too should be suitable for the climate.[16]

Hitler's comments were a belated recognition of the mistakes of the past. The importance of labour by prisoners of war on DGIV and elsewhere had not been properly appreciated and a potentially valuable resource had been squandered. Hitler only recognized the value of prisoners in terms of their temporary ability to labour. He later confirmed that eventually 'all prisoners would be ill-treated and killed anyway'.[17]

Experience of the inadequacy of Soviet prisoners of war as road labourers led the Germans to press into service a large number of Ukranian civilians – possibly 50,000 or so. In 1942 Ukrainians had no long-term future in Hitler's vision of an Aryan utopia, but in the short term, at least, they could be useful as an uneducated labouring class. Indeed, the labour reserves of Ukraine constituted an enormous potential economic asset and there was considerable competition to control its use. The German Labour Ministry wanted substantial numbers of Ukrainians to come to Germany to work in factories, agriculture and domestic service. Promises of a better life in Germany proved hollow for those Ukrainians who were prepared to leave their homeland voluntarily. Only by the use of force could the necessary numbers be rounded up and transported to Germany. However, these deportations threatened to cause difficulties for Organization Todt and other German projects which needed Ukrainian labour in the areas behind the German front. Eventually a deal had to be brokered between the competing ministries in Berlin. The German Labour Ministry undertook not to deport Ukrainians from villages, towns and cities within 25 kilometres of the road. Labour available in the vicinity of the road was reserved for the use of the SS, Organization Todt and the German construction companies working on DGIV.

The actual procedure by which Ukrainians were persuaded or compelled to work on the road is not clear. The use of force was undoubtedly implicit, if not explicit. The nature of the relationship was probably understood on both sides, removing the need for anything other than an informal understanding about the work which had to be completed, and the possible consequences if workers were not forthcoming. In a harsh and uncertain world, work on a road near their own homes must have seemed a far more attractive proposition than being carted off to work in far off Germany. Some tangible rewards were also on offer. Working conditions for Ukrainians were undoubtedly better than those for the prisoners of war and Jews forced to work alongside them. SS Oberführer Jurgen Stroop later recalled:

> The workers were divided into groups made up of men and women from sovkhozy and kolkhozy near the surrounding villages. The crews were paid on a piece-work basis. When the order came to speed up construction, we paid the road construction workers more than the others and they also got more tobacco, sugar, textiles, and metal wares.[18]

The supply of prisoners of war and Ukranian forced labour was still regarded as inadequate for a huge undertaking such as DGIV. Desperate for more workers, the Germans turned towards considering the possibility of using Jewish labour. In the second half of 1941 police units and Einsatzgruppen had murdered thousands of able-bodied Jews who might have supplemented the workforce in Ukraine. In 1942 the Germans were glad that some Ukrainian Jews had survived and could be forced to work on the road. As the ghettos in towns such as Uman were liquidated in the first half of 1942, Jews fit for work were sent off to the work camps servicing DGIV. Those not fit for hard manual labour were murdered immediately. In time, as the Ukrainian Jews succumbed to the harsh conditions under which they had to work, Romanian Jews would also be brought in to labour on the road. All told, some 25,000 Jews would be murdered or worked to death on the Street of the SS, an alternative name applied to DGIV.[19]

One of the most critical areas in dispute between historians concerns the origins and development of the Holocaust in 1941. Some have maintained that, with the invasion of Russia in July, Hitler was ready to move towards his long-held goal of the total extermination of the Jewish population in all areas controlled by Germany. Verbal orders and warnings about the Jews were issued before the invasion. This has led some Holocaust scholars to argue that, from the outset of the invasion, it was German policy to move towards the final solution of the Jewish question. However, so haphazard was the treatment of Jews in the occupied areas of Russia in July–August 1941 that this is open to question. In some areas during this period very little happened to the Jewish population; in others there were certainly mass killings, but not on the scale necessary to effect genocide.

By late 1941, however, a full-scale programme of extermination was in progress in the captured territories of the Soviet Union. The actions of particular individuals such as Friedrich Jeckeln seem to have tipped the balance to a point where Himmler began to give verbal orders to encourage others to put into effect a final solution of the Jewish problem. During late 1941 many thousands of Jews were murdered in Ukraine. At Babi Yar, outside Kiev, almost 34,000 Jews were murdered between 29 and 30 September 1941. The process of killing would go on throughout the following months to raise the murder total to over 100,000. Even so, by the end of 1941, as Berlin received regular reports that parts of Ukraine were now 'free of Jews', Nazi policy was incoherent to the point where there was still some talk of using Ukraine as a dumping ground for the resettlement of Jews from other parts of Europe.

In late November 1941 arrangements were made to hold a conference in a large villa at Wannsee, in the suburbs of Berlin. Attending the conference would be senior figures from the Reich Security Main Office (Reichssicherheitshauptamt, RSHA) and representatives from other relevant government departments. It is probable that the initial purpose of the meeting was to discuss the deportation of German Jews. However, the purpose of the meeting was transformed by Hitler's decision in December 1941 to aim at nothing less than the extermination of the Jewish nation.[20] Thus when the meeting was finally convened on 20 January 1942 the discussions about the Jewish problem and the murder of the Jewish people were extensive and far-reaching. The conference established the principle that, in addition to more direct and immediate methods of murder, large numbers of Jews could be engaged on construction projects. The minutes recorded:

Under proper direction the Jews should now in the course of the Final Solution [*Endloesung*] be brought to the East in a suitable way for use as labor. In big labor gangs, with separation of the sexes, the Jews capable of work are brought to these areas and employed in road building, in which task undoubtedly a great part will fall out through natural diminution [*natuerliche Verminderung*].[21]

Daniel Goldhagen has pointed to three key reasons why the Nazis wanted to employ Jewish labour:

1. Slave labour could provide a means to exterminate large numbers of Jews. In early 1942 the Nazis had not yet fixed on mass gassing as the primary means to effect the final solution of the Jewish problem. Working Jews to death, alongside mass shootings and mobile gas vans, was just one of a number of methods of murder which the Nazis were ready to employ.

2. Anti-Semites would derive some emotional satisfaction in forcing those previously perceived as work-shy to engage in heavy manual labour on behalf of the Reich.

3. There was a practical desire to get from the Jewish community 'the greatest possible economic contribution to the winning of the war'.[22]

In employing Jewish labour the ultimate aim remained the death of all Jews, but a secondary objective would be to utilize, for as short a period as possible, Jewish labour to carry through some key construction projects necessary for the development and defence of the Reich. Rations for Jewish labourers would be kept to starvation level and there would be no medical care. Jewish slave labourers would be worked until they either died of disease, malnutrition and heavy work, or became so enfeebled that they were no longer considered to be worth even their meagre rations. They would then be executed, usually close to their place of forced labour.

The tensions in German policy between productive employment and extermination were never resolved, and it was left to local officials overseeing particular projects to determine which of the two goals deserved a purely temporary priority. One author has concluded that '"extermination through work" . . . [has] little use as an analytical tool'.[23] This area, like much of Holocaust literature, remains contentious.

Even before the Wannsee Conference, German officials in Ukraine had begun to use Jewish labour. A network of camps was set up to house labourers working on the large-scale construction programmes planned for the region. Road construction was considered vital both to the support of the troops at the front and the future economic exploitation of Ukraine. In some places, such as Letichev, the ss would utilize labourers from the Jewish ghettos which had been established in some of the larger towns and cities. The list of camps and ghettos gives some impression of the scale of the undertaking: Friedrichkowka, Pawlikowce, Proskurow, Leznievo, Letichev, Lityn, Gniwan, Winnica, Niemirow, Berezowka, Bugakow, Zarudynce, Czukow, Braclaw (two camps), Raj-Gorod, Nz. Kropiwna, Tarrasiwka, Mikhailowka, Kiblicz, Karabelowka, Narajewka, Krasnopolka, Teplik, Iwangorod, Uditsch, Talajewka, Orodowka, Ostina and Uman.

Within the camps and ghettos the ss ensured that conditions would inevitably destroy the health of the slave labourers. Hard labour, either on the road or in the quarries which serviced it, combined with inadequate food, invariably opened the door to illness and contagious diseases such as typhus. Individual murders of Jews too sick to work were combined with mass actions designed to liquidate ghettos such as Letichev or dispose of substantial numbers of Jews suffering with infectious diseases. Large-scale killings of Jews were usually preceded by the opening of mass graves, dug by the Jews themselves or by Ukrainians.

Remarkably, the Cullompton film features a few frames showing a pit being dug under military supervision. The pit is clearly substantial and the fact that the labourers are working under an armed guard is suggestive. After a few frames showing the pit the screen goes blank. After a few moments of black screen, the action resumes on the other side of the pit as a senior German officer advances on

The pit.

the commander of the guard. There is a sharp exchange of salutes. The passage of events perhaps points to a shouted warning to stop filming and a senior officer's reassurance to a non-commissioned officer that the cameraman is acting under his personal direction. This handful of frames point to both the significance of the pit and the sensitivity of those associated with its excavation.

As Wendy Lower has described, 'Some Ukrainians who lived near the forced labour camps of DGIV brought food to the prisoners and signalled when a massacre was imminent because they saw the death pits being prepared nearby.'[24] Despite the official Nazi anti-Semitism, Jewish labour on the road was highly regarded by some German supervisors. Rudolf Wolters, one of Speer's managers, was very favourably impressed:

> Everywhere along our street . . . work is going on at full speed. The crews of foreigners are working here under the command of the German OT men. In terms of quality, the Jews are in first place. We have been told that some of them volunteer to work two shifts in a row. They know what's at stake now.[25]

The Nazi dream of an empire to provide *Lebensraum* for an Aryan master race had to be modified in practice to cope with the reality of a serious manpower shortage. That problem was not confined to employments, such as road construction, which involved heavy manual labour. Russia was such a huge country that the Germans soon discovered that they had insufficient men for maintaining internal security. Like it or not, the Nazi concept of Aryan perfection and purity had to be broadened to embrace branches of the human race which could not claim to share the full Aryan genetic inheritance. In the Baltic States the Germans had been greeted as liberators and saviours from the evils of Communism. Lithuanian, Latvian and Estonian nationalists were eager to work with the Germans in order to pursue the goal of local autonomy. The German military authorities had been glad to use that enthusiasm to form auxiliary military units known as Schutzmannschaften, usually equipping them with weapons and uniforms captured from the Soviet Army or even dating from the period before the Soviet occupation of the Baltic States.[26]

In addition to the local people forced to labour on the road, some Ukrainians whose sympathies lay with the Germans found themselves acting as guards to the workforce. In Ukraine the German authorities recruited a number of military, police and auxiliary units. No doubt some of these Ukrainians in German uniform joined for a variety of political motives such as nationalism, anti-Bolshevism, anti-Semitism or admiration of Nazism, while others merely calculated the personal advantages of being on what seemed to be the winning side.

> Some of these units were subsequently incorporated into the *Schutzmannschaften der Ordnungspolizei* or '*Schuma*', the auxiliary paramilitary police force recruited to serve under German Higher ss & Police Leaders in the occupied territories . . . There were about 71 Ukrainian *Schuma* battalions in all, raised at different times for anti-partisan purposes, and including some Cossack and artillery units.[27]

The Schutzmannschaften reinforced the unit charged with protecting the 5,000 or so Germans working on the road. That task was delegated to *Polizeisicherungsabteilung an der DGIV*, which was commanded by Major George Muhlmann and later Captain Paul Tillman. The police security department was made up of a headquarters staff and four companies – some 546 men or thereabouts.

Protection was also provided, at various times, by such units such as 444 and 454 Security Divisions and by certain Schutzmannschaft battalions of anti-Russian Lithuanians and Latvians. For example, in mid-1942 Schuma Battalion 4 was based in Stalino, Schuma Battalion 7 in Vinnitsa, Schuma Battalion 8 in Uman, Schuma Battalions 17, 23 and 268 in Dnepropetrovsk, and Schuma Battalions 27 and 28 in Krivoi-Rog.[28] These Schutzmannschaft battalions established a reputation for savagery among the workers.

Security became an increasingly important issue. At the beginning of 1942 scattered acts of resistance across Ukraine were developing into attacks by well-armed partisan bands that controlled increasingly large rural areas. For example, in July 1942 Gruppe Geheime Feldpolizei 721, operating to the north-east of Kiev between Neshin and Konotop, shot 24 partisans and 18 others for aiding the partisans.[29] They also recovered 20 rifles, a light machine gun and a variety of pistols to underline the claim that the dead men were partisans. The following month they shot 18 partisans and 26 people for aiding them.[30] At the same time Gruppe Geheime Feldpolizei 708, operating to the north of 721's area of operation, killed 54 partisans.[31] Both units were struggling to deal with the partisan threat to road and rail communications in their areas. Increasingly, DGIV and the camps which served it would become very tempting targets for the partisan bands.

By 1942, according to an estimate by Richard Breitman, something like 18,000 men were serving in the different Schutzmannschaft battle units.[32] Deployed throughout the occupied territories, the Schutzmannschaften played a key role in supporting the Einsatzgruppen and German security units engaged in the murder of Jews and other groups classed as 'undesirables'. Indeed, imbued with radical anti-Semitism, many Schutzmannschaften were to prove particularly cruel. Their savagery was heightened by the inadequacy of their pay, which they sought to supplement by extorting money or valuables from Jews and other victims. In December 1942 1,000 of the Schutzmannschaften were allowed to join the regular German police battalions, and on 23 January 1943 Hitler gave his formal approval for the formation of Latvian and Lithuanian Legions within the SS. Approval followed for the formation of a Ukrainian (Galician) SS Division, and other SS units were recruited from various anti-Russian nationalities living in the Caucasus.

Wherever the actual battlefront was located during the roller coaster of advance and retreat, DGIV remained a strategically vital artery, and Walter Gieseke and his Einsatzstab, Organization Todt, their various protection units and the army of forced labourers continued playing their essential roles. Increasingly, Soviet partisans menaced road traffic throughout Ukraine, and attacks on the network of labour camps became more frequent. To meet the growing threat, further Schutzmannschaft battalions, Cossack and Ukrainian, were deployed. For example, Schuma Battalion 124 (Ukrainian) was based in Kirovograd, Schuma Battalions 134 (Ukrainian), 135 (Cossack) and 159 (Cossack) in Krivoi-Rog, and Schuma Battalion 160 (Cossack) in Stalino.[33]

In spite of prodigious efforts, progress on the road was considerably slower than the ss had hoped. In 1943 the SSPF for Lvov gave an overview of developments in his area since 1941:

There was, first of all, work on the urgently needed reconstruction of DGIV, which was extremely important for the entire southern section of the Front and which was in catastrophically bad condition. On October 15, 1941, a start was made on the building of camps along the railroad tracks, and after a few weeks, despite considerable difficulties, 7 camps had been put up, containing 4,000 Jews. More camps soon followed, so that in a very short period of time the completion of 15 such camps could be reported to the Higher ss and Police Leader. About 20,000 Jewish laborers passed through these camps in the course of time. Despite all conceivable difficulties that turned up on this project, about 160 km. have now been completed.[34]

That figure of 160 kilometres would, of course, merely have been for the Lvov sector in Poland, not over the complete highway right across to Taganrog.

Constructing the road involved the labour of 50,000 prisoners of war, 50,000 Ukrainians and 10,000 Jews at any one time in 1942. The majority of the skilled labour was provided by 5,000 specialists brought in from Germany. In 1943 the total number of labourers needed on the road fell to around 70,000. They were guarded by

12,000 men from the Schutzmannschaften.[35] A post-war German court estimated that 25,000 Jewish workers on the road were shot.[36] There are no estimates for the number of prisoners of war who must also have perished from shootings, disease, starvation and freezing temperatures while working on the road. In late 1942, as particular sections of the road were completed, some of the labour camps were liquidated and their inhabitants murdered. However, 'a small number of camps (such as that at Tarrasiwka) remained in operation . . . until December 1943.'[37]

In addition to the task of building DGIV, Einsatzstab Gieseke was also made responsible for repairing a dam at Zaporozhe. The dam, which had been blown up by Soviet engineers during their retreat in 1941, had been constructed in the 1930s as part of the Russian Five-Year Plans. It was one of the great triumphs of Soviet engineering, providing hydro-electric power across Ukraine, and it became one of the great symbols of Soviet industrialization.[38] Under Einsatzstab Gieseke the dam was rapidly repaired and brought back into production. One of the wonders of Stalin's Russia became one of the wonders of the new Nazi empire in the east.

Even if he had only been appointed as a result of some confusion of identities in the SS Personnel Office, Walter Gieseke seems to have shown impressive leadership, energy and competence in tackling the important jobs delegated to him, both in road-building and in other construction projects. Nevertheless, Einsatzstab Gieseke encountered

The pit – the salute.

daunting problems in finding enough labour, maintaining the work force in the face of high death rates, a shortage of steel and other building materials, interdepartmental rivalries, partisan attacks and having to rely on a motley collection of guard units which varied as much in quality as they did in nationality.

Coping with those problems would have given Einsatzstab Gieseke enough headaches if they had been working in a very quiet sector, but that was not to be. While Gieseke grappled with his new road-building, Hitler and the German High Command were grappling with the even bigger problems of planning their 1942 summer offensive. The rapid advance of 1941 followed by serious setbacks during the harsh winter of 1941–2, had made them realize that expectations of a speedy total victory over the Russians were not going to be fulfilled. They no longer had the resources to take the offensive at every point along the whole length of the huge Russian Front. Instead, they planned to concentrate their main effort in the southern sector. Ukraine would provide the locations from which the offensive would be launched, and that meant an increase in the volume of traffic along DGIV, as it had to serve as one of the main arteries carrying men and war materials to sustain a renewed drive to the east.

During the winter of 1941–2 the front line in eastern Ukraine had been stabilized. It ran from Taganrog, the planned terminal of DGIV on the Sea of Azov, in a generally north-northwesterly direction to Izyum, Belgorod, Kursk and Orel. After checking a Russian 'spoiling' offensive towards Kharkov in May 1942, the Germans launched their own offensive on 28 June. In the first five weeks they advanced as far as the general line of the river Don from Voronezh southwards, and had taken Rostov, at the mouth of the Don, where they forced a crossing of the river to invade the northern Caucasus. By mid-October the Germans had reached the river Volga at Stalingrad, where they became engaged in an attritional battle in their determination to capture the final strip of smouldering ruins, all that remained of the city named after the Russian generalissimo. Their incursion into the Caucasus had also been greatly extended to take in Maikop, Mozdok and Elista and the Black Sea port of Novorossisk. At the furthest penetration they were over 400 miles from their starting point at Taganrog.

At that time it looked as though, once the Germans finally managed to drive the Russians from the west bank of the Volga at Stalingrad, they would be able to occupy the whole of the river bank as far south as Astrakhan, where the Volga runs into the Caspian Sea. In the Caucasus there seemed nothing to prevent them pushing forward to the western shore of the Caspian down as far as Baku and its important oilfields. Then, isolated from the rest of the Soviet Union, the republics of the southern Caucasus (Georgia, Azerbaijan and Armenia) would be there for the taking. The empire that was to provide *Lebensraum*, coal, wheat and oil appeared to be virtually within Germany's grasp. An optimistic planner might have been forgiven for thinking that, in the long term, DGIV would need to be extended from Taganrog to Baku.

If the Germans could establish a firm defensive front along the Don, the Volga and the Caspian Sea, Hitler hoped to provide security for both the wheatfields of Ukraine and the oilfields of Baku. He reasoned that, with access to both those key resources, Germany would prove virtually impossible for her enemies to defeat. Pursuit of both objectives overstretched his armies to the point where neither objective was attained, however. As more and more troops were drawn into the protracted struggle for Stalingrad, the Germans simply did not have the resources to exploit fully their incursion into the northern Caucasus.

With the onset of winter the Russians, backed by seemingly inexhaustible resources in manpower and weaponry, were preparing their own counter offensive. On 19 November 1942 they stormed across the Don, broke through in a wide enveloping movement, and by 22 November the German 6th Army at Stalingrad was encircled. Forbidden by Hitler to attempt a break-out to the west, the encircled troops suffered heavy casualties within a steadily shrinking perimeter until the 94,000 frozen and starving survivors were finally compelled to surrender to the Russians on 30 January 1943.

The German troops in the northern Caucasus were threatened with a similar fate if their opponents managed to cut them off from Ukraine by breaking through to the mouth of the Don at Rostov. Fierce fighting kept open a corridor, however, while they beat a precipitate retreat. By the middle of February they had completely abandoned the Caucasus except for the substantial '*Gotenkopf*' bridgehead which they still held along the lower reaches of the Kuban river. The bridgehead was intended to provide a convenient springboard for a renewed offensive at some future date, but with their backs to the Black Sea and the Sea of Azov, the German troops would have to rely on supplies being ferried across the Kerch Strait from the Crimea.

The surrender at Stalingrad and the flight from the Caucasus dealt a shattering blow to German forces on the Eastern Front. An army of 250,000 first-class troops, with all their equipment, had been needlessly squandered. They had been betrayed by Hitler's stubborn refusal to yield territory, betrayed by the High Command's reluctance to challenge Hitler's intuitive decisions, and betrayed by Marshal Göring's assurances that the surrounded army could be supplied from the air if necessary. Psychologically these events also had far-reaching significance. The German people began to realize that their confidence in final victory might have been misplaced and their leading generals knew that they had been too trusting in Hitler's military acumen.

By the middle of March 1943 the front line in eastern Ukraine lay roughly where it had been twelve months earlier. Anchored on the north shore of the Sea of Azov at Taganrog, it ran for about 500 miles in a generally northerly or northwesterly direction. In mid-February the advancing Russians had taken the important city of Kharkov and surged forward almost as far as Dnepropetrovsk, location of the headquarters for Einsatzstab Gieseke and the other agencies involved in roadbuilding on DGIV. Just when all seemed lost, a brilliant German counterattack recovered Kharkov and pushed the line back in the direction of Izyum and Belgorod. That success represented a triumph for the tenacity and superb generalship of the German army in adversity. Perhaps victory over the Russians might still be achievable with one more superhuman effort.

SEVEN

THE FILM-MAKERS

A study of the titanic military campaigns of 1942 and 1943 gave me some indication of how the work of Walter Gieseke and his task force fitted in to the sweep of complex events, but there was still a worrying question mark against the short film which had aroused my interest. When had the actual filming taken place? Images of the harvest being gathered in and of sunflowers in full bloom suggested July or August as the months in which the film must have been shot, and 1942 looked to be the most likely year. That was the year of Germany's greatest military successes in Russia. In both 1941 and 1943 the harvest period was marked by fighting in Ukraine. The German officers in the film exuded such self-belief and confidence that it seemed improbable that it could have been shot after the great German defeat at Stalingrad in January 1943. Surely German officers would hardly have appeared so confident after a defeat of such magnitude?

Remarkably, the United States Holocaust Memorial Museum showed me where I might be able to establish the year with certainty. Comparative analysis of the film had already taken me through a considerable footage of German propaganda film shot during the Second World War. That analysis had confirmed that the Devon film was very different from the standard German newsreels. While waiting for the production of documents at the Holocaust Museum, I looked on their electronic catalogue to see whether they had further film footage which I might examine for purposes of comparison. Intriguingly, there was mention of a sixteen-reel film entitled *Ukraine 1943*, the original of which was held at the United States National Archives II at College Park.[1] The reel descriptions indicated that the film had been shot in the same broad area of southern Ukraine as the Devon

One of the film-makers directs a harvest scene.

film. Indeed, in some cases there was clear overlap of locations. Dnepropetrovsk, the site of Einsatzstab Gieseke's headquarters, featured in both films. The catalogue also suggested similarities in theme, with both films making a feature of peasant life and farming in Ukraine.

By the time I had viewed the first four reels I was convinced that *Ukraine 1943* and the reel which had turned up so mysteriously in Reg Whitton's film collection at Cullompton were linked in some way. *Ukraine 1943* had obviously been shot by someone who knew their trade behind the camera. The Devon film was noticeably more uneven in quality but in its best sequences it was of the same standard as the film in Washington. Strikingly similar techniques – from close-ups of peasants through to upward tilting shots of impressive large buildings – had been employed in both films. Even more revealingly, the maker of both films had been interested in artistic shots of fields of sunflowers.

It was established that the Washington film had been shot by two German female film-makers. In several of the shots one or other of the women was visible, taking still photographs or helping to organize the action in front of the cine camera. With this piece of information in mind, I examined the Devon film again with great care; and there, in the corner of one of the shots, was a well-dressed woman directing a scene involving some peasant women gathering in the harvest. Although her face was indistinct, her presence seemed to confirm the likelihood of a link between the Devon and Washington films. The coincidences were too numerous to ignore. Some enquiries in the relevant forums on the Internet soon produced names for the two film-makers: Margot Monnier and Tilde Holz. Holz was the camerawoman and Monnier the director. Both were connected to the Deutsche Frauenschaft, one of the Nazi party's women's organizations.

Their rather scanty personnel files, subsequently obtained from the Bundesarchiv in Berlin, showed that Holz had worked her way up through the cine film industry in the 1930s.[2] Starting as a film processing assistant, she had risen to the point where she had her own business and could become a film-maker in her own right for the National Socialist Frauenschaft (the National Socialist Women's League). In the mid-1930s she had used her connections with the Nazis to get 16mm films processed and prints made (sometimes in quite sizable volumes). Her connection to the Nazi party and its goals seems to have been no more than tenuous, even if it was also commercially useful. Her role in the making of *Ukraine 1943* appeared to be almost exclusively technical, providing the essential skills in handling the camera.

Meanwhile, Margot Monnier, born Hadamovsky on 31 December 1908 and married to Heinz Monnier on 8 July 1938, turned out to be a rather more interesting figure.[3] She had joined the Nazi party in June 1931 (party number 573,627), and she became one of the leading figures in the Frauenschaft, founded in the same year.[4] A key organization within the party, the Women's League was intended to ensure that women were as politically committed and radicalized as men in the new Germany. In practice that meant promoting the message of support for Hitler, the Nazi party and Germany while preserving absolute adherence to the traditional roles of the German *Hausfrau*.

Part of the propaganda mission of the Women's League would be delivered through the use of film. Cine films and projection equipment were available on loan across the regional sub-districts of the Frauenschaft. Films made by the League depicted women's work and lives. In 1942 Monnier and Holz were sent to Romania to make a film about the lives of the ethnic Germans (*Volksdeutsche*) who lived there. From the content of the Washington film, it might be inferred that in 1943 they were asked to conduct a similar exercise in Ukraine, focusing on the lives of German women (both those serving with the

German armed forces and the *Volksdeutsche*). In the Devon film there were several images of women's work and life: peasant women gathering in the harvest; women typists working at Gieseke's headquarters; Gieseke entertaining off-duty German women.

What turned out to be of possibly equal significance was the identity of Margot Monnier's older brother, Eugen Hadamovsky. An early supporter of the Nazis, he had served as assistant to Joseph Goebbels in the party's propaganda machine. He had particular responsibility for radio and he played a leading role in organizing Nazi rallies.[5] His appointment as National Programming Director for German Radio after Hitler came to power in January 1933 was a reward for his efforts and loyalty. He wrote seven propaganda books, including *Propaganda and National Power* in 1933.[6] In 1940 he served for a short time as a war correspondent for the Luftwaffe, earning in the process an Iron Cross (1st Class). From 1942 to 1944 he was chief of staff in the Reichspropagandaleitung (Central Propaganda Office) in Berlin. At the end of the war Hadamovsky joined the 4th ss Polizei Division as an Obersturmführer and was killed in action in March 1945.

It was probably under the authority of Hadamovsky's office that his sister began making the film of Ukraine in 1943. The diary of Joseph Goebbels confirmed his respect for his National Programming Director for German Radio, but it also revealed that by the end of 1942 their relationship had deteriorated over Hadamovsky's ambitions to extend the activities of the Reichspropagandaleitung. The entry for 12 December 1942 highlighted the growing tension:

I talked about the Party's Reich Propaganda Office with Hadamovsky. He is on the wrong track at present since he has no real connection with me. He is trying to set up his own movie production and radio broadcasts in the Reich Propaganda Office. I consider that quite wrong. While the war is on we just can't afford to have both, a production looked after by the Reich and on top of it a production looked after by the Party. We lack the necessary personnel and also the material. Hadamovsky just wouldn't see the point and I had to be pretty tough to bring him to his senses. I must draw Hadamovsky over to my side to get him back on the right track.[7]

Conflicts between the institutions of the party and the German state were one of hallmarks of the Nazi period, but the comment in the diary left open the possibility that Hadamovsky had got his sister involved in an ambitious film project in Ukraine that was part of his ongoing differences with Goebbels. Hadamovsky's ultimate fate, being sent to fight and die on the Russian front, suggests that the difference of opinion between the two men may have led to a dramatic conclusion.

With knowledge of Hadamovsky's involvement, it was not difficult to speculate about how Gieseke might have come into contact with the two women film-makers. Their presence in Ukraine, especially when one of them was so well connected, might very quickly have come to his attention as the man in charge of security along the vital strategic highway DGIV. In addition, they might have requested the help of motor mechanics attached to Gieseke's headquarters. The women's travels throughout Ukraine would undoubtedly have required their vehicle to undergo routine maintenance and repair. In the Washington film there were shots of their car being serviced. After the opening sequence of the Devon film the camera's attention rapidly turns to the motor pool and to images of cars being serviced at Gieseke's headquarters. Gieseke would have felt obliged to extend the hospitality of his command to the two women. It would probably have pleased him that his command would have something of a starring role in the film they were making.

While this hypothetical narrative of events seemed perfectly credible, it was hard to account for the disjunctures:

1. If the film found in Devon really was shot by the two women, why was it not of uniformly high quality? Was it, in some way, a product of Holz's well-honed professional skills combined with some other decidedly amateurish camera work by Gieseke and/or one of his subordinates?
2. If sixteen rolls of film had ended up as war booty in the hands of the US Army in 1945, and later sent back to Washington, how had the canister containing the Devon reel become separated from the main body of the film? Why had that reel enjoyed a separate and seemingly more clandestine life?

3. While the Washington film remained in the form of unedited rushes, the Devon film looked like an edited print.

Hypothetical answers to these questions include the possibility that the film-makers had gone about their task rather half-heartedly in the case of the Gieseke reel. Perhaps The Fat Man had been a rather persuasive but over-demanding host when it came to putting himself and his command before the camera. Perhaps the film-makers decided that the reel was of such poor quality that it could be discarded. Perhaps they decided in 1945 that the Gieseke reel, with its potentially incriminating connections to unfortunate events in the east, ought to be allowed to 'disappear'. Perhaps on return to Germany they cut Gieseke a rough print of what he had asked them to film, either for his own pleasure or to impress his superiors with evidence of his hard work in Ukraine. Perhaps Holz, using her connections in the film processing industry, helped Gieseke to get a print of his film made. Possibly she put into the print some additional footage that she had shot herself while engaged on the film project for Monnier and her brother.

The last possibility was particularly intriguing. Was Gieseke in trouble in some way with those above him? Did he think that he needed to prepare visible evidence of his effectiveness as project man-ager on DGIV? Or was someone above Gieseke taking a personal interest in the affairs of his command? Did someone want to see evidence, other than command reports from Gieseke himself, about progress on the road? Could the politics surrounding Gieseke's command offer any clues as to why our female film-makers might have been given another brief while in the middle of shooting material for the National Socialist Women's League? With unanswered, and possibly unanswer-able, questions such as these spinning around in my head, I needed to look elsewhere for fresh sources of information about Walter Gieseke and his role in Ukraine.

EIGHT

THE ROMANIAN CONNECTION

THE Red Army's westward advance during 1943, not just in Ukraine but all along the Russian Front, began to arouse understandable apprehension among Germany's allies in Eastern Europe. One of the most important of those allies was Romania, a country which had slipped without resistance into the German orbit. During 1940 the connection had not worked out to Romania's advantage. Under German pressure, she was compelled to cede Transylvania to Hungary and southern Dobrudja to Bulgaria, while Bessarabia and northern Bukovina had to be handed over to Russia in the face of threats from that country. Romania lost approximately one-third of her territory as a result of those changes, King Carol abdicated and, under the nominal rule of King Michael, his nineteen-year-old successor, General Ion Antonescu was appointed prime minister with dictatorial powers. Antonescu immediately signed a pact pledging Romania's support for Nazi Germany.[1]

Anti-Semitism was widespread in Romania. In July 1940, as Romanian troops withdrew from the lands that were to be ceded to the Russians, they had taken out their frustration on Jewish communities. One witness to the withdrawal later listed the atrocities he had heard about:

> In Comonesti-Suceava, the Zisman siblings were shot dead after being thrown out of a train. Rabbi Laib Schachter and his two sons were first tortured and then murdered on the edge of the village. The rabbi's wife was shot dead while at prayer. Sloime Mendler was bayoneted in the nape; in Cariniceni (Radauti county), the Aizic siblings and Burah Wassermann were shot dead by a group of

eight soldiers led by an infantry sergeant; Mendel Weinstein, Maratieve and Strul Feigenbaum were murdered in Adancata; Moise Rudich, landowner, in Gaureni-Suceava; M. Hibner, his wife and son, Iosub Hibner, and his four grandchildren were killed by soldiers and peasants in Igesti-Suceava.[2]

Romanian anti-Semitism was given free rein under the Antonescu dictatorship. In January 1941 an organized pogrom in Bucharest resulted in widespread damage to property and the deaths of 125 Jews. The Jewish community was also forced to pay higher taxes and more than 84,000 Jews were compelled to provide free labour to the Romanian state as and when required.

The pogrom was part of wider political developments. On 21 January Antonescu faced an attempted putsch from the Iron Guard, an ultra-right-wing movement, and he only managed to regain control in Bucharest with German assistance. Antonescu was a realist who must have calculated the extent to which he needed to reach an accommodation with the Nazi ss in order to maintain his hold on power. In March 1941 Himmler's personal envoys visited Bucharest to discuss the future of Romania's Jews. In those discussions the Romanian authorities were assured that the Nazis were planning a pan-European solution to the Jewish problem.[3] Antonescu's representatives were happy to indicate Romania's willingness to comply with the German plan and to give assurances about General Antonescu's personal support for the programmes which the ss might wish to pursue. These discussions continued sporadically for the next three months.

Eagerly seizing the chance to recover the territories ceded to Russia a year earlier, in June 1941 Romania marched as one of Germany's willing allies into the Soviet Union. As a reward she not only recovered northern Bukovina and Bessarabia, but also received the Ukrainian lands between the Bug and Dniester rivers, an area known as Transnistria. The Romanian General Nicolae Tataranu and General Arthur Hauffe of the German army signed an 'Agreement for the Security, Administration, and Economic Exploitation of the Territory between the Dniester, the Bug and the Bug-Dnieper'.[4] This drew up the working arrangements between the German and Romanian authorities along the joint border between their respective areas of control.

Systematic acts of violence were perpetrated against Jewish communities as the Romanians, with German support, entered what had been Soviet-controlled territory:

> The attack along the entire length of the Romanian border begins, from Bukovina to the Danube. Simultaneously, a campaign is launched during which looting and slaughter among the Jews occurs on a massive scale along the path of the fascist army. The acts of looting and murder, both individual and mass, are committed by Romanian and German soldiers, as well as civil authorities and local residents. The . . . similarity of the crimes indicate[s] that they were executed in accordance with pre-prepared orders and plans.[5]

As was intended, the violence helped to push Jews and Ukrainians out of the provinces which were regarded as part of Romania proper and into Romanian-controlled Transnistria. It was intended that Transnistria would become home to these displaced peoples, and they were not to be permitted to leave Transnistria. The agreement negotiated between Tataranu and Hauffe specified that the 'evacuation of the Jews across the Bug [and thus into German-controlled Ukraine was] . . . not possible'.[6] The last thing required by Germany's Army Group South, as it advanced deep into Ukraine, was the sudden incursion of tens of thousands of displaced persons in its rear areas.

Large numbers of people from Romania were deported to Transnistria, a land which already had a population of some three million, including 300,000 Romanians, 330,000 Jews and 125,000 *Volksdeutsche*. In August 1941 Hitler personally presented Antonescu with the Knights Cross of the Iron Cross for his support and loyalty.[7] To emphasize the fact that there was no chance of return for those who had been deported from Romania, an order was published on 2 September 1942 specifying the death penalty for anyone who attempted to return.[8] The process of resettlement for the deportees was accompanied by such savagery and brutality that even the Nazis were disgusted at the actions of the Romanian authorities, whose soldiers were guilty of rape, casual murder and theft.

Thousands of Jews were starved to death, while similar numbers succumbed to disease as cities such as Moghilev and Bershad were turned into ghettos. The *Report of the International Commission on the Holocaust in Romania* later concluded:

> The Jews deported from Bessarabia and Bukovina typically died as a result of typhus, hunger and cold. Food distribution was erratic. Many lived by begging or by selling their clothes for food, ending up virtually naked. They ate leaves, grass and potato peels and often slept in stables or pigsties, sometimes not even allowed straw. Except for those in Peciora and Vapniarka camps and in the Rabinta prison, the deported Jews lived in ghettos or in towns, where they were assigned a residence, forced to carry out hard labor, and subjected to the 'natural' process of extermination.[9]

Those in the ghettos were comparatively fortunate compared to those in the work/extermination camps at Peciora and Vapniarka, where cannibalism was not unknown. However, the worst excesses occurred in Golta county. At three camps – Bogdanovka, Domanovka and Akmchetka – together with a network of subsidiary camps, approximately 110,000 Jews from Romania, Odessa and Transnistria were imprisoned and subjected to a regime of sadism and brutal neglect designed to destroy a substantial number of human beings with the minimum of effort.

A further stream of inmates for the ghettos came from Ukraine, as Jews fled from Friedrich Jeckeln's attempt to render Ukraine '*Juden frei*'. The testimony of survivors leaves no doubt as to the horrors which could be encountered in the ghettos of Transnistria. Alexander Kupperman was thirteen years old when he arrived in Bershad with his mother. They had already survived a shooting action at the hands of the Germans at Khashchevatoye in Ukraine:

> What was the Bershad Ghetto like? It included three or four streets no longer than one and a half kilometres, with mostly Jewish homes built back in the eighteenth or nineteenth century. The ghetto was surrounded with three layers of barbed wire, with electric wiring in one of them. There was only one exit from the

ghetto. In the winter of 1941/42, there were over 150,000 Jews in the ghetto, including 25,000 from Ukraine, 75,000 from Bessarabia and about 50,000 from Bukovina. At that time, typhoid and famine began in the ghetto. I was sick with typhoid for over fifty days, and when I got up after the crisis there was nothing to eat. My mum would make me soup from potato peelings. People were dying each day, 150–200 daily. They were not buried but, instead, were put onto a cart and in winter dumped in the fields.[10]

To the cruelties and torture of neglect, overcrowding and disease were added the sadistic pleasures of some of those responsible for the ghetto. The Romanian Jews in Transnistria could only keep up their spirits by clinging to the faint hope that one day they might be allowed home. William Rosenzweig was transferred to Bershad with his Romano-Jewish family:

In Bershad we were isolated without access to radio, newspapers, mail or any other communication. There were always rumours about various things, including repatriation . . . The commander of Bershad, a lieutenant named Ghineraru, was extremely cruel. He sometimes drove around the ghetto on a motorcycle, picked up a young boy or young man, tied him to a motorcycle, and drove at a very high speed over the cobblestone streets. Also in Bershad the bodies of people who were shot were hung for days on telegraph poles.[11]

In addition to inflicting cruelties on people in the ghettos, Romanian killing squads also targeted the tens of thousands of Ukrainian Jews who could call the Transnistria region home. On at least one occasion a trainload of Jews was taken directly into German territory so that they could be disposed of immediately and effectively. The Germans had become alarmed at Romanian policy and the danger that contagion would spread from dead Jews and those dying of disease.

In the late summer of 1942 SS-Hauptsturmführer Franz Christoffel looked on the Jews of Transnistria in a very different light. He was responsible for the construction of the stretch of DGIV near Gaisin.

Senior officers assembling for a meeting. Gieseke is on the left.

The project was hampered by a perennial labour shortage in its efforts to cope with the constant pressure of heavy military traffic. The Jews of Transnistria were not far away, just across the Bug river. Christoffel realized that they might provide a potentially valuable solution to his labour problems. Seemingly on his own initiative, he persuaded the Romanian authorities in Transnistria to allow him access to the camps and ghettos.[12] With promises of good conditions and food he managed to persuade a substantial number of Jews to leave Romanian-controlled territory voluntarily. Some of them, particularly those from German-speaking parts of Bukovina and Bessarabia, probably thought that they would be likely to receive better treatment at the hands of the Germans than they were receiving while under the control of the Romanians.

Other Jews, who were simply handed over to the Germans without any option, fully appreciated that, no matter how bad things were under the Romanians, the transfer to German control amounted to a death sentence.[13]

In August 1942, the prefect of Tulcin, [Colonel] Loghin, sought ... permission to hand over 5,000 Jews to the ss for construction of the Nemirov-Bratslav-Seminki-Gaysin [Gaisin] segment of the highway. The prefect asked that the governor accede to this request from 'the headquarters of the ss squads', since he himself did not need those Jews for any large-scale project in his district and did not want to continue feeding them. Alexianu approved

the transfer. The first 'delivery' consisted of some 3,000 Jews
. . . On August 18, an ss unit headed by ss-Hauptsturmführer
(Captain) Franz Kristoffel transferred them to the German side.
The children and elderly were put to death first, and by October
1943 most of the Jews had been killed – even those still able
to work.[14]

Among the ranks of those deported to German controlled territory was an aspiring artist, Arnold Daghani, and his wife, Nanino.
On 22 February 1909 Daghani had been born into a German-speaking orthodox Jewish family living in a small town called Suczawa, on
the eastern fringes of the multi-ethnic Austro-Hungarian Empire.
He was then known as Arnold Korn, youngest child of Viktor and
Mina Korn, and he had three sisters and three brothers. The family
lived in middle-class comfort, with Viktor making a living by import-
ing manufactured goods until he died in 1917.

The multicultural nature of the Austro-Hungarian empire
ensured that the young Daghani became fluent in several languages.
Of these, German was the most important since it was the language
of the Habsburg court and imperial bureaucracy based in Vienna.
The Bukovina region surrounding Suczawa was particularly marked
by its ethnic diversity, with Romanians, Austrians, Hungarians,
Armenians, Poles, Slovaks and Ukrainians contributing to the ethnic
mix of the region. The population of Suczawa was evenly divided
between ethnic Germans, Jews and Romanians.[15] In the peace settlement after the First World War Romania received Bukovina as a
reward for having fought against Germany and Austria-Hungary.

Daghani adapted to the new political realities. After travelling to
places like Munich, Vienna and Paris in the 1920s, he spent most of
the 1930s in Bucharest, the Romanian capital. By that period he had
already demonstrated some talent as an artist. His time in different
European cities had provided opportunities for visits to some of the
great art galleries, and he was reputed to have attended drawing
classes in Munich. It was while living in Bucharest that Arnold Korn
chose to change his name to Arnold Daghani, perhaps in an attempt
to obscure his Jewish-German origins.[16] A short spell of compulsory military service in the Romanian army during 1931–2 probably

alerted him to the rising tide of anti-Semitic sentiment within Romania. For a time Daghani was apprenticed to a commercial publishing house in Bucharest. Putting his language skills in Romanian, German, English and French to good use, he then worked for an import/export company.

In late 1939 or early 1940 he met his wife-to-be, Anishoara (known as Nanino). Born in the same year as Daghani himself, she came from a Francophile middle-class family whose home was 50 miles or so from Suceava. They were married on 27 June 1940, but their Bucharest home, along with so many other buildings, was destroyed on 11 November 1940 by an earthquake that measured 7.7 on the Richter scale. In face of this disaster and the growing tide of Romanian anti-Semitism, Daghani and Nanino decided to move back to Bukovina, one of the provinces recently ceded to Russia. They made their home in the city of Czernowitz. The decision was a fateful one, for it meant leaving behind Daghani's mother, who died in Bucharest in April 1941. There were, however, even more serious consequences for the young married couple.

Following the launching of Operation Barbarossa in June 1941, Romanian troops advancing into the Soviet Union reached the outskirts of Czernowitz on 5 July. The city had become a refuge for many people escaping persecution elsewhere. A Jewish woman, who had left Krakow after the German invasion of Poland in 1939, later recalled:

Czernowitz became the last place of refuge for Jews from all over Europe. There were German Jews, Czech, Polish, Austrian Jews, and from other countries. Some of them managed to stay alive and find something to eat, but the majority lived in extreme want. But cultural life thrived. Many concerts were held, a daily Yiddish paper was published, and the Yiddish theater gave constant performances . . . I got a job working in a mill. My husband also worked there – as a stoker.[17]

Undoubtedly the German and Romanian authorities wanted to remove this large community of Jews who had gathered from various parts of Eastern Europe. They were destined for destruction. German and Romanian troops entered the city between 4 and 5 p.m.

on the afternoon of 5 July and took up key positions. Killing and looting began as soon as Romanian troops reached the Jewish quarter. In some streets soldiers went from house to house, looting and killing all the occupants. The commercial heart of the city was destroyed as Romanian troops added to the destruction caused by earlier shelling. The massacre continued into the following day until some 2,000 people had been killed.

German troops made demands on the Chief Rabbi of Czernowitz, Abraham Jakob Mark. His wife, Perla, survived the war to appear as a witness at the trial of Adolf Eichmann in Israel in 1961. She recalled the exchanges between her husband and the Germans: 'Who has jewellery?', to which Rabbi Mark replied, 'It is out of the question for the Chief Rabbi of Czernowitz to give the names of people who have jewellery.'[18] Rabbi Mark was taken to the Schwartzer Adler Hotel, which was then serving as the headquarters of Sonderkommando 10B, part of Einsatzgruppe D. They had the task of arresting the leading Jews of the city and destroying the leadership of the community. Arresting and interrogating the Jewish intelligentsia, they eventually killed about 100 people and destroyed the main synagogue. Rabbi Mark, who was one of the Jews temporarily imprisoned in the cellar of the Schwartzer Adler Hotel, was brought up to the roof of a building opposite the synagogue to witness its destruction, as barrels of oil and petrol were used as an accelerant to the inferno. The Rabbi was later executed by German forces.

Even the Germans were appalled at the barbarities being committed around them by their Romanian allies. Their propensity for looting and uncontrolled savagery sickened the killers of the Sonderkommando. The Germans noted how the Romanians also took the opportunity to attack Ukrainians to ensure that the ethnic make-up of Bukovina would henceforth be solidly Romanian. Indeed, the men of the Sonderkommando had to be quickly redeployed from their own murderous anti-Semitic mission in order to protect certain Ukrainian nationalists, whom it was hoped might prove useful in the future of a German-controlled Ukraine.[19] Antonescu had specified the ethnic cleansing of Bukovina and Bessarabia as a goal of the re-occupation forces during a meeting of the Romanian cabinet on 8 July 1941:

This is a time when we are masters of our land. Let us use it. If necessary, shoot your machine guns. I couldn't care less if history will recall us as barbarians . . . I take formal responsibility and tell you there is no law . . . So no formalities, complete freedom.[20]

On the same day that Antonescu was authorizing barbarities in cabinet, the dead of Czernowitz were being stacked on carts and interred in four mass graves in the Jewish cemetery.

Arnold Daghani was lucky to survive the July massacres in Czernowitz, since Romanian forces seem to have made a special point of targeting people who had arrived in the city since the Russian takeover in Bukovina the previous year. After 8 July Daghani and the surviving Jews of Czernowitz were interned in a designated ghetto to await their fate. In the short term that meant being confined to the ghetto unless express permission was given. Jews were required to wear the Star of David; their opportunities for taking part in the commercial life of the city were very strictly limited; and they were only allowed restricted access to two bakeries and four markets within the ghetto.

In the long term the fate of the Jews of Czernowitz involved expulsion to the newly acquired Transnistria. The Jews of Bessarabia and Bukovina were the first to be deported. It was intended that, in time, all of Romania's Jews would be expelled into Transnistria. The first marching columns reached Transnistria on 1 October 1941. The 1930 census for Bukovina had recorded 93,101 Jews resident in the region. Following the deportations, by the census of May 1942 only 17,113 Jews were still resident there.[21] By keeping a very low profile Daghani and his wife were lucky enough to avoid deportation from Czernowitz. He may also have been able to use his personal contacts to obtain special leave to remain from the Romanian authorities.[22]

Their good fortune was not to last. Sunday, 7 June 1942, was a fateful day in the life of the Daghanis:

Four o'clock in the morning. We were awakened by wailing and screams that reached our ears from the house opposite. Going over to the window, we saw just then a person on a stretcher being taken out. Gendarmes at the front door. People with bundles. Deportation had resumed . . . Ten in the morning: Two men in plain clothes entered our room, a gendarme posting himself by the door outside. The two went swiftly over the business: Deportation order. While one of the two was specifying and taking on record the various household things and clothing left, the other – of the police – looked at the rucksack we had between ourselves. Then his glance became arrested by a box of watercolours and sketchbook on top of the wardrobe to be left with the other things behind. Why had we not packed them, too? He wanted to know. Seeing the shrug of my shoulder, he ordered me to open the rucksack and to put the colours and the sketchbook in. I refused stubbornly, saying: 'We're being sent to death, and you expect me to take 'em? To what use?' He asked back, 'They might just save both your lives, one can never tell.' As I went on being refractory, he made Nanino open the rucksack, and both sketchbook and colours were placed on top.[23]

Along with some 2,500 other Jews from Czernowitz, the Daghanis were taken to Transnistria by rail freight car and then by forced march. The callous treatment of the marching columns was particularly horrifying. Little or no provision was made for the people as they trudged across country. The sick, elderly and very young were executed if they fell behind the rest of the column. Indiscriminate killings and acts of brutality were routine, and local peasants would sometimes pay the escorting guards to execute particularly well-dressed prisoners so that they could steal their clothes. The *Final Report of the International Commission on the Holocaust in Romania* later summed up the experience of the deported Jews:

Each convoy was first plundered by the gendarmes. Young women and girls in each convoy were raped, particularly by the officers, who chose stops where they could organize orgies. Gangs of Ukrainians attacked the Jewish convoys as well – killing, looting, and sometimes even stripping hundreds of Jews bare and leaving them to freeze to death. The convoy commanders were not responsible for Jews' lives, only for their transfer – these Jews had no name or identity. Ukrainian volunteers (later called the Ukrainian police) accompanied the convoys, exhibiting even greater cruelty than the gendarmes. Unfamiliar with the area, the gendarmes relied on these volunteers, assigning them partial escort and guard duties.[24]

On their arrival at the camp at Ladyzhinka, near Tulcin in Transnistria, it became apparent to the surviving Jews that the region was a vast execution site. By neglect, by disease, by back-breaking labour, by starvation and by murder the Jews of Transnistria would steadily be eliminated. The Jewish population of towns such as Tulcin increased massively as the marching columns arrived. For some of the newcomers life in the ghetto or the camps of Transnistria would be short; they were taken across the Bug, either for disposal by the Germans or for labour on DGIV and other construction projects. The Daghanis seem to have been included among approximately 3,000 Jews who were sent across the Bug in August 1942 by the Romanian Prefect of Tulcin, Colonel Loghin. These Jews represented a sort of gift from the Romanians to Organization Todt in southern Ukraine.

The labour camp at Mikhailowka, to which Daghani and his wife were sent, was typically unpleasant. Romanian Jew Nathan Segall was one of those taken across the Bug river from the camp at Ladyzhinka. On 21 October 1943 he dictated an account of the setting up of the camp at Mikhailowka and the killings that followed. The account was later smuggled out and eventually found its way to both London and Israel. Segall and the rest of his family were killed when the work camp at Tarassiwka was liquidated on 10 December 1943:

At Mikhailowka, we found a stable, forty-five metres . . . long, which belonged to a collective farm. About four hundred Ukrainian Jews were quartered there. They looked unkempt, tattered and in a brutish state. I applied immediately to the Camp-Commandant, a German police Sergeant whose name was Kiesel, to ask him not to put us together with the louse-starved people, for we were still clean and in possession of our clothing. Instead of quartering us in the stable, I obtained permission for us to be allowed to pass the night in the open air within the barbed wire enclosure. At exactly six o'clock in the morning, our people were indiscriminately sent to labour at road-making. I was appointed leader of the Camp. In this capacity, I had the opportunity to get in touch with some of the O[rganization] T[odt] men under whose control we laboured. They were the only ones who showed any comprehension and sympathy. I succeeded in having the Romanian Jews separated from the Ukrainian ones and obtained a second stable for ourselves. It was absolutely heartless and impossible to pen around eight hundred people together, from whom it was expected they should do hard road-making labour. Until the horses were moved from the second stable, we had to pass four more nights in the open air. Then came the difficulty of cleaning the stable. I lived in that stable from the 22nd of August until the 6th of November.

The first killings at random – killings of the elderly and infirm – followed.

After three to four weeks the first mass killings happened. One morning, before having marched off to work, the people were arranged by fives in rank and file: Ukrainian Jews separately; Romanian Jews separately. At that first mass murder there were twenty-five victims; at the second one, thirty or so, and twenty-four during the third and at the last one, one hundred and six; most of them Ukrainian Jews.[25]

The mass killings at Mikhailowka mirrored actions at other work camps along DGIV. Investigators later uncovered evidence of numerous mass killings connected with the construction of the road:

Gniwan – 40–50 Jews – August 1942
Lityn – 60–70 Jews – summer 1942
Niemirow – 1,800 Jews – November 1941
Proskurow – mass killing of Jews – November 1941
Proskurow – mass killing of prisoners of war – autumn/
    winter 1942
Teplik – 1,000 Jews – May 1942
Winnica – mass killing of Jews – autumn 1941
Winnica – mass killing of Jews – spring 1942

Winnica – 100 Jews – March 1942
Narajewka – shooting of sick Jews – winter 1942–3

The activities of the killing commandos that carried out the mass actions were curbed by severe snow and frozen ground during the depths of winter. Transport of prisoners would be difficult at that time, and the digging of mass graves virtually impossible. Actions like that at Narajewka in the winter of 1942–3, undertaken in order to combat the spread of spotted fever, were exceptional. Most of the killings took place at times of the year when the weather was likely to present fewer problems.

For many of the killings there would be no one to bear witness at a later date. The difference between these killings at various locations along the road and those which occurred at Mikhailowka was that Arnold Daghani was on hand to record the events at Mikhailowka. His evidence as an eye witness is crucial for anyone who wishes to understand the experiences of those unfortunates who laboured to build DGIV under the auspices of Walter Gieseke and his Einsatzstab. Daghani carefully built up a collection of brief dated notes that he would later expand into a diary. Using the paint and paper that a thoughtful policeman had made him take along with him from Czernowitz, he also made a visual record of life in the camp.

He very soon discovered that he could market his artistic skills to German and Lithuanian guards and civilian employees of Organization Todt who worked on the road. He would make sketches, paint portraits or undertake any other artwork that his patrons demanded. Many of his commissions required careful and discreet completion, since they involved painting while he was supposed to be engaged in hard manual work on the road or in the quarry which serviced its construction. He noted in his diary on 25 October 1942:

This morning Pita Mihailowski [one of the Lithuanian guards] wanted me to paint his portrait in water-colours, and allowed me to exchange the pick for the brush. Of course, not when the commandant or the Lithuanians were in sight. After a long while my fingers got numb with cold, and I had to interrupt. Mihailowski gave Anishoara a few pickled apples.[26]

In his diary notes Daghani recorded the paradox of Nazi policy: the neat order and immense demand for labour on the construction of the road contrasting with the casual brutality and waste of human life at the hands of sadistic camp staff. The daily march from the camp to the road involved the deliberate brutalization and humiliation of the Jewish labour force. Guards would be ready with their rifle butts to encourage the less speedy on their journey to the construction site. Daghani described the systematic abuse:

> The goading to and from the road has become hellish. Toiling on the road is small beer compared to the quick march imposed by the guards throughout the time. Uphill, downhill, we get pushed on by roaring guards. As shepherds and cowherds respectively, they would not dare do such things to the entrusted live stock.[27]

While the brutality of the march to work was part of a consciously planned policy, death on the road could also be shockingly casual and unexpected. On 28 September 1942 Daghani witnessed a seemingly arbitrary murder:

> Witsotzkas arrived late on the plot. He alighted from a cart and looked down at a piece of paper in his hand. Then he went up to a woman, the former civil-clerk. Curtly, he summoned her to mount the cart. 'No, no', she cried out. 'For goodness sake, let me live! I do work well! I am sure you won't find fault with my work!' Alas, try as she did, he remained unmoved. 'Come on!' he swore at her. Mother and daughter started to cry, trying their best to persuade Witsotzkas. Impatiently, Serskus joined his fellow-Lithuanian, and giving the woman a violent push in the direction of the cart, encouraged her daughter with the rifle-butt to resume work. Sitting on the cart, the woman kept crying, stretching out her arms: 'My child, do help me!' The cart was moving slowly, and stopped in front of another group. Here an elderly woman was also summoned to join. Lest his grandmother should be beaten, her grandson lifted her up by himself, placing her gently upon the cart. The cart set off under looks of stone, and soon it disappeared into the field . . . Two shots.[28]

Such murders were a feature of life on DGIV. The slightest sign of a decline in the productivity of a particular labourer would lead to their murder.

Two months after witnessing the scene by the cart, Daghani witnessed another death on the road:

> We have still been working at the ditch. The ground is frozen, but we have to dig it. The Lithuanians have a fire for themselves. A man staggered; he was feeling sick. Witsotzkas, keeping a close eye on him, ordered some of a close-by group to dig a grave at the mouth of the ditch ... He then went up to the man summoning him to follow ... Afterwards a young man was told to pull out the gold-crowns from the man's mouth, as he was lying in the grave. Back in the camp, the man's family, mother and son, seriously ill, were only told that he had died of heart-failure.[29]

In addition to recording the violence and horrors of working on DGIV, Daghani also described life in the camps, the appalling conditions in which they were forced to live and the struggle to keep people alive for just another day. Jewish children were especially targeted by the ss, camp guards and Lithuanians. Not only did their murder signal to the Jewish inmates that their kind had no future in

27 Inmates going to work on DGIV.

Hitler's Europe, but children were also among the weakest and most vulnerable section of the workforce. By late April 1943 eighteen-month-old Mucki Enzenberg was the last child remaining at Mikhailkowka. Daghani witnessed the courageous efforts and ingenious subterfuges which were necessary to keep him alive:

> As a rule he would hide himself in the cage as soon as his mother called out, 'Mucki, the commandant!' Today, having acted upon the advice of our doctor and of Segall, his mother administered some drug to him and put him to sleep in a rucksack. Sukerka, knowing of the existence of the baby, was looking for it everywhere, and thus came upon the rucksack. Feeling it, he detected Mucki! Luckily, Sukerka was open to a sound bribe offered by Segall.[30]

Keeping Mucki Enzenberg alive undoubtedly called for a considerable collective effort to hide and protect him, and to furnish bribes when all else failed. Men and women collaborated in that endeavour, even though their own children had been less fortunate. For them, keeping the little boy alive meant individual redemption, and it was a form of active resistance to a system of murder designed to rob its victims of hope and any lingering belief in the possibility of a future for their race. The child represented innocence and purity in a world of evil. He also represented the potential of the community – its future and the possibility of survival. To the Jews in the slave labour camp, Mucki Enzenberg's survival meant much more than just another life.

Daghani's experiences along DGIV were typical of life and labour in the camps which served the road. Ukrainian Jew Avram Rosengraft, born in 1938 at Nemirov in the Vinnitsa *oblast*, was remarkable both as a child survivor of the road and for the length of his incarceration in the various ghettos and camps that housed the work force. He witnessed the process by which Nemirov became a ghetto town serving the needs of the road, and he also witnessed how the Nazis treated the Ukrainian Jewish labour they pressed into service to build it:

> Every day, healthy and able people would be selected from the

ghetto. They worked on the construction of the Nemirov–Gaisin road. The companies Fiks and Schtral were in charge of the technical supervision of the construction. The workers were punished for every little mistake in their work; they were beaten with whips until they were barely alive. Nevertheless, the ghetto prisoners who worked on the road or unloading things were capable of getting some food from the local population and bringing it into the ghetto. Thus, children and old people avoided death from starvation, while being locked in the ghetto for the whole day. After the first *Aktion*, the slaughter of the Jews [in late 1941], the area of the ghetto was decreased by approximately a half. The guards became more severe. Those adults who remained alive were escorted daily to the road works. They would get some food there, while others were left on their own. The houses would not heat. Daily, some child would die. Children and adults who got ill were taken out of the ghetto and killed. The only source of food was whatever our parents managed to bring in secretly from the road works. Thanks to our dad, who seemed to know many local residents of villages nearby, they would leave food products, clothes and shoes for him in designated places. That was how the children in our family survived.[31]

Following the liquidation of the Nemirov ghetto on 26 June, the 200 surviving Jews were transferred to another road-building camp in the Vinnitsa area.

Another child survivor of the road was Grigory Bassovsky, born in 1927 in the town of Olshany. When the Germans occupied the town in 1941 they murdered the adult male inhabitants. In May 1942 the women and children were marched off to work camps:

We were taken to a concentration camp, first in the village of Smelchintsy, Lyssyansky district; then my mum and I were transferred to the village of Nemorozh, Zvenigorodka district. Both camps were located along a highway then under construction. Those that were left (elderly and children) were taken out of town and killed. What was our concentration camp like? It was a yard of a former collective farm [*kolkhoz*], fenced off from the local population with barbed wires. We were put in a pigsty, where we slept on the ground. During the day we worked in a stone quarry, on the highway construction. They gave us food once a day (some watery soup and 100 grams of bread from millet). Every once in a while, they would select weakened people and shoot them. When we returned from work, they forced us to run around the pigsty while beating us with truncheons. After shootings, they brought clothes taken off the dead to the camp and distributed them among us.[32]

Some Jewish survivors confirm Daghani's impressions that many of the civilian German construction staff had some sympathy for their plight. Shelya Polishchuck was ten when the Germans invaded. Her mother's profession as a doctor afforded the family some measure of protection in the camps:

Yozef Wassen, a German construction foreman, was supervising our work. He was an elderly man, and treated us pretty well. Half of the prisoners worked at one end of the village, while the other half worked at the other end. Some prisoners were transferred to another camp, in the village of Smelchintsy. The teams of policemen on guard would change every ten days. One team was relatively tolerable, while the other abused us to the utmost limits: they raped, beat and just tortured us.[33]

Jews forced to join the road-construction gangs might have their spirits lifted once in a while by an encounter with some Ukrainian peasant willing to supply a little food or a pair of old shoes. The remote possibility of meeting a sympathetic German who was prepared to treat a Jew with ordinary human decency might briefly ease their despair at man's inhumanity to man. For the majority, however, the life they were compelled to lead must have been without a single redeeming feature or the faintest glimmer of hope.

NINE

THE END OF THE ROAD

THE campaigns in 1941 and 1942 had followed a pattern by which the Germans showed that they could make very rapid and extensive advances during summer offensives but suffered reverses and had to give up some of the newly gained territory during the severe Russian winters. As spring moved on to summer in 1943 the German High Command still hoped to mount their third successful summer offensive in succession.

North of Belgorod, in the area around Kursk, the Russians held a big salient they had forced into the German front during the previous winter. On 4–5 July 1943 German forces launched Operation Citadel, designed to envelop and overwhelm the Soviet forces in the Kursk salient. The Red Army's response to the German offensive relied on defence in depth, and it demonstrated the increasing effectiveness of Soviet arms. By the end of the first day the German 9th Army and 4th Panzer Army, entrusted with the task of breaking through, were already bogged down. Ten days of large-scale tank battles produced no significant advances for the Germans. Operation Citadel had to be called off. It had cost the German army 70,000 men and 3,000 tanks. In material terms the blow was crushing. Never again would German troops mount a successful major offensive inside the Soviet Union. Psychologically the blow was equally devastating. After the collapse at Stalingrad and the failure of the offensive at Kursk, it was clear to all but the most deluded that Germany would be hard pressed to hold onto her gains in the East.

Daghani and many of the other Jews who were labouring on DGIV in the spring of 1943 realized that, for them, death could only be a matter of time. In June Daghani and his wife were ordered to put their artistic talents to use in Gaisin. There they were set to work creating a garden mosaic, in the form of a German eagle, outside the offices of the Dohrmann construction firm. They decided that this task might offer their best – and perhaps their only – opportunity to make a bid for freedom. With the encouragement and assistance of a sympathetic Jewish cobbler, the Daghanis risked all in staging an escape from their temporary quarters in Gaisin on 15 July. Carrying with them 50 paintings documenting life working on DGIV, they succeeded in making their way to the Bug river. With the help of a guide, they forded the river and reached the relative safety of the Bershad ghetto, where surviving members of the Jewish community would conceal them. While hiding in Bershad they learned that a partisan attack on their former camp at Mikhailowka had caused the Germans to relocate the labourers to the camp at Tarrasiwka. Tarrasiwka was considered less vulnerable to attacks of this kind, which were growing in frequency and intensity.

Hitler having set his face against preparing strong defence lines well in the rear, the German army had to make the best defensive use it could of the wide Russian rivers, but the Russian armies swept westwards inexorably. By the beginning of September they were back once more in Kharkov. A month later the Russians had reached the bank of the river Dnieper above Dnepropetrovsk. All of DGIV to the east of that town through Stalino to Taganrog was by then in Russian hands. The important dam at Zaporozhe was closely threatened, and the troops left behind in the Caucasus had, with Hitler's permission, finally withdrawn from the '*Gotenkopf*' bridgehead and sought safety in Crimea.

By early November the Russians were across the Dnieper on a broad front west of Dnepropetrovsk, and another 70 miles of DGIV had fallen into their hands. They had also swept through southern Ukraine as far as the lower reaches of the Dnieper, an advance which isolated the German forces still holding Crimea. From the Volga at Stalingrad to the Dnieper at Kherson, the Germans had been forced to conduct a fighting retreat of 600 miles in the space of twelve months.

British decodes of German police and SS radio traffic from the Eastern Front add some interesting, if scanty, details about Gieseke's work and the role of his task force. In particular, they show that in

1943 he and his men were involved in certain operations far from the immediate route of DGIV:

> 10 July 1943: A Latvian Schuma battalion attached to
> Einsatzstab Gieseke is engaged in a *Sonder Einsatz* at
> Kerch.[1]
>
> 24 July: Two Schuma battalions attached to Einsatzstab
> Gieseke are engaged in a special operation in the vicinity
> of Nikolayev-Cherson.[2]
>
> 29 July: Gieseke receives authorization for transport, 1 F-*Wagen*
> *mit* PKW, from the main railway station. The destination is
> the Police School for *Rechnik und Verkeer* in Berlin.[3]
> Einsatzstab Gieseke moves to Luzk.[4]
>
> 6 November: Einsatzstab Gieske thought to be at Olyka
> engaged in anti-partisan activity in the vicinity of Rowno.
> Einsatzstab Gieseke thought to have three Schuma
> regiments attached.[5]
>
> 13 November: Order of Battle Report No 3 – Einsatzstab
> Gieseke reported at Olyka on 27 October.[6]
>
> 20 November: Einsatzstab Gieseke clearing railway line vicinity
> of Rowno.[7]
>
> 27 November: Report of two new police regiments forming –
> one under Gieseke.[8]
>
> 5 December: Order of Battle Report places Schuma Battalion 28,
> listed as part of Einsatzstab Gieseke, at Biala-Cerkwa.[9]
>
> 18 December: Order of Battle Report places Einsatzstab
> Gieseke at Kowel in Poland on 7 December.[10]

Through all these turbulent events Walter Gieseke continued in command of the Einsatzstab named after him. His personal dossier provides only the basic details of his war service. On 1 January 1943 he was awarded the War Service Cross, 2nd Class with Swords, and he was promoted to the rank of SS Obersturmbannführer on 21 June.

After the thwarting of the major German summer offensive known as Operation Citadel, autumn 1943 brought further Soviet advances that threatened to cut the route of the road. The Jews in the con-

struction camps had good reason to suspect that the end of the
road would also mean the end for the slave labourers. From their
relatively safe place of refuge at Bershad, Daghani and Nanino hoped
against hope that fate would somehow spare the friends they had
made in Mikhailowka. Their hopes were in vain. As the Red Army
neared the route of DGIV the Germans began killing off the surviving
Jewish labourers in the camps along the road. Who issued the exec-
utive orders for these massacres has never been established, despite
lengthy investigations by West German prosecutors after the war.
Who actually carried out the executions – SS, SD, police or Schuma
personnel – is also shrouded in uncertainty. Many witnesses who were
later questioned by the same West German authorities seem to have
suffered from either a total lack of curiosity or the sudden onset of
amnesia. One man put it very succinctly when questioned about
the liquidation of a particular camp: 'I declare I have no knowledge
of who ordered that killing action, who belonged to the killing-
commando, nor where the killing-commando came from.'[11] Another
insisted: 'Who had ordered that killing-action I didn't learn.'[12]

It is, however, probably easier to answer the question who must have
known about the *Aktions* before, during and after they were carried
out – the senior officers of Einsatzstab Gieseke and the majority of
German personnel associated with running the camps. Preparations
for Einsatzstab Gieseke to retire westwards out of the path of the
advancing Red Army began as early as July 1943. By September it
was apparent that the road would not be completed and that there
would be no further need for the slave labourers. Werner Bergmann,
one of the civilian contractors on the road, later revealed: 'It was
generally known that the area would be captured by the approaching
Russian troops. We understood that the Jews at Tarrasiwka would be
liquidated before we evacuated.'[13]

From Daghani's diary it is evident that the impending end of the
camps was common knowledge even to the Jews who were corralled
there. News of the liquidation of camps in other areas was spread
by Ukrainian civilians, by people with connections to the partisans and
by German sympathizers within Organization Todt. The process of
liquidating the camps was only carried out after careful planning and
preparation. In the case of the Tarrasiwka camp, subterfuge was used

in an attempt to allay the fears of the inmates, to reduce the number of escape attempts and to minimize the difficulties faced by the executioners. The senior SS officer at the camp reassured German civilian construction workers, who had some sympathy for the Jewish labourers, that no *Aktion* was imminent and that shortly the Jews would be transported to other areas where their labour was needed. Nevertheless, warnings were quietly passed to the camp inmates by some of the civilian construction workers. As the hour of execution approached, auxiliary police units, usually recruited from the Baltic States, were deployed around the camp to prevent any mass escape attempt. Friedrich Muehl, a German civilian employed by one of the construction companies, later recalled the liquidation of the Tarrasiwka camp, which finally took place on 10 December 1943:

> During the night we heard some shooting near the camp. I thought it was the partisans who were in the habit of sniping every so often. About to leave my room, I was stopped by the Lithuanian guards and forced back with a rifle. I watched from behind my window as approximately 400 Jews had to assemble in the tree-lined courtyard. There were men, women and children. They were led to a mass-grave which had been dug-out and camouflaged as a defensive position for the Luftwaffe. Members of the Luftwaffe had even been seen measuring the site. However, the Jews had voiced the opinion, 'That's our grave.' . . . The pit was seven by three by three metres. With soldierly precision the Jews descended into the grave and lay down head next to another: in complete composure they were shot dead by two members of the SD [Security Police], who had arrived for the task. The two SD men were standing on the raised edge of the grave, giving instructions and carrying out the shooting with a submachine-gun. After the first layer was liquidated, the next had to lie down on the corpses . . . Before this they had to strip stark naked. I recall seeing the Jew [Heinz] Rosengarten forming up at the rear with his two-year old son [in all probability this would have been Mucki Enzenberg, who was the only two-year-old in the camp] and pass by my window from where I watched everything. I knew many Jews by their names. The little boy waved to me and called

out to me 'Uncle Fritz' – he was happy to be marching with the others.[14]

The distraught Muehl desperately wanted to intervene. It was only with great difficulty that other civilian employees persuaded him to come away from the window and leave their quarters. Bernhard Becker remembered that they had to use 'some force' against Muehl to prevent a confrontation with the Lithuanian auxiliaries.[15] Muehl later visited the execution pits and, according to Becker, put an end to the suffering of some of the mortally wounded who had been left to a slow, agonising death among the corpses of their fellow workers.

In addition to the murders at Tarrasiwka, which the Daghanis heard about a few days later, further camp liquidations involving another 350 people took place at Ovadovca, Teklayevka and Krasnopolca. Daghani and his wife were among the small number of former road labourers who had been lucky enough to survive the camps. They were not the only ones, however. Grigory Bassovsky managed to escape the slaughter when his camp was liquidated on 23 August 1943. He and his mother made good their escape, only for the mother to be betrayed by a Ukrainian villager as she tried to get food and help. Grigory had to

Mass grave, Tarrasiwka.

continue alone. Along the route of DGIV the survivors from the closure of the camps hid in forests, joined the partisans, were hidden by sympathetic Ukrainians or tried to find a way to escape into the relative safety of Romanian-administered Transnistria.

Among them was sixteen-year-old Sophia Palatnikova, who had been living in Teplik, Vinnitsa *oblast*, when the Germans arrived. Along with other Jews aged between thirteen and 45 who were assessed as being capable of hard work, she had been taken to a construction camp at Raigorod in April 1942. The remaining Jews of Teplik had been murdered, although Sophia's parents escaped to hide in the forest. The camp at Raigorod served a quarry that produced stone for the construction of DGIV. When Sophia and her sister Tanya escaped from the camp in 1943 they knew that Transnistria might be the only place where they would have some hope of surviving. Like the Daghanis, they managed to reach the Bershad ghetto where, although famished with hunger 'and living 14 of us in two rooms', they were able to survive the next few months.[16]

The murder of so many Jewish labourers along DGIV conformed to the irrational patterns of the Holocaust: the Nazis appear to have been motivated by an obsessive compulsion to humiliate and kill Jews even while the whole German war economy was in desperate need of additional labour. With German forces hard pressed on the Eastern Front, the workers along DGIV could have been usefully redeployed in digging static defences. Indeed, even within Einsatzstab Gieseke's own operational sphere, the need for Jewish manual labour had not completely disappeared, but rather than transfer people from some of the work camps along DGIV, the Germans again combed the ghettos of Transnistria for the labour needed.

In the spring of 1943 Einsatzstab Gieseke was given additional responsibility in connection with the building of a bridge at Nikolayev. Building the bridge over the Bug between Trihaty and Nikolayev was a major and very difficult undertaking, but it was essential to improve lines of communication between Romania and Ukraine and provide better access to Crimea if the peninsula were to be held and built up as a base for future offensive operations.

In constructing the bridge the Germans eventually employed 4,000 Jews who had been turned over to the ss by the Romanians. These

Jews were held at three camps (Trihaty, Varvarovka and Kolosovka) on the Romanian side of the Bug and two on the German side (Kurievka and Matievka). In addition, more Jewish labourers were brought in daily from some of the camps and ghettos in the locality of Trihaty and at the Romanian end of the bridge. William Rosenzweig was one of the Romanian Jews rounded up in the process:

> In winter 1943 the Germans requested able-bodied men to be sent to Nikolaev to build a bridge. This was one of the biggest demands. It was an extremely cold day. I was caught wearing a light jacket and practically no shoes. On the way to the *comandatura* [the local police command post] my brother – who was then only fourteen – saw me freezing in the convoy. He wanted to run back to our place to bring me the only coat that our family possessed, but I screamed at him not to do it. Fortunately, however, my Romanians did not choose me because they figured that I would freeze on the way. My luck! The work in Nikolaev was very harsh. The people had to work in freezing water and many died. In addition, if some of the work was not done according to the Germans' plan, they would line the people up and execute every tenth person. By following a local Jew who lived in the same quarters, I discovered a type of catacomb system under the town's streets that could be reached by crawling through a typical Russian oven and reaching a passage at the back leading to underground tunnels. We hid in these tunnels from time to time.[17]

The Germans eventually managed to get their bridge built, but it later had to be blown up to deny its use to the Red Army. When Soviet engineers tried to put their own bridge across the southern Bug they understood the difficulties that had faced the Germans at Nikolayev:

> No job was ever more arduous than the building of the bridge on the Southern Bug. The sappers only had a tiny strip of land on the western bank to work on and the enemy was pressing hard. So the sappers had to build the bridge amidst the bursting shells. A heavy northern gale helped the enemy. The level of water dropped suddenly one and a half metres. The mire seemed

bottomless. A test pile sank down into the doughy mess for eleven metres. But the bridge was built.[18]

Einsatzstab Gieseke would have been able to say, with equal pride, 'but we also got our bridge built'. By the time the Germans had managed to overcome all the difficulties and complete their bridge its main strategic value no longer lay in carrying men and equipment for a renewed offensive; instead it offered a possible line of retreat for German forces in southern Ukraine. That change in strategic role was a sign of the dramatic way in which the war had turned against the Germans, not only in Ukraine, but also in the central and northern sectors of the vast Eastern Front. As Alan Clark has described so graphically:

By the late summer of 1943 the morale of the whole Wehrmacht, from top to bottom, had suffered permanent change. Its courage and discipline were unimpaired. But hope was tainted, and human-ity, where vestiges of it remained, was extinguished. August came in stifling heat; then September, the days crisper but with an evening fog. The old battlefields of 1941 rose and receded – Bryansk, Konotop, Poltava. To the rattle of machine guns, as a few last scores were settled with the local population, and the thud of demolition charges, the German Army retreated across European Russia, leaving a trail of smoke, of abandoned vehicles and loose-covered shallow graves.[19]

For the remaining Jews who were hiding in Transnistria and else-where, the possibility of salvation arrived early in 1944. In January the Romanian dictator, Marshal Ion Antonescu, anticipating the immi-nent arrival of Russian troops in his country, publicly protested that Jews had not been deported from Romania. The following month the Pope sent financial aid for the Jews in Transnistria, and Soviet troops entered the area in March, bringing an end to the anti-Semitic horrors there. In the same month Arnold Daghani and Nanino, still carrying the paintings completed at Mikhailowka, returned to Bucharest after the Romanian government had lifted the restrictions on Jews return-ing from Transnistria.

The Daghanis could count themselves extremely fortunate to have survived. Between June 1941 and March 1944 approximately half of Romania's Jews had perished. At every turn the statistics made grim reading. In 1930 the Jews in Romania numbered 756,930, about 4.2 per cent of the population. Some 170,000 Jews had been living in the Russian-occupied former Romanian provinces of Bessarabia and Bukovina at the start of 1941. During the Romanian re-occupation of those provinces in June 1941, between 45,000 and 60,000 Jews were murdered. In the following months most of the remaining Jews had been deported to Transnistria. Between 105,000 and 120,000 Jews died in Transnistria between 1941 and the end of 1943. Einsatzstab Gieseke and the construction of DGIV had made an appalling but comparatively modest contribution to the 'final solution' of the Jewish problem in Ukraine and Romania. By November 1943 only some 50,000 Jews remained alive in places like Bershad and Moghilev. In total, between 280,000 and 380,000 Jews had perished in territory under Romanian control.[20] From 1945 onwards, however, to the disgust of Daghani and others, the Romanian state would continue to deny any responsibility. The pogroms, the massacres, the deaths from neglect or casual brutality, the hard labour on DGIV, the camps along its route and its victims would continue to be subject to the collective amnesia of the post-war Communist state, which wished to deny the role of Romanian people in the Holocaust.

The abandonment of the DGIV road-building project and the ruthless 'disposal' of the slave labourers described by Arnold Daghani and others had been largely completed by the end of 1943. At that time the entire eastern half of the great highway from Taganrog through Stalino and Dnepropetrovsk and as far west as Kirovograd (except for the section near Krivoi Rog) lay in areas overrun by the advancing Russian armies. In the new year almost the entire western half of DGIV was also directly threatened by a renewed Russian offensive south and southwest of Kiev. By the end of January 1944 the Russians were only 35 miles from the important road centres of Uman and Vinnitsa and, further west, they were within 45 miles of Proskurov and about 60 miles from Tarnopol.

By the end of March the complete length of DGIV was in Russian hands, except for about 50 miles immediately east of Lvov. Hitler's advice to Albert Speer in February 1942, that the road need only be built 'in the most primitive way' with a surface to last '2–3 years', showed remarkable prescience.[21] After just two very eventful years, if the road could be said to serve any strategic purpose it was as a supply route supporting the final Russian advance across Poland to Berlin.

The Russians also made significant advances along the Black Sea coast of Ukraine. By mid-April 1944 they had taken the important ports of Nikolaev and Odessa, while further inland they were already fighting on Romanian soil. German troops were still trying to cling on to Crimea, which had once been envisaged as the 'jewel in the crown' of the planned *Lebensraum* for the Aryan master race. They had strongly fortified the Perekop isthmus and also managed to contain two small Russian bridgeheads, one on the north coast and the other on the Kerch peninsula. Despite the advice of his generals that prolonged defence of Crimea would serve no useful purpose, Hitler obstinately refused to sanction withdrawal from the area.

The Russians began their offensive on 9 April, breaking through the Perekop defences and breaking out from the two bridgeheads they had established earlier. Within a week they had swept through Crimea and the Germans were retreating into the fortress city of Sebastopol, which they were forced to abandon in an emergency evacuation, with Hitler's grudging approval, between 9 and 13 May. Of approximately 65,000 men who made up the final garrison, almost 27,000 had to be left behind to become prisoners of war. In all, the defence of Crimea incurred the loss of 80,000 German troops.[22] Hitler must then have realized that his dreams of building an Aryan utopia in the east had collapsed under the assaults of a Russian army he had expected to defeat in a few short weeks and the capacity to wage total war shown by a political system whose resilience he had underestimated.

As the German army was driven from Ukraine, and DGIV came to serve a Russian, rather than a German, strategic purpose, Walter Gieseke continued in command of Einsatzstab Gieseke, but the unit was no longer in a position to carry out the purposes for which it had originally been set up. Gieseke's men and the Schuma battalions working with them simply got caught up in anti-partisan operations in eastern Poland and in carrying out whatever military tasks the harrassed German command chose to allocate to them in areas behind the battlefront.

In January 1944 Gieseke received the Eastern Front Service Medal, and the following month he was decorated with both the Iron Cross 1st Class and the Infantry Assault Badge in Silver. These decorations suggest that his superiors must have been satisfied with his work and that, in 1944, he had become personally involved in the increasingly intense battles on the Eastern Front. On 21 March a report on his personnel file showed Gieseke in command of Police Regiment Gieseke (3 battalions), and on 2 April an Order of Battle Report stated that he had been at base (*Stutzpunkt*) Sedziszow on 8 March.

By spring 1944 the end of the Second World War in Europe seemed almost in sight, but the final German surrender was to be delayed for more than 12 months. Much hard fighting lay ahead – in Italy, in the Balkans, in the Anglo-American invasion of Normandy, in the strategic air offensive and in the Russian advance through the Balkans, the Baltic States, Poland and Germany itself – before Hitler committed suicide and Russian and Anglo-American forces were able to extinguish the last vestiges of German resistance. During those final battles, as concentration camps such as Auschwitz, Sobibor, Treblinka and Belsen were liberated, the full extent of the Nazi 'final solution' was revealed. They had gone to great lengths to organize nothing less than the extermination of Europe's Jews on an industrial scale.

What could have happened to Walter Gieseke during the final year of hostilities? Having discovered his identity and established the relationship of the scenes shown in the Devon film to the work of Einsatzstab Gieseke in Ukraine from 1942–4, I hoped to round off the research by finding out what became of him. To my intense disappointment, after 2 April 1944 references to Gieseke in both the British decryptions and German records ceased. The awards received by him in early February suggested an increasingly front-line role, and his last known location, Sedziszow near Debica in southern Poland, was known to have been the scene of particularly heavy fighting in early 1944. The area's large Jewish population had been murdered by then, but German troops were busy fighting the partisans of the 'Polish Home Army'.

Sedziszow and Debica were both important railway towns on the route to Lvov. An attempt by partisans on 2 February to blow up a train carrying Hans Frank, the Nazi Governor of the so-called Government-General of Poland, led to large-scale reprisals. At Debica 50 Poles were murdered by the side of the railway track. Otto Schimek, a young German soldier, courageously refused to participate in the murder of civilians. He was put on trial before a military court, convicted and sentenced to death.

The fighting was intense, confused and conducted without mercy by both sides. I presumed that Walter Gieseke had most likely been one of the casualties in this struggle, or of some very similar action during the spring or summer of 1944. Perhaps his remains lay in some unmarked grave, like so many of the unfortunate Jews and other labourers of various nationalities who had been employed against their will in the construction of DGIV. But words like 'presumed', 'most likely' and 'perhaps' are not very satisfying for a historian whose curiosity must forever remain unsatisfied by their inconclusiveness. I felt impelled to continue the search.

TEN

THE CRY FOR JUSTICE

IN the closing stage of the Second World War there was a widely shared assumption that, after victory had been finally secured, the victorious powers would mount an unrelenting campaign to identify, track down and put on trial enemy nationals who had participated in actions which violated the laws and usages of warfare.[1] After the war, the actual investigations into allegations concerning possible war crimes were initially handled by the American, Russian, British and French authorities in their respective zones of occupation in Germany and in the camps holding the very large numbers of prisoners of war who had fallen into their hands.

The Allied powers continued to stage war crimes trials until the end of the 1940s, but the overall number of convictions was modest and the majority of those convictions resulted in relatively light sentences. Over one-third of the accused who were found guilty and condemned to death had their sentences instantly commuted to life imprisonment, and the actual period spent behind bars was often dramatically shortened at a later date. The majority of those who were convicted of war crimes would be out of prison before the end of the 1950s. Henry Friedlander has calculated that 'altogether, the western Allies convicted more than 5,000 Nazis, sentencing over 800 to death, and executing almost 500'.[2]

At government level the desire for vengeance against those who had been responsible for terrible atrocities and the resolve to administer truly deterrent sentences did not persist for very long after the winding up of the International Military Tribunal, set up in Nuremberg to try the major war criminals – the men who had been at the very heart of the Nazi regime. Throughout Europe, ordinary people whose family and friends had been victims of war crimes might still cry out for justice; but their leaders found it convenient to forget. The main war criminals – Hitler, Goering, Himmler and Goebbels – had all escaped the noose by suicide. At a lower level, in many cases the accused or key witnesses had themselves not survived the war; others had made good their escape to neutral countries. In a world with so many problems of reconstruction, people began to ask whether it was really worth spending time, money and energy in pursuing lesser war criminals whose offences could, with the passage of time, begin to look relatively minor compared with the monstrous guilt of the Nazi leadership. Perhaps the Allied governments also began to wonder how their own carpet bombing of German cities, the unrestricted submarine campaign waged against Japan, some of the assassination and sabotage operations of the French Resistance or partisan actions behind the lines in Russia might be assessed when the history of war crimes eventually came to be written.

In some cases deals were done with the accused. Erich von dem Bach Zelewski escaped prosecution for his role in the Holocaust because of his willingness to take the stand at Nuremberg as a prosecution witness. He was later imprisoned, however, for political murders committed in Germany during the 1930s, including his involvement in the 'Night of the Long Knives'. He died in prison in 1972.

Erich Koch, former head of Reichskommissariat Ukraine, was tried in Poland for crimes committed on Polish territory. In 1959 the court sentenced him to life imprisonment rather than invoking the death penalty, seemingly because of his willingness to assist the Polish authorities. He died in prison in 1986.

In addition to prosecutions for offences which could actually be classified as war crimes, the Allies also claimed the right to ban anyone tainted with a Nazi past from holding a position of authority in the administration of post-war Germany. The Americans went to fairly elaborate lengths to implement this policy of denazification in their occupation zone, but the British and French occupation authorities were rather more relaxed about the pre-war careers of many of those they appointed to senior positions in their respective zones.

In 1946 the British occupation authorities drafted an ordinance creating special denazification courts (*Spruchkammern*). With three 'judges' presiding, the courts were empowered to impose punishments on anyone identified as a key member of the Nazi party or supporter of the Hitler regime. Punishments could include a term of imprisonment of up to ten years, forfeiture of property and payment of a fine. Members of the Nazi leadership corps (*Gauleiters* and others) were identified as being the most guilty, with members of the Sicherheitsdienst (SD) and Gestapo second in order of guilt. Ordinary members of the SS, including 'members of the different police forces who were members of the SS', were placed third in culpability.[3] Simple membership of such organizations did not lead to an automatic finding of guilt or to an automatic sentence. The British, not wishing to be accused of repeating the injustices of the Nazi legal system, recognized the legitimacy of a plea that an individual might have been 'drafted into membership by the State in such a way as to give them no choice in the matter'.[4] However just and however practical the setting up and operation of the *Spruchkammern*, the courts were to have important repercussions for postwar Germany and the search for justice in respect of war crimes committed during the years of National Socialism.

Kurt Schumacher, chairman of the German Social Democratic Party, visited Hannover in May 1946. Situated squarely in the British zone not far from Walter Gieseke's place of birth, and formerly a place familiar to Friedrich Jeckeln and other leading Nazis, Hannover was then a ruined city which both the occupying power and the surviving German inhabitants were struggling to rebuild. As a man on the left wing of German politics, Schumacher had spent ten years in concentration camps. Eavesdropping on the conversations of the policemen assigned to protect him during his visit, Schumacher realized that several of them had tainted pasts. Subsequent investigations showed that, of the five men tasked with protecting him, four were former members of the SS.

The issue provoked a wider enquiry into the background of Hannover's police force. It emerged that the city's chief of police, Lieutenant-Colonel Adolf Schult, had formerly been head of personnel for the German police in the Netherlands. A former SS man,

Schult had been expelled from the organization as a result of his involvement in large-scale dealings in the Dutch black market. Thus not only was Schult a former senior official of the Third Reich, but he was also known to be corrupt. After the German defeat in 1945 Schult had been given the job of creating the new police force for Hannover. The British had asked few questions about him and his background, and seemingly even less about the careers of the men he accepted for enrolment in the police force. Many of them turned out to have been former members of the Ordnungspolizei.

The scandal over the police force in Hannover was by no means an isolated instance. A number of complaints were made to the British authorities about the make-up of the new German police. On pragmatic grounds the British were minded to ignore such complaints, except where the row threatened to attract too much public attention. In 1946 an official in His Britannic Majesty's Foreign Office explained the dilemma: 'It is fairly clear that if denazification of the police is carried to extremes there would be no police force left.'[5] Himmler had done an exceptional job in the 1930s in building a police force wholly loyal to him. By the end of the Second World War it was remarkably difficult to find anyone with a background in policing who was not tainted in some way by past associations. In the embryonic stages of the Cold War with Russia, when difficult living conditions in cities like Hannover might be conducive to the growth of both criminal activity and Communist subversion, the British authorities regarded ensuring public order as a priority, even if that meant employing policemen who had learned their trade under the Nazis.

The Hannover case underlined the limitations of denazification in the British zone, and highlighted how quickly the relationship between former adversaries had changed. Old enemies during two world wars were beginning to be regarded as potential new friends. It was thought essential to build this new relationship for the security of the whole of western Europe, but some of the consequences were perhaps open to question. The tainted careers of members of the Hannover police force mattered on more than just a superficial level, however, and the failure to denazify the police was mirrored by failures in other fields, including the judiciary and the legal profession.[6] Old friendships and old loyalties were very enduring among the people responsible for administering justice and those given the job of investigating the criminality of men alongside whom they had once served in the occupied lands of Hitler's empire.

In 1949, on the unification of the British, American and French zones to form the Federal Republic of Germany, responsibility for investigating and punishing war crimes was passed to the West German police and the network of justice ministries in the individual German states. Following the trial in 1958 of Gestapo and SS officers accused of war crimes committed in Lithuania, it was recognized that the system was inadequate for investigating the large number of crimes committed beyond Germany's borders. As a result, in December 1958 the justice ministries of the eleven German States agreed to form the Zentrale Stelle der Landesjustizverwaltungen zur Aufklärung Nationalsozialistischer Verbrechen (Central Office of the State Justice Administration for the Investigation of Crimes Committed during the National Socialist Period). At first the Central Office, based in Ludwigsburg, was only charged with investigating crimes committed against civilians outside Germany. Later its remit was extended. It was expected to carry out initial investigations before handing over promising cases to the justice ministries of individual West German states.

During the late 1950s there was increasing opposition among the people of West Germany to the staging of further war crimes trials. Such trials could not bring back the dead and they only served to damage the international reputation of the new West German state by highlighting the complicity of a substantial number of German people in Nazi war crimes. Nevertheless, in 1960 the abduction and trial of Adolf Eichmann in Israel refocused attention internationally and within Germany on the war crimes issue.

While a majority of the West German public hoped that the unhappy memories of Hitler's Germany could quietly be allowed to fade, the Holocaust remained an unforgettable day-to-day reality for the men and women who had suffered in the camps. Holocaust survivors could never escape the memories, images, smells and emotions of their ordeal. Survivor guilt was commonplace. Surviving members of murdered communities had tangible physical reminders in their own health problems, tattooed prison numbers, faded photographs, abandoned Jewish cemeteries, former synagogues converted to other purposes and grassed-over mass graves. A certain restlessness and rootlessness among survivors was only to be expected. Among their ranks were Arnold Daghani and his wife. In 1958 they left Romania for Israel. Two years later they moved to France, and in 1970 they moved again to Switzerland. From 1977 until his death in 1985 Daghani was resident in Hove, near Brighton, on the south coast of England.

Two things animated Daghani from 1945 until his death – the determination to remember and the fight for justice. He was implacably resolved to remember and memorialize those who had suffered in the ghettos of Transnistria and the work camps along DGIV, especially at Mikhailowka. For Daghani, the hours of darkness could conjure up nightmare visions of the long-dead inmates of Mikhailowka and their German tormentors. During the day he would turn these visions into works of art. The walls of his flat in Hove became adorned with the nightmarish images which continued to plague him. He saw his art as an extension of himself, and he found great difficulty in parting with paintings and drawings which he felt were expressing the depths of his own consciousness. In addition to this deeply personal work, he earned an income by painting religious themes or lighter subjects associated with the circus, music and literature.

Daghani also hoped to keep alive the memories of Mikhailowka by publishing an account of life in the camps along DGIV. In 1944, when he reached Bucharest, he had begun to transcribe the collection of notes he had made during his time at Mikhailowka and Gaisin. Those notes had been originally jotted down in the form of English shorthand. If the fact that Daghani was keeping some kind of diary had been discovered by the guards at Mikhailowka, it would probably have led to his execution. Using the brief notes originally made at such great risk, Daghani set out to turn his memories into a literary diary. It was first published in Romania in 1947, but it attracted little attention. The book was a remarkable publication, nevertheless. In Edward Timms's opinion:

The Grave is in the Cherry Orchard owes its effect to the chilling precision with which events are described and the sober simplicity

Working on the road.

of Daghani's style, even in passages of reflection. His distinctive achievement, both in the text and in the accompanying illustrations, is to give a human face to the sufferings which the Nazi system inflicted on slave labourers. The description of events at Mikhailowka provides a microcosm of the system of mass murder, with the precise dates and details of mindless atrocities. In place of the impersonal machinery of 'the holocaust', we are presented with the names and ranks of individual perpetrators, the individual characteristics of their victims, and the identities of the bystanders – officials of the construction company who colluded with a system of institutionalized barbarism.[7]

The diary was also published in German as *Lasst mich Leben* (Let me Live) in 1960. In May 1960 Daghani, recovering from a mental breakdown, was contacted by the Central Office of the State Justice Administration in the Federal Republic of Germany.[8] They were ready to set up an investigation into the murders detailed in the diary. Daghani was greatly encouraged by the prospect of obtaining justice at last for those to whose sufferings he had borne witness. In fact, the German authorities had already begun to look at the issue of DGIV even before the publication of the diary. Early in 1960 the Central Office, from its headquarters in Ludwigsburg, had begun preliminary investigations with a view to bringing prosecutions against some of the men of Einsatzstab Gieseke. Men who had served in the command were tracked down and interviewed, as were the handful of traceable survivors from those who had been forced to work on the road. With great care the Central Office team had built up a detailed picture of Einsatzstab Gieseke, construction work along DGIV and life inside the camps. These investigations had established that several men who served in the Einsatzstab were already dead and several more had disappeared. The fate of everyone who could be connected with the road was thoroughly investigated. One of the first people the investigation team called on was retired Oberstleutnant of the gendarmerie Walter Gieseke.

The man who had aroused my curiosity when I first saw the reel of film on the screen at a Baptist church in Devon – the man to whom I had attached the nickname The Fat Man following a comment by my son Edward – had not, as I had tentatively assumed, met his death in southern Poland in 1944. Somehow he had survived the war. Apparently, like thousands of German troops from Army Group North, Gieseke had been trapped in the Kurland pocket in Latvia when the Russians isolated that province from East Prussia by driving through to the Baltic Sea in October 1944. Despite the apparent hopelessness of their position, the German troops besieged in Kurland were able to hold their ground against the Russians until the final German surrender in May 1945. During those final battles, only a limited evacuation of German troops took place from Kurland, since Hitler was certain that what he called Army Group Kurland was tying down vast numbers of Red Army troops that would otherwise be available for the drive on Berlin. Walter Gieseke must have been among the fortunate few who were evacuated by sea from Kurland in time to reach one of the north German ports. Gieseke had returned to Germany just in time for the final surrender and for the relatively safe fate of life behind the barbed wire of a British prisoner-of-war camp. The 135,000 German soldiers in Kurland who had to surrender to the Russians after 9 May 1945 were not so fortunate.

In 1960 the German war crimes investigators found that Gieseke was living at 6 Market Place, Burgdorf. He was then married and living in retirement with his wife Helene in that pleasant town to the east of Hannover, a few kilometres from his birthplace in Hohenhameln. His brother Otto was living in Hannover. Walter Gieseke's quiet retirement was disturbed, however, when the investigators called at his home to question him on two occasions in 1960. During those interrogations Gieseke was shown wartime documents signed by him and photographs of some of the senior figures in Einsatzstab Gieseke. Some of these signed documents were intended to prove that Gieseke had exercised authority over certain men who stood accused of involvement in war crimes. The questioning was also intended to define Gieseke's place in the chain of command and his relationship with the Higher ss and Police Führer for South Russia. During his first interrogation Gieseke was also questioned about war crimes committed near Rowno, where Einsatzstab Gieseke had relocated after they had been forced to withdraw from Ukraine.

At the first interrogation Gieseke told his questioners:

It is true, that I was appointed as leader of Stab DG IV in the Ukraine. According to my memory, I took over leadership of the Stab only at the end of 1942 or start of 1943. In May or June 1943, but it could have also been April, I was IA with the Stab. Back then Prützmann was the Higher ss and Police Leader. Part of my official position involved participation in numerous meetings. The building of the road demanded that meetings were held with the Wehrmacht, the OT [Organization Todt] and other units. I would have taken part in meetings, which would have been led by Prützmann. I cannot recall if I took part in the . . . meeting

(May or June 1942). It is also possible that the meeting in question was a senior management meeting.

I cannot recall Prützmann saying that the 'relocation of Jews' caused a great stir abroad.

To carry out the security tasks, a police battalion was subordinate to me . . . This battalion was called the security battalion . . . I do not know another name for it . . . Apart from this battalion, several units of Ukrainians and Cossacks were used, each of which had a German link officer. I cannot recall the name of these officers, they also changed frequently.

I can also recall that there was a Lithuanian and an Estonian battalion. These units were used for security at the DG IV, and for no other tasks.

I can only recall by name, of my former officers, my former IA and later link officer with a Cossack battalion, Hauptmann Moldenhauer. At the moment he is Major with the border control in Bonn . . .

I neither saw nor heard about Jew executions during my appointment from April 1942.

I do not know the names read out to me. I do not know what the local SD leader or the commander of the POW camp in Rowno were called.

I cannot make a statement in response to whom I would hold responsible for the Jewish executions, since, as I told you, during my being stationed there, none were carried out. I want to mention that Rowno was not my [base quarters], which was in Dnjeperpetrovsk [Dnepropetrovsk]. The stay in Rowno was forced by the thaw period. I cannot make any further statements on this subject.[9]

During this first interrogation Gieseke offered as little information as possible. He was not about to incriminate either himself or the officers and men alongside whom he had served in south Russia and Poland. While giving every appearance of cooperating with the authorities, he was careful to deny any personal wrongdoing or any link with the wrongdoing of others. His selective memory allowed him to mis-remember key dates such as that of his appointment.

Phrases such as 'I cannot recall' or 'I cannot remember' constituted Gieseke's first line of defence against the questions being put to him. His interrogators undoubtedly realized that the former policeman was well versed in the protocols and practices of interrogation.

Six months later, in June 1960, armed with fresh information to try and break him down, the investigators returned to question Gieseke again. On that occasion the retired policeman was forced to be more forthcoming:

As I already explained during my police interrogation, I was the leader of the 'Stab Durchgangstrasse IV' in the Ukraine. I can't remember exactly when I took over the leadership of this Stab . . . You can look this up. I had the rank of major back then. Before that I took part in the France campaign. After that I was ill for some time and was in a field hospital. Following this I was leading a police school in Berlin.

It was from there that I was appointed to the Stab . . . The Stab was back then in Dnjeperpetrovsk [Dnepropetrovsk]. In spring 1942 I learnt that the organization 'Todt' was given considerable tasks in this area. This included among other things the extension of the Durchgangstrasse IV . . . that is the planning of this road. The road was 2000km long and reached from the Polish border to Taganrog. Planned was the further extension to Rostow [Rostov-on-Don]. The tasks of the organization included the renewed usage of the dam at Zaporizha [Zaporozhe], bridge building over the sound/strait at Kertsch [Kerch], bridge building over the Bug at Nikolajew [Nikolayev], rebuilding the industrial area of Slawiansk. The leadership of the OT was also in Dnjepropetrovsk and was subordinate to Professor Bruckmann. Back then, the organization Sauckel was engaged in recruiting workers from the Ukraine for work in Germany. But since the organization Todt now also needed local workers for the organization's tasks, an agreement was reached that Sauckel's organization was not to operate within 50km either side of the new road. The whole road was divided into sections . . . Viniza [Vinnitsa], Kirowograd [Kirovograd], Kriwoi-Rog [Krivoi-Rog], Dnjepropetrovsk and Stalino . . . In each of the named locations there was a section

leader of the OT and in addition a higher SS leader. The workers
. . . needed by the OT were now gathered by the section leader of
the OT together with the SS leader . . . Significant difficulties did
not arise as far as I know. The Ukrainians naturally preferred to
work in their own land rather than in Germany. The workers
were taken from locations/villages near the construction areas.

Subordinate to our Einsatzstab were so called security forces.
As the name states, they were responsible for securing the work
of the Organization Todt against external influences (partisans,
sabotage). To my knowledge, the presence of the security forces
was enough, so that their deployment was not needed, especially sabotage did not happen . . . Taking into account the huge size
of the territory and the physical distance between the construction areas, these security forces were not sufficient. Therefore,
additional battalions of volunteers (so called Hiwi) were created.
These units were led by their own officers. Each battalion had
just the one German officer with a few men as contact (link) officers. There was a Cossack battalion and another time there was
a Ukrainian battalion. How many battalions there were I cannot
recall. It could have been three or four.

Our Einsatzstab had no influence on the technical work.
Neither the number of workers, nor the set up of the work norms
or working times, nor their accommodation . . . was our responsibility. All of that was solely the responsibility of the OT . . .
My task as leader of the Stab was the leadership of the deployed
battalions (from the respective countries) and the deployment of
the security forces at the different work places. The requisitions
were made from the OT (Professor Bruckmann). That's how
far I worked with Prof. Bruckmann. I don't know his first name
or residence.

The security forces, which I made available for a particular
construction section, were led . . . by the SS leader responsible for
this section. This SS leader was appointed by the Higher SS and
Police Leader in Kiev. In each case it was a SS-Brigade or
Oberführer. They were by nature not subject to my orders.
Rather, the leader of the security forces unit in question was subordinate to the responsible SS section leader. I was not involved

with the work of the security forces in the construction sections. Considering the huge distances, it would have been impossible to carry out such duty. My task was limited to making available the requested security forces and keep them ready for deployment (equipment, food, clothing etc.).

I am aware that, among others, Jews were used as workers, and I know that from one location in the section Winiza [Vinnitsa]. I can't recall who told me and how. Officially, I was not, as I said, involved with that. I just heard about that occasionally. During the whole time I never heard about Jew shootings (executions). I can't therefore comment on who ordered these shootings. I had, as I stated, nothing to do with the deployment and treatment of the workers and would have had, therefore, no possibility to influence events. As I said, 3 organisations were active at the same time, the OT, the ss and our security forces. I am stressing again, that in the construction areas in question the responsible ss leader also had to handle the work of our security teams. I had nothing to do with that. I did not take care of, and could not have taken care of, the work of the individual [security forces]. I am distinctly stressing that I did not know anything about the deployment or involvement of security forces in Jew shootings . . . I only knew that workers were used for the work and that in one case Jewish workers were also used. Even if I had known everything, I would not have had an opportunity to change anything. But I am stressing again strongly, that I did not know about this. In my Stab was just one ss leader, an Untersturmführer. Why he was appointed to me, I can't say . . . I don't know about work camps in Mikhailowka, Braslaw, Tarrasiwka, Krasnapolka, Kublicz and Nemirow. As I said, I didn't even know that there were camps at the construction sites.

Already, after my police interrogation I named Hauptmann Moldenhauer, who at the time was part of my Stab. In the meantime I remembered:

Hauptmann Hensel, who then led a company and is today with the police;

Oberleutnant Stender, who then led the communications train, I am sure he is on police service again, since he visited me some years ago. His address I do not know;

Brigade leader von Alrensdorf or similar, section leader in Viniza [Vinnitsa];

Brigade leader Strob, section Kirowograd [Kirovograd].

Further names I cannot at the moment recall.[10]

Gieseke's affidavit amounted to a further flat denial of any personal involvement in wrongdoing in respect of the building of DGIV. He portrayed himself as an office-bound minor figure having no place in the SS chain of command – just a simple police officer responsible for security matters along the route of the road. The SS were responsible for accommodation, conditions of labour and any execution of prisoners. Gieseke seems to lay some blame at the door of the SS officer attached to the Einsatzstab, a reference to a certain Untersturmführer Jaeger.

To jog Gieseke's memory, the interrogators showed him his own signature on appraisal and promotion documents that related to SS men. Gieseke insisted that he had no memory, or only very weak memories, of the men and the circumstances in which he might have been signing such documents. His memory, although apparently much improved on some matters since the first interview in January, was still poor when it came to identifying other senior figures involved in the construction of DGIV. Ludolf von Alvensleben became 'von Alrensdorf'. SS Brigadeführer Jurgen Stroop, who headed the Kirovograd Construction Office, became Strob.[11] Walter Brugmann, architect and manager of Organization Todt in south Russia, became Professor Bruckmann. In any case, identifying them correctly would not have mattered. Alvensleben was safe in South America and Stroop had been executed on 6 March 1952 as punishment for his brutal role in helping to quell the Warsaw uprising of 1944. Untersturmführer Jaeger had also been killed in action before the end of the war and Walter Brugmann had died as a result of injuries incurred in an aircraft crash in 1944. Gieseke was obviously well versed in the strategems by which an accused could lay false trails and otherwise provide the minimum of useful information while appearing to be cooperative.

Gieseke suspected that the investigating authorities did not know he had also been a member of the SS. His involvement in the promo-

The Fat Man inspecting conditions for Red Army prisoners.

tion and appraisal of other ss men was a direct reflection of his close working relationship with that organization. He must have been hoping that no further documents would come to light to disprove any of his assertions or explanations.

One piece of evidence which he may have hoped would stay quietly lost for ever would have been the film that eventually turned up in Cullompton, Devon. That short, silent film would have torn enormous holes in Gieseke's account of events in Ukraine. The camera shows that, far from being a desk-bound administrator, Gieseke liked to get out in the field to examine conditions for himself and to talk to the men of his command. Was it really credible for him to maintain that he was unaware of the existence of the Jewish labour camps and the treatment of the Jewish slave labourers on the road? He was probably involved, at least to some extent, in supervising conditions in the camps. He is seen personally inspecting the accommodation to be occupied by a group of Russian prisoners of war employed as labourers. He had the most cordial relations with some of the most senior ss officers in Ukraine and Crimea, men whose names he later had such trouble in recalling, and he was in no way inferior or subordinate to the ss. Indeed, his body language in the film suggests a man enjoying considerable authority in overseeing one of Himmler's pet projects. Finally, Willi Jaeger, the man I had initially nicknamed 'Lemon Head' on account of the shape of his face, was very much subordinate to Gieseke. Appearing in the film almost as often as Gieseke himself, Jaeger is every inch the aide-de-camp to the policeman. Gieseke could count himself lucky that the film was to stay hidden for a further 45 years.

Before that second interrogation took place, the Central Office staff had handed over the cases against Gieseke and the men of his Einsatzstab to the public prosecutors in each of the cities where the accused were resident. The Department of Public Prosecution in Hildesheim had formally instituted legal proceedings against Walter Gieseke on 4 May 1960. Justice would not be swift, however. Wrangling over issues concerning overlapping jurisdictions and the need to bundle cases together blighted the next four years.

On 10 August 1964 the Department of Public Prosecution in Hildesheim decided to drop the proceedings against Gieseke, but that was not the end of the matter. In 1968 he was questioned again, this time by the public prosecutor for Lubeck. During the course of investigations into Einsatzstab Gieseke, the public prosecutor at Lubeck had heard evidence from at least three witnesses that Gieseke had been aware of the executions of Jews. The 1968 interrogation, which lasted over three and a half hours, focused on the central question of Gieseke's precise position in regard to the ss chain of command. Once again, evidence that Gieseke had appraised ss men was used to suggest that he had carried greater responsibility and wielded more authority in his relationship with the ss than the former police officer had previously admitted. Cleverly and subtly Gieseke shifted his ground yet again to claim that he had only carried out the appraisals on the delegated authority of the Higher ss and Police Führer for South Russia:

If I did their appraisals, as shown by the evidence shown to me, these appraisals were done on order of the HSSPF. It follows from practical necessity that I did these appraisals since I was in contact with these people at the DGIV. I could only report any complaints to the HSSPF, who then had the possibility for disciplinary action.

Things were different for the area of 'giving orders'. I was put in place by the HSSPF as the responsible officer for the construction of the DGIV. To fulfil this task, I necessarily had to be in a commanding position. I therefore could give orders, within the framework of the tasks of the DGIV, to the administration of the main construction zones [*Oberbauabschnitte*] and their leaders. These main construction leaders now had to carry out these orders and instructions within their main construction section and within their discretion/judgement. In other words, I only gave framework orders.

I didn't have any direct influence on the construction section administrations. That also follows the military hierarchy, that as leader of the Stab you turn to the next lower office and only in special circumstances contact directly the offices concerned. It is correct that I visited on my inspection rounds also the construction section administrations and the bases of my police officers, to enquire about the general situation and the provision; and to check the relationship between the police and the OT on the one hand, and between the police and the SS on the other hand.

It is also correct, that the main construction zones sent reports on the progress of the work to my Stab at certain intervals, which I then summarized with my Stab and sent on to the HSSPF. This way of reporting was not, however, planned from the beginning. At first the main construction zones were to report directly to the HSSPF . . . When I am asked about the Jew executions in the main construction zone Winniza [Vinnitsa], I can only say, that I didn't know anything about such measures. I did know, due to the incoming reports, that Jewish workers were used there, and I also saw such a camp along the road while driving past on inspection round. [Translator's note: He really means a glimpse from his car as he was driving by.] I cannot recall today anything about the strength of these Jewish workers.

I have heard today for the first time, to what an extent Jews were shot in this area and that members of the I Company and members of the construction section administration took part in such measures. I assure you that I never heard about this, either in private or officially. I cannot explain on which order Ettenhuber and his men had to take part in such measures. Partly, I explain it, that the orders of the higher SS leaders in the eyes of my people seemed binding, since they were instructionally subordinate to them. Even as a higher leader of a Stab, you hardly had an insight into the internal SS hierarchy of orders [in

the sense of who passed orders to whom and in what succession].
It is possible that these measures were ordered directly by the
security police, thus by-passing the responsible Stab; and our
people were simply presented with a fait accompli.

Even shown the statements given by witnesses Mannhaupt,
Moser and Schenck, according to which I knew about the Jew
executions, I have to insist on my description of events. I do not
believe, that I would have behaved in such a way in the situation
described by Mannhaupt. I would have immediately taken care of
these things, would have not treated the administration officer
of the 1 Company in such a way (if only for disciplinary reasons),
and would have undertaken the presumably useless attempt [to
go to] Prützmann, to prevent such actions.[12]

Gieseke's protestations of innocence were cleverly coupled with
finely nuanced assurances about the limits of his authority. In his
testimony he traced managerial boundaries that the public prosecutor
would not find detailed in any document. If he only gave orders
within a certain framework relating to the construction of the road,
that would have been the result of informal understandings between
him and Prützmann. He was forced to shift a little ground from his
earlier testimony. He had to admit making tours of inspection and
receiving reports from the different sectors. Earlier attempts to por-
tray himself as a desk-bound administrator, blissfully unaware of any
wrongdoing, were dispelled. Indeed, his involvement with the bureau-
cratic paperwork was in danger of proving a liability. Gieseke's
apparent myopia, both on his tours of inspection and in his examination of the paperwork coming across his desk, lacked credibility.
Nevertheless, knowledge of criminal acts and being held responsible
for them were not really the same thing. Although proceedings against
lower-ranking officers within Einstatzstab Gieseke would continue
for several years, in the case of Walter Gieseke himself, the Public
Prosecutor concluded:

The accused Gieseke due to his official position not only knew
about the use of Jewish slave labourers, as he admits himself, but
also knew about the measures directed against them. The testi-

monies do not, however, contain sufficient concrete evidence that
Gieseke actively participated in the killing of Jewish slave labourers by giving related orders . . . The alleged phrase from Gieseke:
'who does not work gets shot' does not mean that Gieseke himself gave the order for the shooting; it may have been solely a
statement of facts . . . on which the accused had no influence.[13]

The available evidence left the Public Prosecutor with only one
possible course of action:

> It is not possible to sustain the allegation against the accused
> Gieseke, despite his influential position as leader of the Einsatz-
> stab Gieseke, which was responsible for DGIV . . . that he direct-
> ly or indirectly participated in the killing of Jewish slave labour-
> ers through the giving of related extermination orders.
> Therefore the proceedings against Walter Giesecke are to be
> dropped.[14]

The decision not to prosecute was taken in spite of the fact that,
after lengthy investigations, the authorities had felt able to reach a
number of very significant conclusions about the building of DGIV.
They concluded that the Higher SS and Police Leader for South
Russia was ultimately responsible for building the road and that
orders for mass executions of Jews probably originated from his
office. That finding transferred potential guilt from Gieseke to Hans
Adolf Prützmann, who was beyond reach of the law, since he had
been dead since 1945. After interviewing a large number of men who
had served in Einsatzstab Gieseke, however, the authorities felt
certain that a set of operating procedures for dealing with Jewish
slave labour had been in use within the unit. A written order detailing the procedures was not found, but it was felt that, by one means
or another, orders had been given to the following effect:

1. Jews unable to work are to be shot. [This included the
   elderly, sick and very young.]
2. Captured Jews are to be shot.
3. For each escaped Jew, every tenth Jew of his/her working

gang, or ten hostages of his/her home village, are to be shot.

4. Escaping Jews are to be shot without warning.[15]

The investigators could not produce any proof of who actually gave the order and by which chain of command it reached the ss and police units (responsible for the building project) and the offices of the security police and the sd (responsible for the shooting of slave labourers). In other words, the prosecutors were content to view Gieseke's authority as quite limited, and seriously circumscribed by the ss chain of command. Franz Christoffel, an officer in the ss, alleged that Gieseke and Prützmann had drafted orders for killings, but the prosecutors considered that the only thing about which they could feel absolutely certain was that Gieseke had been informed about the killings linked to DGIV. They could not establish his direct personal involvement in the murder of Jews, despite the evidence of several witnesses that the killings had been openly talked about in Einsatzstab Gieseke.

The prosecutors may have given some credence to one favourable piece of evidence which came to their notice. In summer 1942 an inspector with one of the police units under Gieseke's command had refused to take part in a mass shooting of Jews. Gieseke had been involved in the ensuing disciplinary procedure. The inspector, Hauptmann Ettengruber, was examined by an ss doctor who declared him medically unfit for further front-line service. Ettengruber was promptly transferred back to a desk job in the police administration office in Königsberg, East Prussia. According to one witness, Gieseke had used his influence to protect Ettengruber. Some elements of the story were confirmed in Ettengruber's own testimony, but he claimed that his return to Königsberg was due to his age and the need to release younger police officers from administrative duties so that they could be made available for front-line service.

The failure of the case against Gieseke was of relatively little significance to Arnold Daghani. His prime concern was to bring to justice German officers such as ss Unterscharführer Walter Mintel, camp commandant at Mikhailowka, whose crimes he had witnessed personally. Daghani cooperated fully with the prosecuting officials. For example, in 1965 Dieter Joachim, Public Prosecutor for Lubeck, wrote to Daghani to ask him to make a legal deposition. Daghani was happy to spend two and a half days drawing up his statement.

In 1971 Joachim sent him four volumes, totalling 741 pages, of evidence and conclusions in the cases against the men of DGIV.[16] Daghani used this documentation to trace certain old acquaintances. He wrote to some of the civilian staff of August Dohrmann, the civilian firm responsible for building the road near Mikhailowka. Daghani had last seen Werner Bergmann (boss of the works) and Joseph Elaesser (foreman) in 1943. Like many other Jews at Mikhailowka, Daghani had had a fairly positive relationship with the civilian construction staff. In the 1970s he exchanged over 50 letters with the two men, and he met Elaesser in 1974. Both Elaesser and Bergmann died in the late 1970s, by which time Daghani had begun to suspect that Elaesser might himself have been involved in the murder of Jewish slave labourers.

At every turn of events Daghani was angered and depressed at the slow pace of the investigations. On 8 March 1972 he met Hans-Joachim Roehse (Counsel for the Hamburg County Court), the Hamburg Public Prosecutor and Walter Mintel's defence lawyer to go over the accusations against Mintel.[17] A trial seemed imminent. Four years later, Roehse finally wrote to inform Daghani that the investigation had not been able to locate any witnesses to substantiate a charge of murder against Mintel.

Of particular importance to Arnold Daghani was the investigation of the murders he had witnessed at Mikhailowka and the eventual liquidation of the camp at Tarrasiwka. In the case arising from the liquidation of the camp at Tarrasiwka the prosecutors eventually concluded: 'The accused Karl Burger is dead. The members of the execution-commando are unknown. There are no clues for a search. As a result the proceedings are to be quashed. The search goes on for the leader of the commando, allegedly called Froehlich.'[18]

Allegations against the Lithuanian security forces that had acted as guards along the road foundered on an almost complete lack of information; even their names could not be established with any certainty. By the early 1970s Daghani realized with dismay that there would be no justice in the case of DGIV, despite an ostensibly thorough investigation. According to a news report which had appeared in the *Jewish Chronicle* on 7 April 1967, 1,500 people had been interviewed in Germany and a further 100 in Israel.[19] Noting from the prosecutor's report that several serving members of the police force in West Germany had served in Ukraine with Einsatzstab Gieseke between 1941 and 1943, Daghani came to view the investigations 'as merely a farce, a meaningless gesture'.[20]

Bitterly depressed by the failure of the West German authorities to bring the men of Einsatzstab Gieseke to justice, Daghani spent his final years going over the prosecutor's report time after time. He continued to do what he could to advance the cause of justice, publicly attacking Walter Mintel in an article in *Stern* magazine on 8 September 1980, when they carried an article on the poetess Selma Meerbaum-Eisinger, who had died in Mikhailowka.[21]

Daghani was probably unaware of the wider context in which the investigation of Gieseke and others had taken place. When the justice system of the Federal Republic of Germany was created in the late 1940s there was a specific rejection of the idea of creating laws retrospectively by which to try the crimes of the past. The Federal German State would not recognize the 'crimes against humanity' specified by the London Charter and put into operation by the International Military Tribunal at Nuremberg in 1945. In West Germany crimes committed between 1939 and 1945 could only be tried under the conventional criminal law in force at that time. That, in turn, presented a further difficulty. The German definition of the crime of murder differed significantly, in some respects, from definitions in, say, the USA or Great Britain. German law defined a murderer as someone who kills another person – treacherously, cruelly or by means endangering the community – from love of killing; from sexual motives; from covetousness; from other base motives; or from desire to conceal another crime. Usefully, the German Supreme Court (*Bundesgerichtshof*, BGH) determined that anti-Semitisim or racism constituted 'base motives' but the legal definition of murder still made it difficult for the authorities to bring to justice men who could reasonably claim to have been carrying out the official policy of the German state at that time.

Although the defence of 'only obeying orders' was rejected by the West German courts, as it had been at the Nuremberg trials, the claim nevertheless remained relevant since the German definition of murder placed a heavy emphasis on the motives of individuals. In emphasizing his own role as just another cog within the official machine, Gieseke seems to have been very well aware of the framework in which his wartime actions would have to be judged. As a result of the definition, it was easier for the authorities to prosecute lower-ranking perpetrators, who could perhaps be shown to have acted with deliberate malice or personal sadism, than responsible, middle-ranking command figures like Walter Gieseke, who had not personally pulled triggers or ended up with Jewish blood on their hands and polished boots.

Even if the case against Gieseke had been allowed to continue as far as a verdict, fortune would probably have continued to smile on him. Omar Bartov has shown that, in the 1950s and '60s, courts in the Federal Republic of Germany were ready to convict sadists from the margins of German society: they were much more reluctant when it came to convicting Germans from respectable backgrounds. The latter raised just too many uncomfortable questions about the complicity of ordinary Germans in the final solution of the Jewish problem.[22] Interestingly, in the case of events along DGIV, the investigations pressed with greatest persistence were into allegations against Oskar Friese and Walter Mintel, both of whom had been born in Danzig, the port city administered by the League of Nations from 1919 to 1939. They could be regarded, therefore, as coming from the fringe of mainstream German society.

Other factors were also at work. During the first year of its existence the Central Office initiated 400 investigations. The first director of the Central Office was Erwin Schüle, a Wehrmacht veteran who had served on the Eastern Front.[23] Searching for fresh leads and new war crimes worthy of investigation, in 1960 Schüle spent time in Washington going through the German archives captured by the Americans at the end of the war. The pace of prosecution in the early 1960s was frantic, and towards the end of that decade the Central Office was handling over 600 investigations at the same time. The Office appeared eager to bring a significant number of cases to trial, but there was criticism of their work in some quarters. Their investigations may have looked zealous, but in the mid-1960s suspicions were aroused when evidence emerged that Schüle had been a member of both the Nazi party and the SA. Questions about the effectiveness of the Central Office were also raised because of the small number of prosecutions which were actually pressed to a successful conclusion in West Germany. A Dutch researcher, who has analysed the work of the Central Office from a statistical basis, has argued:

Up to 1992, 755 persons stood trial for their war-time involvement in the systematic persecution and killing of Jews. In 283 instances, these trials ended with the acquittal of the defendants, the dismissal of charges for other reasons, or because no punishment was imposed. In 472 cases the defendants were convicted and punished. In one case a death sentence was imposed, while 113 others received life imprisonment, and 358 were punished with a temporary sentence running up to a maximum of 15 years. Thus, of all convictions for Nazi crimes pronounced by West German courts during the past 5 decades, little over 7% actually related to the mass killing of Jews. Assuming . . . a total of 100,000 persons originally involved in these crimes, slightly more than 7 out of 1,000 saw the inside of a courtroom, while not even 5 of them eventually met with a punishment. From a quantitative point of view, then, the record of West Germany's prosecution of its most serious Nazi offenders does not look particularly impressive. In fact, as the above statistics reveal, the German judiciary hardly scratched the surface in this respect.[24]

To a large extent the failure to secure justice in so many cases, and specifically in cases relating to the construction of DGIV, resulted from no failure on the part of the Central Office or of its personnel, no matter how tainted their pasts. In the post-war period, under West German law, a statute of limitations came into operation with a series of deadlines for prosecuting war crimes. Under its provisions, cases potentially punishable by a jail sentence of five years could no longer be brought after May 1950. In 1955 the limitation was extended to crimes punishable by up to ten years imprisonment. Five years later, crimes punishable by terms of imprisonment of up to 15 years for such offences as manslaughter, grievous bodily harm, mistreatment leading to death and robbery could no longer be brought to trial. By 1960 the statute of limitations meant that only 'unqualified murderers' could be brought to court.[25] There was a firm expectation in many quarters that the rolling statute would place all Nazi war criminals beyond the reach of justice by 1965, but the Eichmann trial in Israel meant that the West German government felt unable to put a final end to the possibility of bringing even the most notorious war criminals to trial.

For most of the men who had served with Einsatzstab Gieseke the statute of limitations provided assurance that they would never be prosecuted. True, there could be little argument about their responsibility for working people to death, allowing them to succumb to starvation and disease, depriving them of their liberty and administering brutal beatings. After 1960, however, the statute of limitations meant that only those involved most directly in actual murders were still liable to prosecution before a West German court. The publication in German of Daghani's diary and the investigations of the men of Einsatzstab Gieseke amounted to no more than a painful charade.

The abortive prosecutions of the men of Einsatzstab Gieseke led Daghani to conduct his own investigations. At Yom Kippur Daghani and Nanino would say Kaddish for the dead of Mikhailowka, reciting their names one by one. Daghani channelled his frustrations into his art. Incorporating text and evidence from the prosecutor's report, along with extracts from his Mikhailowka diary, he eventually produced two illuminated manuscripts which were a reflection on the failure to secure justice for those who had died along DGIV. According to Deborah Schultz: 'Until his death in 1985, Daghani would continually return to his experiences of this period, rewriting the text, often painstakingly by hand, and reworking the images.'[26] His wife Nanino died in 1981 and Arnold Daghani followed her on 6 April 1985. To the end he was troubled by the failure to obtain justice. As one of his biographers noted shortly after his death, the fulfilment of justice was 'what he wanted most'.[27]

Remarkably, following Daghani's death there was little interest in the fate of his artwork, partly as a result of its diversity, its form and the fact that much of it had been painted after 1945. The Imperial War Museum in London and several repositories in Israel declined to accept the offer of the collection. Daghani had earlier made a substantial donation of material to Yad Vashem, the official Israeli memorial to the victims of the Holocaust, but he had fallen out with that institution after they refused to add the name Mikhailowka to the list of extermination camps. Hopes of exhibiting the art collection in the artist's own flat in Hove foundered on lack of public interest. In 1987 the collection at last found a home. The Arnold Daghani Trust donated over 6,000 works, including the two illuminated manuscripts, to Sussex University Archive.

Daghani's life had ended in failure as his crusade to obtain justice for the dead of Mikhailowka and Tarrasiwka came to nothing. His personal inquest into the tortures of the past had brought him only frustration and further misery. At some point he had, for example, made rather more progress than the German authorities in establishing the identity of the ss Untersturmführer who commanded the execution detail at Tarrasiwka in December 1943. Identifying him as Heinrich Froehlich, Daghani was staggered to learn that he was one of the *Volksdeutsche* from Neuzuczka, in Bukovina. At Tarrasiwka and elsewhere, Froehlich had been murdering some of his own neighbours.

Daghani's illuminated manuscripts, featuring details from the investigations into the men accused of crimes along DGIV, reveal his mounting frustration and resentment at the failure to secure justice. That failure was not total, however. In May 1945 the Americans had captured in Rottau, Bavaria, ss-Brigadeführer Jurgen Stroop, former head of the Kirovograd construction office on DGIV. Armed with false papers and disguised as an infantry officer, Stroop knew that Allied military police would be looking for him. His responsibility for crimes committed along the route of DGIV was overshadowed by his responsibility for the brutal liquidation of the Warsaw ghetto. He also bore responsibility for the summary execution of Allied airmen in his area of command in Germany. It took two months of interrogation to extract an admission from Stroop that he was not Captain of Reserve Josef Straub. Convicted by an American military tribunal of involvement in the murder of Allied airmen, Stroop was sentenced to death on 21 March 1947, but the sentence was not carried out. Instead, he was handed over to the Polish authorities to answer for his actions in Warsaw in April 1943.

Stroop spent the best part of five years in a Polish jail, first as he awaited trial and then waiting for the sentence to be carried out. His last days were spent with a fellow German officer and Kazimierz Moczarski, a political prisoner and former member of the Polish underground. After his own release from jail, Moczarski set down an account of his conversations with Stroop. They are deeply revealing. They show that Ukraine continued to exercise a powerful hold over the mind of the condemned man. In his prison cell he would remember warm nights in Ukraine. Gazing out from his cell window at a rising full moon, one evening in November 1949, he waxed lyrical:

I remember a moon like that over the Ukrainian steppe in 1942 . . . We were on horseback, not far from our garrison. It was so peaceful that I forgot the war for a while. I can't describe what I felt when I saw that great red moon – I'm a soldier not a poet – but I'll never forget the way it rose over the quiet countryside.[28]

Stroop had longed to settle in Ukraine and in prison he would daydream about the great estate of 5,000–10,000 acres which would have been his after a complete German victory:

I often dream of that beautiful countryside with its rich black earth . . . Imagine what it would have been like for us there after we'd won the war, *Herr* Moczarski. I can picture it so clearly . . . A summer evening . . . lights streaming from the windows of my manor house . . . my wife supervising the butler as he lays the table for dinner . . . porcelain, crystal, silver, candles. *Sehr* elegant! Olaf and me in the courtyard, back from a ride . . . not a sound except for the buzzing mosquitoes and the hum of . . . machinery pumping water into the melon patch.[29]

Even from a prison cell, Stroop could still feel the power of that idyllic vision of the future – centred on ambitious plans for creating an Aryan empire in Ukraine – which had been put before him and other ss officers. Completed and upgraded, DGIV was intended to become a vital artery in nourishing that vision and converting it into a reality, with all that would have meant in terms of personal and national enrichment. It was not to be. Stroop was eventually executed on 6 March 1952.

He was not the only person connected to DGIV to face trial. In 1966 the public prosecutor for Stuttgart brought two groups of cases to court. The cases related to the most westerly section of the road, between Lvov and Tarnopol. Eighteen thousand Jews had lived in Tarnopol before German forces reached the city on 2 July 1941. The Germans instigated a full-scale pogrom, with the synagogue becoming a place where Jews were murdered. Ukrainians also participated in the pogrom. They attacked men, women and children as well as Jewish property. They also targeted Jews in the rural areas around the city. In all, some 5,000 Jews died between 4 and 11 July 1941. Subsequently a ghetto was established in Tarnopol and a network of labour camps was set up. Some of those camps serviced the building of DGIV, and the quarries that produced stone for the new highway.

By April 1943, at the approach of the Russian army, the Germans decided to liquidate the ghetto. The Jews in the ghetto knew that the end was approaching and those in the labour camps realized that their end would also not be delayed. A letter, dated 7 April and written by one of the women in the ghetto, gives an insight into the desperation of the surviving Jews of Tarnopol. The letter would later be found among the pile of clothing left by those who perished a day or two later:

My beloved! Before I leave this world, I want to leave behind a few lines to you, my loved ones. When this letter reaches you one day, I myself will no longer be there, nor will any of us. Our end is drawing near. One feels it; one knows it. Just like the innocent, defenceless Jews already executed, we are all condemned to death. In the very near future it will be our turn, as the small remainder left over from the mass murders. There is no way for us to escape this horrible, ghastly death. At the very beginning . . . some 5,000 men were killed, among them my husband. After six weeks, following a five-day search between the corpses, I found his body . . . Since that day life has ceased for me. Not even in my girlish dreams could I once have wished for a better and more faithful companion. I was only granted two years and two months of happiness.[30]

Those in the ghetto were placed in cattle wagons destined for the concentration camp at Belzec. Many jumped from the wagons and were killed by the fall or by bullets fired from the guards on top of the wagons.

Following the destruction of the ghetto during April and May 1943, the slaves in the work camps prepared for the moment when they too would face execution. That moment came on 12 July, but this time the victims were prepared and ready to resist. One of the survivors later explained:

After they liquidated the ghetto, the Germans started tearing down the labour camps around Tarnopol. On 12 July 1943 panic broke out in the Hlobocek camp, where everyone expected it was about to be liquidated. Many Jews broke out and ran into the woods. Obersturmführer Rokita heard the Jews had run off, and postponed the liquidation of the camp for a few weeks. When General Katzner's aide, that murderer Hildebrand, arrived from Lemberg [Lvov] at the end of July 1943, we knew the time had come to act. After we finished work, the camp was locked up and no one was let out. At four in the morning, large groups of SS and Gestapo, together with the Ukrainian militia, surrounded the camp and started firing at the people inside. We resisted. There was a resistance unit in camp and we'd been organized. Germans were killed, but the resistance was broken in the end. The remaining inmates were led off to the Petrikow Forest and shot. The executions went on for three days until the 2nd of August, 1943, when an announcement was posted for all Jews left in the camp to report for work registration and they wouldn't be harmed . . . A few days later, Rokita came and promised all kind of privileges to those who registered for work. Many people were talked into it and did like he said. Before they were marched to the station, they were given rations of white bread, butter, jam and marmalade; they were also allowed to take their things along. The Germans sent them to the trains unguarded. After boarding them into the wagons, the doors were bolted shut. Suddenly trucks were driven up, the people were chased from the train into the trucks, they were sped off to the Petrikow Forest and shot to a man.[31]

About 200 Jews from the labour camps around Tarnopol were kept alive until August in order to sort through the belongings of the dead. When that work had been completed, the last 200 were in turn murdered.

In 1966 justice caught up with some of those connected with the events at Tarnopol. The first case featured ten individuals, three of whom were acquitted and four sentenced to terms of imprisonment of ten years or less. Two men, Hermann Müller and Paul Raebel, were sentenced to life imprisonment.[32] Later the same year the Stuttgart prosecutor brought a further case involving fifteen people accused of crimes in Tarnopol and its work camps. Ernst Epple was convicted and received a life sentence, while five men were either acquitted or received no sentences.[33] The other nine men were given prison sentences ranging from two and a half to five years.

The handful of men who were brought to trial in the 1960s, and the smaller number who actually received prison sentences, amounted to a disappointing result compared to the thousands who were questioned, and the tens of thousands who had toiled and died on DGIV. Undoubtedly, in the public perception, the suffering of those who had slaved for Nazi Germany had been overshadowed by the industrial level of killings and the evils of human experimentation which had taken place in the huge extermination camps. While the scale of mass murder committed at Mikhailowka, Tarrasiwka and elsewhere had been appalling, it paled by comparison with the hundreds of thousands who were murdered and incinerated at Auschwitz, Belzec and Treblinka. Nevertheless, the camps along DGIV cannot be said to have been any less dedicated to the task of exterminating the Jewish people. The infamous conference at the Villa am Wannsee in 1942, which decided on the genocide of the Jews, specifically countenanced the working to death of Jews as a 'legitimate' method of disposal.

During the later stages of his life Arnold Daghani perceived that, in a public consciousness dominated by appalling images of Auschwitz and Belsen, there was little room for remembering the dead of Mikhailowka and Tarrasiwka. He could see that the road, the victims and the perpetrators were quietly slipping into complete oblivion. As the years went by, he and the other survivors would pass away, leaving no one to bear witness. Only the silent, hidden graves in Ukraine would remain.

ELEVEN

BEYOND EARTHLY JUSTICE

IT is amazing just how small a plot is required for a mass grave capable of holding several hundred people. Judging by the normal standards of civilized humanity, it might be expected that a plot the size of a couple of tennis courts would be required for the interment of 1,000 corpses. That would be hopelessly wrong. Those who carried out the killings in Ukraine from 1941–3 were not guided, even loosely, by the normal standards of civilized humanity. The killers had not even recognized their victims as human. A plot big enough for two tennis courts could easily suffice for the slaughter and burial of 10,000 victims. Ukraine is dotted with such mass graves.

As I stood before the grave outside Berdichev in July 2009, little had apparently changed since the days of execution in late 1941. Before the war the town had been home to 30,000 Jews. They were employed in many of the town's factories, such as the Ilyich tanning plant, and Berdichev was renowned as a Jewish centre within Ukraine. In 1941 only around 10,000 of Berdichev's Jews managed to escape eastwards ahead of the advancing German army. Those who stayed behind were victims of a series of mass murders during August, culminating in a general liquidation in September. Friedrich Jeckeln was the author of this particular atrocity.

The mound before me had been heaped high since 1941, when 12,000 to 15,000 dead and dying people had been dumped into the grave. Since then, trees and other vegetation have colonized the site, which is set in pastureland outside the town. A small stone memorial at one end of the rectangular grave was almost hidden in the undergrowth; at the other end a Jewish prayer shawl had been draped in the branches of one of the trees – signs of neglect and signs of remembrance. The stone memorial at the roadside referred to '18,640 Soviet Citizens' who had been killed by the Nazis 'in and around this spot'. After the war the Soviet authorities had not wished to foster division by recognizing the scale of the Jewish tragedy under the Nazi occupiers. The murders of Jews could be quietly subsumed into the wider horrors of the German assault on the USSR.

If one stands by the roadside marker, and looks towards the site of the mass grave some 200 metres away, the geography of the killing is easy to reconstruct. The Jews of Berdichev were herded out along the road on foot, families, women carrying babies and the elderly struggling to keep up. Most of the younger Jews (those who might have been best able to resist) had already been disposed of in earlier murders. Anyone unable to keep up with the column was murdered where they fell. It was a hot day; fatigue and thirst would have added markedly to apprehension about what might be about to unfold. At a discreet distance from Berdichev, at the edge of a convenient pasture, the column was halted, resting briefly under the shade of trees which lined the road. In groups the Jews would have been led the 200 metres to the grave site. Flat land with minimal cover reduced to an absolute minimum the chances of anyone being able to make a successful escape. As the grave pit filled with bodies, blood had flowed across the pasture. After the killings the grave had been quickly covered with earth, but a few grievously wounded survivors were still managing to dig themselves out for several days afterwards. Some of them succumbed to their wounds as they crawled away, so their unburied corpses had littered the pasture around the grave.

Over 65 years after the slaughter the scene was tranquil but strangely disturbing. The pasture land around the grave site was still farmed. Butterflies enjoyed the abundance of nectar from the incredible array of wild flowers that grew amid the long grass. Justice somehow seemed to demand that nothing should thrive for a hundred years at the scene of such terrible cruelty and suffering; nature clearly did not agree.

Nature had also done her best to reclaim the old Jewish graveyard in Berdichev. The grave sites of the ancestors of the people murdered in 1941 had remained undisturbed during the German occupation and in the post-war years. The dead Jews commemorated in that graveyard had been more fortunate than most: elsewhere in Ukraine, Jewish headstones were systematically desecrated or, indeed, used as a source of stone for road-building. When I visited the site in 2009 small sections of the graveyard had been cleared of the vegetation that had all but overwhelmed the massive stones. Walking along the paths, I encountered two well-dressed people who seemed strikingly out of place in the abandoned graveyard. On the chance that they might be Americans engaged in some family history enquiry, I engaged them in conversation. They turned out to be German. 'What brings you here?' I enquired. 'To see what we did', was the pained and shockingly honest response. I found it impossible to deal meaningfully with such candour, which left me stumbling over a few clichés such as 'It was a long time ago and a very different Germany from today.' The problem was that time had stood still in the grave-yard in Berdichev since 1941. The scars of genocide remained brutally obvious. The murder of millions of people had created a powerful vacuum in the places where they had once lived. I felt it, and so did the young Germans.

Further along the path I met the people responsible for clearing parts of the site: an old lady, a man in his fifties and a man in his twenties. They made a poor living by doing their best to maintain and clear the site and accepting donations from visitors to the graveyard. I had already met a number of people like them, living on the mar-gins of post-Communist Ukrainian society and struggling to survive amid the supposed benefits of capitalism. I gave them a small dona-tion. Who could have refused? They looked after the dead whose murdered families could not tend the graves.

Berdichev was just one of the stops between Kiev and the route of DGIV. From archival research I had learned as much as I could about the old reel of film I had seen in Cullompton and about such men as Walter Gieseke and Arnold Daghani. To learn more I felt it was nec-essary to turn to landscape archaeology to examine Gieseke's journey, as featured in the film, and to see if I could deepen my understand-ing of the story of DGIV and its victims. After flying into Kiev, the capital of Ukraine, I planned to drive along sections of what had been DGIV and through the locations which it had been possible to identify in the film – a road trip of some 3,500 kilometres. Everywhere around

The Jewish cemetery at Berdichev.

me in Ukraine would be the remains of the shattered empire of Soviet Communism: abandoned buildings belonging to former collective farms; ruined factories harking back to the days of Stalin and Krushchev; and decommissioned missile silos and the other military facilities of Cold War days. In addition, there would be new memorials to the dead of the 1930s famine caused by Stalin's collectivization of agriculture, sometimes within yards of abandoned war cemeteries containing the dead 'Heroes of the Soviet Union' who had fallen in the liberation of Ukraine in 1943. The creation of new memorials and the abandonment of the old each testified to the emergence of Ukraine as a separate state from the midst of the wreckage of the old Soviet Union.

Walking through the graveyard in Berdichev and finding the mass grave outside the town confirmed a hunch. The history of events almost 70 years earlier was much more alive in Ukraine than in the West. The years of Communism, rural poverty and a degree of social conservatism had preserved the past in a particularly effective way. Cities, towns and the countryside had not been changed beyond recognition by the multiplication of new roads, urban redevelopment, signature buildings and out-of-town shopping centres. Moreover, in an independent Ukraine that enjoyed an uneasy relationship with Russia, the past mattered very much to the present. Who had done what to whom, when and where, was one of the driving forces of the separate nationalisms that had emerged following the collapse of Communism in 1989.

Throughout central Ukraine, reminders of the war were everywhere: Soviet-era war memorials, atrocity sites, old battlefields, cemeteries for the war dead. Berdichev was by no means exceptional. I could only hope that there would be traces of DGIV and the network of camps along its route. Driving south, my first point of contact with the road was at the city of Uman. An important route centre and key staging post along DGIV, Uman was home to a large Jewish population in 1941. After the arrival of the Germans in August, events had followed a similar sequence to those which occurred in other cities and towns in Ukraine: speedy elimination of Jewish community leaders; the killing of hundreds in random and savage ways in order to terrorize; formation of a ghetto; liquidation of the ghetto and the extermination of all but a handful of Jews who somehow contrived to survive against all the odds. In the case of Uman, most of those survivors had ended up working in the camps along DGIV.

Esfir' Abramovna Kotliar and Mania Mordkovna Fayngold, who had been aged thirteen and 20 respectively and living in Uman when the Germans arrived in 1941, confirmed the anti-Semitic atrocities. Visiting them in their Soviet-era apartments in Uman was a deeply moving experience. Esfir' had fled the city as the general round-up of Jews was taking place. Mania had been taken, along with the other members of her family, to the market area in Uman. 'But what crime had the Jews committed to be dealt with in such a manner?' I asked both women. I knew that there was no crime but I wanted to know just how far they understood the impulses of those set on murdering them. The younger woman could give no answer beyond a shrug. To my surprise, the older woman said that she had asked the same question to the SS men and police herding her family into the market place. 'Because you people want to take over the world', was the response. Realizing the Germans' murderous intent, Mania Fayngold broke through the cordon of security men. As she ran across the road and up the street no one fired at her for fear of hitting the German drivers

waiting with their vehicles. She managed to make good her escape
from the town. In hiding that night, she could hear the continuous
rattle of small-arms fire that would account for her family and the
majority of Uman's Jews.

The two young women had not remained at liberty for long.
Following the general action, both women were rounded up and sent
to a work camp at Ivangorod, near Uman. There they met each other
for the first time. Their experiences of working on the construction
of the road mirrored those described by Arnold Daghani – exhaust-
ing labour, inadequate rations, random individual killings, more
systematic multiple killings, the cruelty of Ukrainian and Lithuanian guards in the pay of the Germans. The road labourers' direct
dealings with the Germans were, in fact, minimal. 'They didn't get
their hands dirty' was one particularly telling comment which had a
strong resonance. In his post-war interrogations Gieseke had said
much the same thing.

In 1942 Mania had been taken to the camp at Mikhailowka. She
remembered the arrival of the Romanian Jews and confirmed the
picture of camp life presented by Daghani in his diary. While she did
not remember Daghani, she did mention, without prompting, some
of the characters mentioned in his diary. She could remember both
Nathan Segall and Mr Hammerling. She recalled how Hammerling
had shown the Germans documents proving that he had been trained
in Berlin. He had protested that there must have been some mistake
in bringing him there; his captors, unimpressed with assertions of
his good ancestry, simply tore up the documents. There was to be
no reprieve for him or his wife. The degree of recall by both Esfir'
and Mania was astonishing. For them the scars of the war years
remained livid.

West of Uman, the old route of DGIV runs parallel with the Bug
river, which once marked the border between Transnistria and Reichskommissariat Ukraine. It is surprising how little has changed. I soon
began to see direction signs to the small communities which once
housed work camps along the route of the road. Other signs pointed
across the Bug to some of the larger settlements which had been the
location of ghettos and receiving camps for the Jews of Romania.
Horse-drawn transport is still a routine sight, and the condition of

the road left much to be desired in 2009, as it had in 1941. Although the road was now tarmacked, it was badly rutted and pot-holed. At the point where side roads ran off the old route of DGIV, the surface was either dirt track or the kind of cobbled surface that had been laid by the slaves working for Einsatzstab Gieseke. Some of those cobbled roads led directly to the sites of the former work camps. Those roads had probably been laid first to enable the construction machinery based at the camps to reach the route of DGIV without difficulty, even in the worst of conditions. They were solidly constructed, even if the nature of the road surface made them uncomfortable and noisy at even the slowest speeds. Driving slowly along the old tracks, I wondered about the hands that had laid each stone carefully in place, settling it into the bed of the road, twisting it to get the best fit with the neighbouring stones, before moving onto the next few inches of road. Each stone in the bed of the road constituted an anonymous memorial to the camp inmates who had toiled on constructing the Nazi empire in the east six inches at a time until their services and lives were considered dispensible.

I was fortunate in receiving further information about life at the camps from three elderly men who had lived in Mikhailowka when they were boys. Even today Mikhailowka remains tiny, little more than a one-street village surrounded by farm land. Chickens roam freely along the verges of the dirt-track road that counts as the main street. Horses and carts are as numerous as motor vehicles. As boys the three men had lived and played in the fields and woods around the village. They had spent their adult lives there and now in old age they would sometimes sit on the tree-shaded benches along the verge of mainstreet and exchange reminiscences of their youth.

They recalled the strange relationship with the 'outsiders' who had been kept penned in the old stables during the war. Those stables had been demolished in the 1960s, but one of the men instantly recognized them from the print of a Daghani watercolour that I showed him. The men recalled how they were forbidden to fraternize with the Jews, but had managed some surreptitious contacts with them, nevertheless. Each day they would watch the labour gangs march off to work. Every so often they would hear sounds of executions being carried out. One of the boys, with a friend, had once

Interviewing at Mikhailowka, 2009.

followed an execution party. Climbing trees to see what the Germans were up to, the boys had witnessed Jews being shot. One of the boys began to cry. After spotting them in the trees, the execution party had begun firing at the two boys, who lost no time in scrambling to the ground and running away.

The place of execution for the Jews of Mikhailowka lay a mile from the site of the old stables. Set in open woodland, the burial humps lay scattered between the pine trees. It was a lonely and yet beautiful location. More than 65 years after the last murder at Mikhailowka, it remains a haunted place. Below the soil, in front of my feet, lay the remains of hundreds of men, women and children who had toiled on the road, only to meet their end in one of the periodic large-scale executions or almost random individual killings.

At least at Tarrasiwka a large memorial marks the spot where the lives of Mucki Enzenberg and others had come of a bloody end. Tarrasiwka had been little more than a large collective farm in 1943 and, in the aftermath of the collapse of Communism, the memorial appears forlorn among the decaying buildings of the old collective. The German empire in the east had collapsed in 1944. The memorial to its victims had been placed there by another empire that in turn had collapsed at the end of the twentieth century. Seeing the memorial at Tarrasiwka encouraged me to think more carefully about the process of liquidating the camps and the murder of their inhabitants.

The closure of the camp at Tarrasiwka had been part of a systematic closure of camps along DGIV at the end of 1943. It is clear from the testimony of Daghani and the two women in Uman that by late 1943 an assortment of individual sympathizers was ready to give some limited assistance to the Jews in the camps. They helped Daghani and others to escape. They also passed information to the Jews in the camps, and they were sometimes prepared to trade food in exchange for other goods. Sympathizers included some Ukrainian peasants and German civilians employed by contractors working on the road. The former, often living a marginal existence themselves, may have instinctively sympathized with people struggling to exist in even worse circumstances. In towns the flames of Ukrainian anti-Semitism might still be fanned by jealousy at the pre-war success of Jewish businessmen; in poorer rural areas the plight of the Jews might have been viewed more sympathetically.

By late 1943, as the Red Army advanced across Ukraine, there was widespread expectation in the camps that final liquidations would soon take place, but the authorities continued to make reassuring noises about the slave labourers 'being moved to other construction projects'. Was there some truth in those reassurances or were they simply blatant lies designed to prevent mass panic or a mass break-out? The whole German war effort was crying out for labour in 1943, but that did not save millions of Jews and other potential workers from perishing in Auschwitz and the other killing camps. Was there, however, a specific need for labour in the east? Did something happen to reduce that need in late 1943, thus leading to the dissolution of the camps and the extermination of the workers housed there?

Without a doubt, the Germans did their best to conceal preparations for mass murder from their intended victims. One of the ladies in Uman told me that preparations for the liquidation of one of the nearby camps had been disrupted by the commandant telling his lover (one of the camp inmates) what was going to happen. The warning allowed her and others to escape. After that, the Germans took more elaborate steps to deceive the inmates. Fearing, nevertheless, that camps were being liquidated one after another, Mania Mordkovna Fayngold escaped from her camp at Teklayevka. She made her way to the camp at Ivangorod to find out whether rumours of a final action against the Jews working on DGIV were correct, but she arrived one day after the camp had been liquidated. In a remarkably brave act, she returned to Teklayevka to tell her fellow inmates that the rumours were true. She persuaded a few to escape with her before Teklayevka was similarly visited by an execution squad.

The closure of the camps was brutal and systematic. It left few survivors. A formal official order for the final dissolution must have been given; Einsatzstab Gieseke must have known about it, and so must Walter Gieseke himself. I wondered whether the film in some way touched upon it. What had been the real purpose of Gieseke's journey in 1943? Could it offer clues to the final act on DGIV?

A journey of 3,500 kilometres across Ukraine in 2009 emphasized for me the practical difficulties which must have faced Gieseke in 1943. The roads of the Ukaine do not make for a pleasant or speedy driving experience, even in a modern 4 x 4 car. Gieseke's journey would have been infinitely slower than mine. He would have done well to maintain an average speed of 30 kilometres an hour. Attacks by partisans would have been an ever present danger, and the need to find secure lodgings for the night an absolute imperative. All I had to cope with was the watchful interest of the Ukrainian police, always ready to pull over the unfortunate motorist in order to come to some sort of 'arrangement' (a bribe equivalent to US$10) for some minor 'infringement'. They were at least ready to venture information for free on the road and Jewish grave sites on the four occasions when I enjoyed the pleasure of their company at the roadside.

Gieseke had clearly broken his journey regularly, as he drove south from his headquarters at Dnepropetrovsk, and at several of the stops the cine camera had been brought into action to record the visit. Thus security points, key strategic crossroads, churches and an out-of-the-way police station at Nowy Bug featured in the film. The journey must have taken several days, as Gieseke slowly progressed towards the final destination shown in the film – Kerch, in Crimea. Along the way Gieseke had taken in some of the key projects with which his command was involved, including bridging operations at Nikolayev.

The length of the journey, and its potential dangers, imply that there must have been a significant need for him to have made the journey.

Driving southeast from Ukraine into Crimea, I began to see the landscapes that featured in the film which had been the starting point for my research – from the steppe lands north of the Perekop isthmus to the immense fields divided by windbreaks in northern Crimea. Now a favoured spot for tourists from Eastern Europe, Crimea had been Hitler's preferred location as the cradle of the new German civilization which was to spring up in the east. The peninsula had been fought over bitterly. The Russian naval base at Sebastopol had withstood a lengthy siege during 1941–2 before it fell to the Germans. At the eastern end of Crimea stood the port of Kerch. It had been taken by the Germans in 1941, seized back by the Russians in December 1941, retaken by the Germans in 1942. From Kerch in September 1942 the German 17th Army had crossed the Kerch Strait to begin their conquest of the Caucasus. One year later they recrossed the strait in defeat. It was to Kerch that the film found in Devon seemed to lead. It contained scenes of Gieseke on a boat, talking to another ss officer in Kerch and carrying out inspections. Once I reached Kerch, I hoped to piece together the final part of the story of Gieseke and the film.

As the Nazi empire in the east reached its apogee, Hitler had added one last undertaking to the responsibilities of Walter Gieseke and his task force. A grandiose engineering project, it would be a crowning achievement of the Third Reich in the east. It can also now be seen as evidence of the increasing gulf between the military realities of the Russian front and Hitler's dreams. A bridge, some three miles in length, was to be built across the Kerch Strait to link Crimea to the Taman peninsula on the opposite shore in the Caucasus. From DGIV a spur would run through the Perekop isthmus, and across Crimea to the bridge. That spur and the bridge would carry the German army to the gates of Asia and the oil of the Caucasus.

Albert Speer was informed of the Führer's intention early in 1943. The head of Organization Todt reminded Hitler that they were already constructing a cable car system across the Kerch Strait to relieve the burden imposed on the German navy by the need to ferry men and material backwards and forwards from Kerch to Taman.

When it opened on 14 June, the cable car system proved highly effective, capable of carrying 1,000 tons each day to meet the supply needs of the German 17th Army. Hitler was not content with this, however, and he decreed that a planned combined road and rail bridge must be thrown across the strait. By this stage the defeat at Stalingrad had undermined Germany's whole position in the Caucasus, but Hitler hoped that the bridge would open up new opportunities for German troops to take the offensive there.

In March 1943 Dr Ertl, who had been appointed head of the Kerch bridge project, prepared a report detailing the resources that he required in order to bring it to completion. Ertl was recognized for his expertise as a 'specialist in bridge building projects'.[1] His report emphasized the enormity of the undertaking: 1120 Organization Todt specialists would be supported by 7,000 *hiwis* (Soviet nationals who had volunteered to collaborate with the German forces). They would need to be further supported with labour from Russian prisoners of war. The number of POWs was not detailed, only the floor area of the accommodation which would house them – 8,250 metres squared. Further accommodation would have to be built for the Organization Todt specialists, *hiwis*, machinery, workshops and all manner of other purposes. As with DGIV, German construction firms would supply specialist workers and specialist machinery such as the pile-drivers that would be essential for work in the Kerch Strait.[2]

The bridge would stretch from Chuska on the eastern side of the strait to Kolonka on the western side. Road and rail spurs would connect the bridge to the existing road and rail networks. The bridge would be carried on a number of piers spaced across the strait. The piers would consist of hollow steel piles driven into the subsoil. Concrete would be poured into the piles and around their base. A lattice work of girders would rise from the piles. Each pier would be joined to the next by a bridging section made of girders. Assembled on shore, the bridging sections would be brought out on barges to the piers they were intended to connect. They could then be raised into position before being bolted to the supporting piers. Finally, a bridge deck would be laid across the top. Ertl's plan for the bridge was in line with the design ethos that had marked the pre-war Nazi autobahns.

The bridge was not meant to impose and dominate; it was meant to flow across the landscape, complementing its curves – an example of nature and structure coming together harmoniously. From the Kolonka side the bridge would begin to cross the strait at a height of 9.4 metres above sea level. As it approached the Chuska side the bridge would gradually and smoothly slope down to five and then two metres above sea level. That would place it at the same height as the surrounding flat coastlands.[3]

On 11 April Hitler and Speer discussed the bridge project. As with so many other major undertakings, the Führer wanted to place his stamp on the bridge:

The Führer agrees to the requisition of iron for the bridge at Kerch. His order therefore stands that this bridge is to be constructed of iron. The bridge is to be protected . . . by bastions, by booms against enemy speedboats and searchlight installations. On the bridge itself some 3.7 cm flak . . . must be installed. Nets against floating mines to be provided: piles for these must be driven.[4]

It was perhaps typical of Hitler that the more his regime started to crumble, the more he enjoyed planning monumental architectural projects to mark its greatness. In 1945, besieged in the Führer bunker beneath the Chancellery in Berlin, he still played around with his plans for the redesign of Linz, even as he contemplated his eventual suicide. In the opinion of Frederic Spotts:

Lord of the world. Such was what Hitler dreamed of being. Through political and military means he hoped to achieve it. And through architecture he intended to manifest it . . . For Hitler architecture had a variety of purposes – self-gratification, self-glorification, social indoctrination and nationalistic self-assertion.[5]

Hitler's bridge at Kerch would be all these things. He also saw himself in direct competition with the architectural achievements of the USA. As early as 1939, Hitler toyed with the idea of constructing the world's largest bridge in Hamburg. In February 1939, addressing a group of Wehrmacht soldiers, he proclaimed: 'I would still build the biggest bridge in the world in Hamburg so that Germans, coming or going abroad and comparing Germany with overseas, will think, "What is America with its bridges? We can do the same."'[6] The straits at Kerch would give Hitler his opportunity to build a bridge signifying German achievement and ambition: a kind of Golden Gate bridge between Europe and Asia. They would push forward with the project, which involved a massive expenditure of manpower and material, even as it became increasingly apparent that German forces in the east could not maintain a secure defensive front against the Russian army.

As the bridge project developed, it began to suck in ever greater resources. For example, between 11 July and 8 August 1943 twelve trainloads of material were brought to Kerch from the Reich.[7] In the summer months *Einsatz* Kerch would require 600 tons of coal a month. In the winter that would rise to 800 tons.[8] Across southern Ukraine, in places like Nikolayev, different units struggled to gather and process the timber requirements for the bridge.[9] A flotilla of boats was requisitioned from all parts of Germany in order to meet the water transport needs of the construction teams.[10] To supplement the more modern means of transport, 800 horses and 350 wagons were requisitioned from across Ukraine.[11] The investment in the bridge project was indeed massive.

The construction work on the bridge was supplemented by other activity around Kerch, as Crimea was hurriedly turned into a fortress which was intended to be impregnable against any further advance by the Red Army:

> The Führer is very pleased with the performance of the Todt Organization in having built a funicular railway across the Kerch [Strait]. He considers this . . . extremely valuable and stresses again that no authority whatsoever must be allowed to interfere with the bridge building schedule for the Kerch [Strait].[12]

By late June 1943 Organization Todt was able to report good progress on the bridge: 'Details of the visit to Kerch and Kuban bridge head reported to the Führer. He thinks such visits useful and agrees to further visits by me [Speer].'[13]

Organization Todt's report to Hitler was, however, less than full and frank. Despite the heavy investment, there remained a critical shortage of labour. On 24 June Dr Ertl wrote to Walter Brugmann, head of Organization Todt in south Russia. He reminded Brugmann that in March he had asked for 2,000 construction specialists before commenting on the small number of workers that he had actually received. Pointedly, he asked Brugmann *Wo bleiben die restlichen 1630 Mann?* (Where are the other 1,630 men?)[14] Ertl called the situation a catastrophe and said that he could not work under such conditions.

Walter Brugmann was asked to report in person at the July meeting between Hitler and Speer. Ertl's complaints had clearly had their effect. Before the meeting Reichskomissariat Ukraine and Fritz Sauckel, the Minister of Labour, had been asked to make available over 4,000 workers from towns such as Halbstadt and Berdiansk for labour on the bridge.[15] This extra manpower seems to have been enough to stave off a Hitler tantrum about the problems at the bridge: 'The Fuhrer took note of the report on the Kerch bridge and at the same time the assent of Gauleiter Sauckel to make the labour speedily available in order to avoid further delays.'[16]

One of the justifications in Hitler's mind for the construction of the bridge, even though it swallowed up such vast quantities of scarce material resources and manpower, was that it would enable the build-up of troops and equipment for a future offensive in the Caucasus. Meanwhile, the German generals on the spot were expressing grave doubts about their ability to cling on to the '*Gotenkopf*' bridgehead on the Taman (Kuban) side of the Kerch Strait, and they were completely convinced that a future offensive there would not be feasible. It was clear that the Russians were massing for a renewed offensive of their own. With some trepidation Speer reported these concerns:

When I reported these fears to Hitler he said contemptuously: 'Nothing but empty evasions! [General] Jänicke is just like the General Staff; he hasn't faith in a new offensive.' Shortly afterward, in the summer of 1943, General Jänicke, commander of the Seventeenth Army, was forced to ask Zeitzler to recommend retreat from the exposed bridgehead. He wanted to take up a more favourable position in the Crimea to be ready for the expected Soviet winter offensive. Hitler, on the other hand, insisted even more obstinately than before that the building of the bridge for his offensive plans must be speeded.[17]

By late August the bridge's future looked increasingly uncertain as Russian troops made significant advances. Walter Brugmann again arrived from Crimea to report directly on progress:

It is possible that the bridge to span the Kerch [Strait] will not be built. A decision will be taken in the next few days. Immediate investigations are however to be made in the steel construction industry as to how far work on the individual bridge elements has advanced, and only those that are nearly finished will be completed.[18]

By September progress on the bridge was further affected by the growing numbers of desertions by the *hiwis*. As the Red Army continued its advance, the Russian *hiwis* knew that, after collaborating with the Germans, they could expect summary execution as traitors if captured.[19] On 4 September Hitler, who was notoriously reluctant to sanction any retreat, finally agreed to a withdrawal from the Kuban on the grounds that it would free up units for other urgent tasks.[20] In October the German 17th Army completed its withdrawal across the Kerch Strait, and at the end of the month Soviet forces landed and seized a bridgehead near Kerch itself. By mid-November the Russian bridgehead was secure enough to put paid to German optimism that it could be speedily crushed. German operations to destroy the cable car link and the partially constructed bridge were compromised when the Russians seized the materials and equipment which had been amassed for completion of the bridge.

The coincidence in timing was striking and thought-provoking. In October 1943, when construction work on DGIV was being progessively closed down and the Jews in the work camps began to fear that final liquidations were imminent, German officials were giving reassurances that the slave labourers would shortly be moved to other projects. Was that merely an empty promise intended to discourage mass escapes or was the promise made in good faith? Is it possible that the urgent need for labour on the Kerch bridge might have proved a potential lifeline for the inmates of Tarrasiwka, Ivangorod and elsewhere, if only the Germans had been able to carry the bridge project through to completion?

The contradictions in Nazi policy, which involved eliminating millions of people while Germany was handicapped by a shortage of labour, are well known. Nevertheless, as long as the Kerch bridge remained under construction, the slave-workers on DGIV might have been regarded as still having potential value. To a certain extent they stood outside the principal mechanisms by which the final solution was being effected. In accounting terms, they were already dead. With slave labourers death was guaranteed in the long run: it was simply a matter of time. Special *Aktions* or transport would not be required. This would have made it a relatively straightforward matter for the Jewish labourers on DGIV to be transferred to another project involving the same command.

The bridge project was undoubtedly encountering long delays and scarcity of labour was the principal problem. These problems may well have provided the reason for Gieseke's visit to Crimea in the late summer of 1943, as shown in the film. Images of him inspecting living conditions for Soviet prisoners of war suggest that the man in overall charge of the building of DGIV was well aware that labour shortages were holding back progress on the Führer's bridge. The images of Gieseke carrying out his inspections also suggest that he probably had much more responsibility for conditions in the camps along DGIV than he was subsequently willing to admit to war crimes investigators. In the person of Gieseke there was a credible link between the need for labour at the bridge site and the fate of the Jews in the slave labour camps along the Bug river. This, in turn, suggests that Gieseke would have been fully aware of, and perhaps authorized, the liquidation of the work camps along the road, once it became clear that the bridge at Kerch was not going to be completed.

The problems of the bridge and the politics surrounding its construction might also explain why Gieseke had his trip to the Crimea recorded on film. The film shows him being proactive, dealing with problems and taking responsibility. The bridge was the Führer's project; DGIV was Himmler's road and he was locked in a fierce battle over the future of the German construction industry with Albert Speer. Did Gieseke want the film as an insurance policy in case his masters decided to take issue with him over the progress of the bridge? Might Himmler have wanted progress on the road filmed, possibly to place in front of the Führer? Hitler loved film and it would demonstrate to him the total commitment of the ss to the construction of the road and to building the bridge across the Kerch Strait. This was Hitler's bridge, which he had played a role in designing, and on whose progress he demanded regular updates. What better way to show Hitler that the ss were getting the job done, despite enormous difficulties, while the head of Organization Todt conspired with the army generals to drag their heels and delay the project? Thoughts of the possible audience for the film might explain why Alvensleben was so nervous of the camera's presence and why Gieseke was so determined to perform before the cameras. Speculation about the potential audience for the film is intriguing, but definitive evidence to prove or disprove the hypothesis has not come to light.

If the Soviet landing on the Kerch peninsula in November 1943 robbed the Jewish workers on DGIV of a possible lifeline, then at least it represented an important, even if ironic, step on the road to victory in Berlin in May 1945. Following the Soviet attack, the Germans attempted to bomb the cable car system which the Russians were trying to use to supply their own troops in the bridgehead at Kerch. With a similar destructive objective, German ships were sent to attack with depth charges the foundations and suspension masts of the cable car system and the piers for the unfinished bridge.[21] A badly damaged transcript of a meeting between Hitler and his generals in April 1944 implies that Soviet forces succeeded in making some use of the partially completed bridge for supplying their troops in the Kerch bridgehead. In response to a discussion about Soviet use of the bridge, General Kurt von Zeitzler, the chief-of-staff of the German army (OKH), retorted dismissively that it was: 'a crossing . . . one can hardly call it a bridge'.[22]

After the Russians drove the Germans from the Crimea in April to May 1944, they decided to complete the bridge over the Kerch Strait. The Soviet army had captured enormous quantities of bridging

The Kerch Strait.

material and machinery and it was recognized that completing the bridge would allow the transit of supply trains from the Caucasus to the Southern Front. Under the direction of K. S. Silin, an engineer who was to have a distinguished career after the war, Russian construction work on the bridge lasted from April to October. From October onwards the bridge carried train after train loaded with badly needed supplies for the Russian troops at the front.

During 1944 ten hammer-blow offensives had driven the German army and their satellite allies out of the Soviet Union. By late 1944, however, the Russians were tiring. Reinforcements and munitions had to be moved over massively lengthened supply lines and the Red Army required a period of rest and recuperation before resuming the drive on Berlin. That period of grace occupied the winter of 1944–5 and led to suspicions about Stalin's motives. As General Shtemenko, their Chief of Operations from 1943 to 1945, later argued:

> The very limited successes we had attained in October [1944] indicated that we had to reinforce the troops advancing to the south, to give some rest to the divisions which had not been relieved for a long time, to re-deploy, to strengthen our logistics,

and to stockpile the materiel we needed for the breakthrough and the subsequent development of operations.[23]

To the Western Allies the inactivity of the Red Army appeared to be a conscious ploy to ensure that the Anglo-American armies weakened themselves in a fight to force a crossing of the Rhine while Soviet forces conserved their strength and waited for the opportunity to seize as much as possible of Eastern and Central Europe. In particular, after the Second World War Western writing was very quick to condemn the failure of the Red Army to speed to the rescue of the Polish Home Army's rising in Warsaw in August 1944. More than 35 years after the event, the great Winston Churchill's grandson complained:

> After a remarkable advance of 250 miles in five weeks, in which they annihilated no fewer than twenty-five German divisions, the Soviet Red Army had reached and crossed the river Vistula immediately to the East of Warsaw . . . [They] made no attempt to continue their advance or to support the Polish resistance with supplies of food and ammunition.[24]

Even in 1944 the apparent betrayal of the Polish Home Army was seen as part of a calculated plan by the Kremlin to secure European domination.

While political considerations undoubtedly played their part in the Russian decision-making process, there can be no doubt about the problems facing the Soviet war machine in late 1944. Above all else, Stalin was not prepared to run risks. Soviet superiority had to be overwhelming to ensure that the German army was not presented with the faintest chance to strike the kind of hammer blow that they had managed against Anglo-American forces in the Ardennes in December 1944. Each Soviet offensive required careful preparation and logistical build-up before it could be launched. It was logistical rather than political considerations that were the real reasons for the Red Army's temporary inactivity in late 1944 and early 1945. Without the bridge over the Kerch Strait, the delay in restarting the drive on Berlin would have been even more protracted.

The presumed remains of Hitler's bridge.

In Russian hands the bridge played a key role in tackling the fundamental difficulty of the Red Army in the winter of 1944–5 – over-extended supply lines.

The life-span of the bridge in Russian service was comparatively short, however. In the winter of 1944–5 ice and storms began to take their toll. On 18 February 1945 about 10 metres of the bridge were destroyed and it began to break apart. By that stage the bridge had done its job of supporting the advance of the Soviet armies. It was allowed to collapse into the strait, although it was not until 1968 that the last of the piers was demolished as a hazard to shipping. The bridge that was intended to carry German troops into the heart of Asia had played an important role in getting the Red Army to Berlin. Hitler had been at least partially right in his view that the bridge could help win the war. Justice lay at the heart of that irony.

EPILOGUE

D GIV was planned to bring about the destruction of Nazi Germany's enemies in two ways. Strategically, the road would improve the flow of reinforcements and supplies to the German armies striving to destroy the armed forces of the Soviet Union; and many Jews, Soviet prisoners of war and other groups classed as 'undesirable' would pay for its construction with their lives. The infamous Wannsee Conference specifically identified the heavy manual labour of road-building as an acceptable method of killing Jews; and life inside the construction camps – marked by starvation, humiliation and sadism – directly reflected the murderous intentions of the influential Germans who sat around that conference table in 1942. Food rations for inmates of the camps were very meagre in order to minimize costs and to ensure that, over time, the debilitated inmates would become more susceptible to illnesses or disease. Arnold Daghani recorded in his diary that, for the first eight days he spent in the labour camp, the ration amounted to one portion of pea soup. Only after that did they receive any bread.

There was callous readiness to accept that large numbers of deaths would be the inevitable consequence of the onerous work of road-building by undernourished labourers in difficult conditions of climate and terrain. Indeed, the deaths were seen as the eugenically essential extermination of 'undesirables' in accordance with the declared racial goals of the Nazi regime. From a victorious Germany a stream of new, 'genetically approved' settlers would eventually flow along the road to build the planned Aryan empire in Ukraine and Crimea. In time the road would facilitate the construction of model homes for model Aryan families, in model settlements, set up in model regions. Like the long-term vision it was intended to serve, the road ultimately crumbled under the impact of the Red Army – but not before it had played a small role in speeding Soviet forces towards the German capital.

Building the road required the cooperation of a number of different German agencies in Ukraine, including the Wehrmacht, the SS, Organization Todt, police and civilian construction companies. The degrees of guilt differed considerably between the various agencies and between individuals. Germans like Friedrich Muehl, who had been ready to fight for the life of little Mucki Enzenberg in 1943, were guided by a completely different set of principles and values from those held and practised by the hardened trigger-men who carried out the numerous killings. For the various agencies and individuals involved, however, collaboration in the road-building was a clear and inescapable patriotic duty, even if it involved collaborating to some extent in implementing policies which eventually led to the extermination of the Jews of Ukraine and Romania. Yet in 1945 only one of the agencies associated with the road came to be classed as a criminal organization: the SS.

In the post-war period concerted efforts were made to pin the blame for the 'final solution' on the narrow shoulders of a small minority of Germans, the leaders of which were either dead or had undergone trial and punishment by the Allies. The legal processes of denazification and war crimes trials could be pointed to as evidence that the guilty minority had been brought to justice. Unfortunately, as the story of DGIV shows, the question of guilt extended well beyond the narrow confines of the SS and senior members of the Nazi party.

The question of guilt also extended beyond Germany. It extended to Marshal Antonescu and the Romanian servicemen whose bestial behaviour towards the Jews in Transnistria shocked even the Germans. It extended to Hungary and Italy, as the Romanians supplied young Jewish women for the sexual gratification of the military units of both nations serving on the Russian Front. It extended to those South American countries which willingly gave shelter to the likes of Ludolf von Alvensleben and other Nazis who were clever enough or lucky enough to put themselves beyond reach of both justice and retribution. It even extended to the British and Americans who knew about the slaughter of the Jews from 1941

onwards and did not speak out. After 1945 the Western Allies gradually became more concerned about preparing for a Cold War
against the Soviet Union than about meting out proper justice for
the wrongs committed under the Nazi regime. The Holocaust was
a pan-European event with many nations, and millions of individuals, complicit in the murder of six million Jews.

If the Nazis had had their way, the slaughter would not have stopped
at six million. The drive on Stalingrad and the advance into the Caucasus in 1942 would have opened up fresh areas to be cleared of Jews and
other potential enemies. Hitler's bridge over the Kerch Straits was the
Third Reich in microcosm. Built as a means of expanding German
influence, it was the product of brutality, of suffering, of inter-agency
competition and of blind will to push the project to completion, whatever the cost. The construction of the bridge at Kerch and filming the
operations of Einsatzstab Gieseke were typical exercises in self-decep-
tion. Even though the Red Army was advancing into southern Ukraine,
the smiles of Gieseke and others who appeared before the camera con-
veyed a confidence in the future of Germany's eastern empire that
belied the actual position on the battlefield. Alvensleben's more nervous
glances at the camera betrayed the inner thoughts of a man who recognized the realities of the situation, and who would shortly make his own
arrangements to ensure that he did not become trapped in Crimea.

If the film which in due course turned up so surprisingly in Devon
was intended to be seen by senior members of the Nazi hierarchy, in
all probability it was never actually screened before the intended audience. Events on the Eastern Front conspired to render the film, perhaps processed with the help of, and incorporating some footage shot
by, Tilde Holz, an embarrassing reminder of ruined dreams. Perhaps
a print of the film, picked up as a souvenir somewhere in the wreckage of Nazi Germany at the end of the war, ultimately came into the
hands of Devon haulier Reg Whitton, film-loving elder of the Baptist
Church in Cullompton.

Research, inspired by curiosity about the film and the people and
activities shown in it, left one major question unanswered. What had
happened to the dominating figure in the film – the man provision-
ally nicknamed by me as The Fat Man – retired Oberstleutnant of
the gendarmerie Walter Gieseke? I had to know.

Hohenhameln, Gieseke's birthplace.

Gieseke's former
headquarters at
Dnepropetrovsk,
2009.

The Market Place, Burgdorf.

After arriving in Hannover in April 2009, my first visit was to Hohenhameln, the place where Gieseke had been born in 1901. The town was as charming as its people. Many of the buildings were half-timbered; the people were pleasant, prosperous and relaxed. The town had not grown much since 1945, and Gieseke would easily have recognized it as home. The war memorial by the church bore witness to the sufferings of Hohenhameln in two world wars, the name Gieseke appearing twice. The cemetery also contained the graves of other members of the family. Walter Gieseke's grave was not among them, however.

I could not help wondering how welcome he would have been in Hohenhameln after 1945. Would he have been hailed as a prodigal son who had miraculously escaped the fate of many loyal Germans in Russia, or would he and his brother Otto have been reviled as senior officers in a movement which had brought such suffering to Hohenhameln, to Lower Saxony and to the whole of Germany? Would there have been resentment that he and Otto had survived to return home while many other boys from Hohenhameln would forever remain listed among the missing? Would they ever really have been able to go home?

From Hohenhameln the trail of Walter Gieseke led me to Burgdorf, a town to the east of Hannover. Burgdorf is larger than Hohenhameln, and located on one of the principal routes into Hannover. Number 6 Markt Platz, Burgdorf, was the last address I had for Gieseke. It was there that he had first been questioned by war crimes investigators in 1960. His former home, a large building now divided into flats, was easy enough to find. How long had this been his home? Had he died there? I decided to check the cemeteries, of which there are several, in and around Burgdorf. At the first cemetery I drew a blank. Walking to the second cemetery, I could not help noticing the pavement studs commemorating the names of citizens of Burgdorf who had been deported to the death camps in the east.

The Uetzer Strasse Cemetery is both impressive and beautiful. The visitor is immediately faced with several rows of war graves: memorials to the victims of a bombing raid on 24 February 1945. Most of the graves are immaculately tended with short hedges between them. The cemetery also contains an impressive range of specimen trees which add to the beauty of the site. Flowers adorn many of the graves, and benches are provided for contemplation and rest. Nevertheless, trudging from gravestone to gravestone is a tiring business on a warm spring day. Three-quarters of the way around I was more and more tempted to conclude that I had embarked on a fool's errand.

I headed out of the sun towards a shady bench by a particularly attractive tree. In front of it was the grave of Walter and Helene Gieseke – a simple polished black granite slab with a low hedge dividing the plot from its neighbours. I had stumbled by chance on the very grave for which I had been searching. Walter Gieseke had died in 1974 and his wife in 1983. Then I noticed the precise date of Gieseke's death – 15 April. I had entered the Uetzer Strasse Cemetery exactly 25 years to the day after Gieseke's death. Some would call it fate, of which I had seen enough not to doubt or question it. As I looked through the camera viewfinder I could see my reflection in the polished granite of the headstone: a peculiar and highly symbolic joining of the living and dead through the medium of a camera lens.

Standing there before the grave of the man in the film, I was reminded of other, more anonymous graves in far-away Ukraine.

Gieseke had lived a full and long life: those who had laboured on the road had not been so fortunate. The Christmas wreath on Gieseke's grave showed that there were still those who remembered him and grieved for him. I wondered who still grieved for Mucki Enzenberg and those who had been murdered at Tarrasiwka in 1943. My feelings were of sadness rather than anger, however. Much as I wanted to hate the policeman whom I had now 'run to earth', I felt that right really belonged to others.

I wondered what Arnold Daghani would have made of Gieseke's grave, if he could have lived to stand at my shoulder that April day. I sensed that Daghani was a man who had wanted to understand – and possibly to forgive – but never to forget. The mortal remains of Walter Gieseke, under whose supervision thousands had toiled in suffering unto death – the man whose eyes I had looked into a thousand times on the screen – were here before me. It was difficult not to see his face in my mind's eye and imagine him wanting – like any human being – to be respected, loved and remembered. Would Daghani have accorded him any part of that? I felt that he probably would, given his post-war relationships with some of those who had worked alongside the ss and Organization Todt. I suspected that he might have agreed with Shakespeare: 'The evil that men do lives after them./ The good is oft interred with their bones.'

Gieseke's grave.

Daghani would not have closed the door on some form of redemption for Gieseke, and neither could I. He must have found life in post-war Germany far from easy, and the period of investigation as a possible war criminal must have caused him and his wife acute anxiety. There must have been some good in him – another side to his personality not evident in the film. As one former committed National Socialist wrote after the war: 'Amongst . . . the executors of the "Final solution to the Jewish Question" . . . there were demonstrably affectionate fathers of families who grew flowers in their spare time and were particularly fond of animals.'[1] This apparently stark contrast, between the nature of some of those investigated for war crimes after 1945 and the crimes of which they stood accused, was identified by the head of the Central Office of the State Justice Administration for the Investigation of Crimes Committed during the National Socialist Period: 'Before the court stand carefully dressed fathers of families, apparently harmless citizens, most of whom live respectably and are well thought of by their neighbours. They appear to be fully normal people, who look so utterly different and behave so utterly differently from common murderers.'[2]

Perhaps to the end of his life Gieseke remained unrepentant about his actions in the 1930s and '40s, presenting an image of respectability while lying his way out of trouble with those tasked to investigate the crimes of the National Socialist era. Did he remember frequently his days of authority on the fringes of the German empire in the east? Did his life end with him revelling in the romance of a lost cause and the camaraderie of men who had been part of the same crusade? Or had Gieseke been a man who, after 1945, experienced some stirring of personal guilt for the terrible events in which he had been involved? Had he been unable to return to Hohenhameln and a community which viewed him and his brother with suspicion or hostility? Had he settled in Burgdorf, finding a wife and making a new life for himself in a town which remembered both its own war dead and its Jewish citizens who had been victims of the Holocaust?

How affected might Gieseke have been by the sights of post-war Hannover and Brunswick? Before the war both cities had been cradles of National Socialism. Brunswick, in particular, had tried to position itself as the most German of cities, only to come second to Nuremberg. Nazi electoral victories in Brunswick allowed Hitler to become a minor official in the free state of Brunswick: that, in turn, opened the door to his gaining German citizenship and eventually contesting the Presidency of the Reich. The ss-Junkerschule in Brunswick had trained some of the most significant and fanatical figures in the organization.[3] In addition, the free state had been the scene of Friedrich Jeckeln's rise to power in the ss, and he was elected by Brunswick to the Reichstag during the 1930s. It was from Brunswick in 1938 that Jeckeln arrived in Hannover to take charge of the Kristallnacht pogrom.

After 1945 both Brunswick and Hannover were wastelands of broken buildings thanks to Allied bombing. Half of Hannover's housing stock had been destroyed and only 1 per cent was entirely undamaged. By 1945 the population of the city had fallen to 217,000 from a 1939 high of 472,000.[4] It would take until 1954 to clear the rubble and basic reconstruction would not be complete until 1961. The rubble of the city would slowly give up 17,000 war dead. How did Gieseke feel about half of Germany being under the control of the Russians or the ethnic cleansing to which the *Volksdeutsche* were subjected across Eastern Europe? Did he feel any sense of personal responsibility for what had taken place under National Socialism? In short, was the ageing Gieseke a symbol of the old Nazi Germany, longing for the good old days, or of a new Germany that was struggling to come to terms with a dark past coated with blood? How deep did his sense of personal responsibility run? His answers to investigators in the 1960s suggested a less than frank acknowledgement of past wrongs, but how far did he admit them in private? Finding the answers to some questions is beyond the power of the historian.

I wondered what Gieseke had made of the pursuit of war criminals in lower Saxony in the post-war era. British military investigators had given way to those of the new German state. The crimes of the past continued to be unearthed. Many of the men brought to justice had followed a similar career pattern to Gieseke, moving from the sa to the police after Hitler's accession to the Chancellorship of Germany in January 1933. Most notably, in the late 1940s and early '50s there had been a large investigation into the Rieseberg murders committed in Brunswick.[5] The murder of thirteen Communists had been carried out by local Nazis on the night of 4–5 July 1933, with Friedrich Jeckeln handily placed as Brunswick's Chief of Police to prevent any effective investigation of the crime. Did Gieseke, in Burgdorf, wonder how long it would be before investigators, or possibly a Jewish revenge agent, came knocking on his door? Had he lived in fear, troubled by ghosts from the past, or had he realized that his chances of conviction were growing slimmer with each passing year? In the case of Brunswick, between 1945 and 1961, investigations into 1,580 persons led to 310 prosecutions.[6] In only 165 of those cases would prison terms result, and in only 25 cases out of the 165 would the term of imprisonment be for more than five years.

As I wondered about the real Walter Gieseke whose grave lay before me, I understood that these questions could have applied to the majority of German adults after 1945. They went right to the heart of the modern German state. The life, times, prejudices and dilemmas of Walter Gieseke summed up the history of Germany during the middle years of the twentieth century. I also realized the impressive scale of the German people's achievements since 1945.

Allied and German attempts after 1945 to bring to justice those involved in war crimes could be viewed as almost a charade when compared with the magnitude of the crimes. Thousands of guilty men escaped punishment. Likewise, the denazification process run by the Allies was hopelessly flawed. Yet Germany had denazified, even if some figures from the Third Reich managed to find their way back into public life in the 1950s and '60s. The exchange with the young German woman in the Jewish graveyard at Berdichev came back to mind. She was there 'to see what we did'. In her comment was an explicit acceptance of responsibility for the Holocaust; in her tone was an expression of disgust at National Socialism. Her honesty and genuineness had shocked me at the time, but she was by no means unrepresentative. In that context, those five words – 'to see what we did' – indicated just how far Germany had come since 1945. Germany had not denazified just because the Allied powers had imposed a process with punishments for the guilty. Germany had denazified because it was the will of the German people. They had, in some cases gradually and by stages, turned their backs on the dark years of Hitler. The process had been neither easy nor perfect, and for many ordinary Germans it meant accepting the crimes of neighbours who otherwise 'dressed respectably' and were 'well thought of'. No doubt some of the guilty, and perhaps Gieseke with them, made their own personal journey in coming to terms with a past dominated by National Socialism.

I felt that I had to leave some symbol at the grave to show that I had visited it and to mark the end of the quest which had begun with that film show in Cullompton Baptist Church. On the headstone I placed a Euro 5-cent piece featuring images of oak leaves, symbolic within German culture of the passage of time, the process of healing and of regenerative strength. I also left a small stone at the grave – a traditional Jewish practice demonstrating that a visit had been made and serving as a sign of permanence. I hoped that whoever still tended Walter Gieseke's grave would understand. The present needed to make its peace with the past and the pursuer with his prey. I hoped also that, before his death, Gieseke had made his own peace with the past and that, on some spiritual level, the policeman could be reconciled with a Jewish artist he had never met. As I left the cemetery I knew that my search had reached some sort of conclusion which would allow me to write this book: what had begun with a dead end had ended with the dead.

REFERENCES

1 MARCHING EASTWARDS

1 R. L. Koehl, *The SS: A History 1919–45* (Stroud, 2000), p. 209.
2 J. R. Angolia, *Uniforms, Organization and History of the German Police* (San Jose, CA, 2004), vol. I, p. 55.
3 Ibid., p. 75.
4 C. Browning, *The Origins of the Final Solution: The Evolution of Nazi Jewish Policy, September 1939–March 1942* (London, 2005), p. 251.
5 R. Gellately, ed., *The Nuremberg Interviews: Conversations with Defendants and Witnesses* (London, 2007), p. 277 (observation by Leon Goldensohn, US Army psychiatrist, 26 January 1946). See also C. Hamilton, *Leaders and Personalities of the Third Reich* (San Jose, CA, 1996), vol. II, p. 131.
6 Browning, *The Origins of the Final Solution*, p. 231.
7 *The German Police: Report by Supreme Headquarters, Allied Expeditionary Force Evaluation and Dissemination Section* (Eastbourne, 1945), p. 1.

2 THE ARYAN IMPERIAL DREAM

1 F. Taylor, trans. and ed., *The Goebbels Diaries 1939–41: The Historic Journal of a Nazi War Leader* (London, 1983), p. 414, entry for 16 June 1941.
2 Cited in W. L. Shirer, *The Rise and Fall of the Third Reich: A History of Nazi Germany* (London 1987), p. 217.
3 Adolf Hitler, *Mein Kampf* (London, 1939), p. 532.
4 Ibid., p. 533.
5 Ibid.
6 Ibid., p. 126.
7 H. Lichtenberger, *The Third Reich* (Freeport, NY, 1969), p. 163.
8 C. Kruszewski, 'International Affairs: Germany's Lebensraum', *The American Political Science Review*, XXXIV / 5 (1940), pp. 964–75.
9 A. Smith, 'The "Golden Age" and National Renewal', in *Myths and Nationhood*, ed. G. Hosking and G. Schöpflin (London, 1997), pp. 36–59.
10 W. L. Shirer, *Rise and Fall of the Third Reich* (New York, 1959), p. 87.
11 R. Breitman, *The Architect of Genocide: Himmler and the Final Solution*

(London, 1991), p. 213.

12 Adolf Hitler, speech at Berdichev, August 1941, in W. Lower, *Nazi Empire Building and the Holocaust in the Ukraine* (Chapel Hill, NC, 2005), p. 173.

3 THE MASTER RACE IN CONTROL

1 P. von Boeselager, *Valkyrie* (London, 2009), p. 107.

2 A. Beevor, *Stalingrad* (London, 1999), p. 29.

3 Seventh Army Interrogation of Heinz Guderian, 28 May 1945, US National Archives, RG 263, Entry Z217, Box 4.

4 Document 1519-PS, 'Notes on the Guarding of Soviet Prisoners of War', 8 September 1941, in *Nazi Conspiracy and Aggression* (Washington, DC, 1946), vol. IV, pp. 58–65.

5 Document NOKW-1605, excerpt from 'Ten-Day Report' from Rear Area Army Group South to the High Command of the Army, 20 December 1941, in *Trials of War Criminals Before the Nuremberg Military Tribunals* (Washington, DC, 1947), vol. XI, p. 31.

6 Ibid., pp. 32–3.

7 P. de Mendelssohn, *The Nuremberg Documents: Some Aspects of German War Policy* (London, 1946), p. 277.

8 D. Pohl and A. Angrick, 'Einsatzgruppen C and D in the Invasion of the Soviet Union', *Holocaust Educational Trust Research Papers*, 1 / 4 (1999–2000).

9 Statement recorded by Leon Goldensohn, US Army Psychiatrist, 1 March 1946, in *The Nuremberg Interviews: Conversations with Defendants and Witnesses*, ed. R. Gellately (London, 2007), p. 389.

10 B. Zabarko, *Holocaust in the Ukraine* (London, 2005), p. 172.

11 Cited in A. V. Prusin, '"Fascist Criminals to the Gallows!": The Holocaust and Soviet War Crimes Trials, December 1945–February 1946', *Holocaust and Genocide Studies*, XVII (2003), pp. 1–30.

12 TNA: HW1 / 135, for the Prime Minister – German Police (Assorted Special Messages), 12 October 1941.

13 R. Breitman, 'Himmler and the "Terrible Secret" among the Executioners', *Journal of Contemporary History*, XXVI / 3–4 (1991), pp. 431–51.

14 H. Höhne, *The Order of the Death's Head: The Story of Hitler's SS* (London, 2000), p. 367.

15 Document R-102, Activity and Situation Report No. 6 of the Task Forces of the Security Police and SD in the USSR, in *Nazi Conspiracy and Aggression*, vol. VIII, pp. 96–103.

16 *Ridna Zemlya*, 17 May 1942, reproduced in A. Butsko, *This Can't Be Forgiven* (Kiev, 1988), p. 14.

17 *Nazi Conspiracy and Aggression*, vol. VIII, pp. 96–103.

18 Father P. Desbois, *The Holocaust by Bullets: A Priest's Journey to Uncover the Truth Behind the Murder of 1.5 Million Jews* (New York, 2008), p. 107.

19 Erich Koch, born 19 June 1896; Reichskommissar for Ukraine 1941–4; arrested by the British May 1949; extradited to Warsaw 1950; sentenced to death 1959; later commuted to life imprisonment; died 1986.

20 Alfred Rosenberg, born 12 January 1893; joined Nazi Party 1919; sentenced to death by the International Military Tribunal at Nuremberg 1 October 1946; executed 16 October 1946.

21 W. L. Shirer, *The Rise and Fall of the Third Reich* (New York, 1959), p. 939.

22 Ibid.

23 V. Grossman, *The Years of War* (Moscow, 1946), p. 321.

24 Document 084-PS, Interdepartmental Report of Ministry for Occupied Eastern Territories, 30 September 1942, in *Nazi Conspiracy and Aggression*, vol. III, pp. 130–46.

25 Document 1381-PS, Secret Report of the Reich Ministry for the Occupied Eastern Territories on Political and Economic Situation in these Territories, December 1942, in *Nazi Conspiracy and Aggression*, vol. III, pp. 932–58.

26 Louis P. Lochner, *The Goebbels Diaries* (London, 1948), p. 89.

27 Ibid., p. 182.

28 Hitler-Speer Conference, 11 November 1942, TNA: FO1078 / 71.

29 See C. Gerlach, *Kalkulierte Morde* (Hamburg, 1999).

30 R.C.K. Ensor, *Mein Kampf* (Oxford, 1939), p. 13.

31 A. Clark, *Barbarossa: The Russian-German Conflict, 1941–1945* (London, 1994), p. 59.

32 Road signage in the Reichskommissariat Ukraine, 25 May 1942, in State Archives of Ukraine (Kiev), Reichskommissariat papers.

33 Order by Reichsminister for the Eastern Lands Rosenberg, 21 December 1942, (including Verordnung über das Verhalten im Strassenverkehr), in State Archives of Ukraine (Kiev), Reichskommissariat papers.

34 Hitler-Speer conference, 7–9 September 1942, TNA: FO1078 / 71.

35 G. Sereny, *Albert Speer: His Battle with Truth* (London, 1995), p. 266.

36 Albert Speer, *The Slave State: Heinrich Himmler's Masterplan for SS Supremacy* (London, 1981), p. 297.

37 Ibid., p. 298.

38 F. Kersten, *The Kersten Memoirs* (New York, 1957), pp. 132–3, cited in H. Pringle, *The Master Plan: Himmler's Scholars and the Holocaust* (London, 2006), pp. 230–31.

4 PUTTING NAMES TO FACES

1 German Government, *Dienstaltersliste der Schutzstaffel der NSDAP, April 1942* (Berlin 1942), p. 8.

2 P. von Boeselager, *Valkyrie* (London, 2009), pp. 64–5.

3 R. Smelser and E. J. Davies II, *The Myth of the Eastern Front: The Nazi–Soviet War in American Popular Culture* (Cambridge, 2008).

4 Ibid., p. 157.

5 A. Schulz, G. Wegmann and D. Zinke, *Die Generale der Waffen-SS und der Polizei* (Bissendorf, 2003), vol. I, pp. 254–8.

6 R. Blanke, Book review in *Slavic Review*, LIII / 3 (1994), pp. 954–5.

7 Schulz, Wegmann and Zinke, *Die Generale der Waffen-SS*, pp. 16–21.

8 Report on activities of the German Police, 1 November–1 December 1943, TNA HW16 / 6.

9 Operational Situation Report USSR, No. 178, Office of the Chief of the Security Police and Security Service, Berlin, 9 March 1942, in *The Einsatzgruppen Reports: Selections from the Dispatches of the Nazi Death Squads' Campaign Against the Jews, July 1941–January 1943*, ed. Y. Arad, S. Krakowski and S. Spector (New York, 1989), pp. 308–9.

10 'Death Sentences at Kharkov', *The Times*, 20 December 1943, p. 4.

11 'Ex-SS Men Gaoled for Executions', *The Times*, 13 April 1965, p. 9.

12 M. C. Yerger, *Waffen-SS Commanders: The Army, Corps and Divisional Leaders of a Legend* (Atglen, PA, 1997), vol. I, p. 276.

13 Schulz, Wegmann and Zinke, *Die Generale der Waffen-SS* (Bissendorf, 2005), vol. II, pp. 343–55.

14 'Herr Hitler and German Citizenship', *The Times*, 26 February 1932, p. 11.

15 'Nazis and the Stahlhelm: The Brunswick Incident', *The Times*, 29 March 1933, p. 13.

16 'Brunswick Unified', *The Times*, 26 April 1933, p. 15.

17 R. Breitman, 'Friedrich Jeckeln', in R. Smelser and E. Syring, *Die SS: Elite unter dem Totenkopf* (Paderborn, 2003), p. 268.

18 'The Blond Nonsense', *The Times*, 19 June 1937, p. 14.

19 [Heinrich Himmler], entries for 1941: 13 January, 3 March, 20 June, 4 December, and 1942: 25 January, 3 February, 9 February, 20 March, 6 June, 24 August, in *Der Dienstkalender Heinrich Himmlers 1941 / 42* (Hamburg, 1999), pp. 107–525.

20 C. Browning, *The Origins of the Final Solution: The Evolution of Nazi Jewish Policy* (Lincoln, NE, 2004), p. 291.

21 On Jeckeln's development of killing techniques see also A. V. Prusin, '"Fascist Criminals to the Gallows!": The Holocaust and Soviet War Crimes Trials, December 1945–February 1946', *Holocaust and Genocide Studies*, XVII (2003), p. 19.

22 A. Angrick, 'The Escalation of German-Rumanian Anti-Jewish Policy and the Attack on the Soviet Union, June 22, 1941', pp. 24–5, at www1.yad-vashem.org, accessed 15 February 2009.

23 Prusin, '"Fascist Criminals to the Gallows!"', p. 18.

24 Operational Situation Report USSR, No. 97, Office of the Chief of the Security Police and Security Service, Berlin, 28 September 1941, in *The*

Einsatzgruppen Reports, ed. Arad, Krakowski and Spector, pp. 164–5.

25 Father P. Desbois, *The Holocaust by Bullets: A Priest's Journey to Uncover the Truth Behind the Murder of 1.5 Million Jews* (New York, 2008), pp. 83ff.

26 See G. H. Bennett, 'Exploring the World of Second and Third Tier Men in the Holocaust: The Interrogation of Friedrich Jeckeln – Engineer and Executioner', *Liverpool Law Review*, XXXII / 1 (2011), pp. 1–18.

27 Jeckeln Interrogation, 30 December 1945, USA, Holocaust Memorial Museum, Central Archives of the Federal Security Service [former KGB] of the Russian Federation; Records relating to war crime trials in the Soviet Union, 1939–1992, RG-06.025.

28 Jeckeln Interrogations on treatment of Soviet prisoners of war, 27 December 1945, and use of poison gas, 31 December 1945, USA, Holocaust Memorial Museum, Central Archives of the Federal Security Service [former KGB] of the Russian Federation; Records relating to war crime trials in the Soviet Union, 1939–1992, RG-06.025.

29 Yerger, *Waffen-SS Commanders*, p. 274.

5 THE FAT MAN IDENTIFIED

1 Reichsrangliste (RRL.) Der Offiziere der Ordnungspolizei, 2 Teil, Oberstleutnant, stand vom 1 October 1943, courtesy Polizeiakademie Niedersachsen.

2 A. Schulz, G. Wegmann and D. Zinke, *Die Generale der Waffen-SS und der Polizei* (Bissendorf, 2005), vol. II, p. 378.

3 Officer Personnel Files, Letter from Race and Settlement Office on File of Walter Gieseke, 14 September 1942, US National Archives, Washington, A3343 Series SSO, Microfilm Publication, SS.

6 *DURCHGANGSTRASSE IV*: HIGHWAY OF THE SS

1 S. H. Newton, *Panzer Operations: The Eastern Front Memoir of General Raus, 1941–1945* (Cambridge, MA, 2003), pp. 2–3.

2 *The Times*, 19 August 1941, p. 3.

3 A. Beevor, *Stalingrad* (London, 1999), p. 36.

4 A. Angrick, 'Forced Labor along the "Strasse der SS"', in *Forced and Slave Labor in Nazi-Dominated Europe*, ed. Center for Advanced Holocaust Studies (Washington, DC, 2004), p. 84.

5 Earl F. Ziemke, *Stalingrad to Berlin: The German Defeat in the East* (Washington, DC, 1968), p. 240.

6 W. Lower, *Nazi Empire Building and the Holocaust in the Ukraine* (Chapel Hill, NC, 2005), p. 144.

7 A. Angrick, 'Annihilation and Labor: Jews and Thoroughfare IV in Central Ukraine', in *The Shoah in the Ukraine: History, Testimony, Memorialization*,

ed. R. Brandon and W. Lower (Bloomington, IN, 2008), pp. 205–6.

8 Observation by Leon Goldensohn, US Army Psychiatrist, 4 June 1946, in *The Nuremberg Interviews: Conversations with Defendants and Witnesses*, ed. R. Gellately (London, 2007), p. 395.

9 Letter of appointment, Reichsführer SS Heinrich Himmler to Dr Hans Kammler, undated, SS Personnel File (frame 183), US National Archives, A3343 Series SSO, Microfilm Publication.

10 Hans Adolf Prützmann, SS Personnel File, Reel 550, 395A (frame 285), Reichsführer SS to Alle Hauptamtchefs, 7 February 1942, US National Archives, A3343 Series SSO, Microfilm Publication.

11 [Heinrich Himmler], *Der Dienstkalender Heinrich Himmlers 1941/42* (Hamburg, 1999), p. 355.

12 For the lower figure see Angrick, 'Annihilation and Labor: Jews and Thoroughfare IV'. In the spring of 1942 it was reported that 110,000 people were labouring on the road. Even with the workforce declining to 70,000 by 1943 there must have been a substantial influx of fresh labour given the death rate, particularly amongst Soviet prisoners of war.

13 'Investigations versus Friese and others for Murder', Lubeck Public Prosecutor's Report, 3 Js 1428 / 65 StA Itzhoe (FM268), Sussex University Library, Arnold Daghani Collection, p. 81.

14 K. Berkhoff, *Harvest of Despair: Life and Death in the Ukraine under Nazi Rule* (Cambridge, MA, 2004), p. 90.

15 Angrick, 'Annihilation and Labor: Jews and Thoroughfare IV', p. 202.

16 Hitler-Speer conference, 19 April 1942, TNA FO1078 / 71.

17 Hitler-Speer conference, 7–9 September 1942, TNA FO1078 / 71.

18 Angrick, 'Forced Labor along the "Strasse der SS"', p. 87.

19 H. Kaienburg, 'Jüdische Arbeitslager an der "Strasse der SS"', *Zeitschrift für Sozialgeschichte des 20 und 21 Jahrhunderts*, XI / 1 (1996), p. 38.

20 C. Gerlach, 'The Wannsee Conference, the Fate of German Jews, and Hitler's Decision in Principle to Exterminate All European Jews', *Journal of Modern History*, LXX/4 (1998), pp. 759–812.

21 *Trials of War Criminals Before the Nuremberg Military Tribunals* (Washington, DC, 1952), vol. XIII, pp. 210–17, Document NG-2586-G.

22 D. Goldhagen, *Hitler's Willing Executioners: Ordinary Germans and the Holocaust* (London, 1996), p. 409.

23 D. Bloxham, *Extermination through Work: Jewish Slave Labour under the Third Reich* (London, 1999–2000), p. 26.

24 Lower, *Nazi Empire Building and the Holocaust*, p. 134.

25 Angrick, 'Forced Labor along the "Strasse der SS"', pp. 87–8.

26 R. Breitman, 'Himmler's Police Auxiliaries in the Occupied Soviet Territories', Museum of Tolerance Multimedia Learning Center, Simon Wiesenthal Center, at http://motlc.wiesenthal.com, accessed 5 June 2008.

27 P. Abbott and E. Pinak, *Ukrainian Armies 1914–55* (Oxford, 2004), p. 38.

28 'Investigations versus Friese and Others for Murder', Sussex University Library, Arnold Daghani Collection, p. 81.

29 Gruppe Geheime Feldpolizei 721 Arbeitsbericht July 1942, 26 July 1942, US National Archives, Microfilm T349.

30 Arbeitsbericht August 1942, 25 August 1942, US National Archives, Microfilm T349.

31 Gruppe Geheime Feldpolizei 708 Arbeitsbericht August 1942, 26 August 1942, US National Archives, Microfilm T349.

32 Ibid.

33 'Investigations versus Friese and Others', p. 87.

34 From the Final Report on the solution of the Jewish problem in Galicia by Katzmann, Commander of the SS and Police in the District Of Galicia, at www1.yadvashem.org, accessed 12 October 2007.

35 Angrick, 'Forced Labor along the "Strasse der SS"', p. 89.

36 C. Browning, *The Origins of the Final Solution: The Evolution of Nazi Jewish Policy, September 1939–March 1942* (London, 2005), p. 509.

37 A. Angrick, 'The Escalation of German-Rumanian Anti-Jewish Policy and the Attack on the Soviet Union, June 22, 1941', at www1.yadvashem.org, accessed 15 February 2009, pp. 32–3; A. Schulz, G. Wegmann and D. Zinke, *Die Generale der Waffen-SS und der Polizei* (Bissendorf, 2003), vol. I, pp. 441–57.

38 Sir Walter Citrine, *I Search for Truth in Russia* (London, 1938), pp. 187ff.

7 THE FILM-MAKERS

1 *Ukraine 1943*, 16 reels of film, US National Archives, RG 242, ARC Identifier 44307, Local Identifier 242-MID-6039u.

2 Reichsfachschaft film file for Holz, Germany, Bundesarchiv Berlin Document Centre.

3 Personalfragebogen Margot Monnier, 8 June 1939, Germany, Bundesarchiv Berlin Document Centre, Monnier Personnel File.

4 Ibid.

5 C. Hamilton, *Leaders and Personalities of the Third Reich* (San Jose, CA, 1996), vol. II, pp. 194–5.

6 Eugen Hadamovsky, *Propaganda und Nationale Macht* (Oldenberg, 1933). His other works include *Dein Rundfunk: Das Rundfunkbuch für alle Volksgenossen* (Munich, 1934); *Blitzmarsch nach Warschau: Frontberichte eines politischen Soldaten* (Munich, 1940); *Hitler kämpft um den Frieden Europas. Ein Tagebuch von Adolf Hitlers Deutschlandfahrt* (Munich, 1940); *Hilfsarbeiter Nr. 50000* (Munich, 1940).

7 Louis P. Lochner, *The Goebbels Diaries* (London, 1948), pp. 238–9.

8 THE ROMANIAN CONNECTION

1 C. Hamilton, *Leaders and Personalities of the Third Reich* (San Jose, CA, 1996), vol. II, p. 221.

2 M. Carp, *Holocaust in Romania: Facts and Documents on the Annihilation of Romania's Jews 1940–1944* (Safety Harbor, FL, 2000), p. 163.

3 *Final Report of the International Commission on the Holocaust in Romania, presented to the Romanian President Ion Iliescu* (Bucharest, 2004), p. 26, at www.ushmm.org, accessed 20 December 2010.

4 Referred to State Attorney Bach, transcripts of the trial of Adolf Eichmann, session 48, part 8, 23 May 1961, at http://adolfeichmanntrial.com, accessed 25 September 2009.

5 Carp, *Holocaust in Romania*, pp. 164–5.

6 *Final Report of the International Commission on the Holocaust in Romania*, p. 42. See also State Attorney Bach, transcripts of the trial of Adolf Eichmann, session 48, part 8, 23 May 1961.

7 Announcement from Führer Headquarters, 6 August 1941, in M. Domarus, *Hitler: Speeches and Proclamations 1932–1945* (London, 2004), vols. I–IV, p. 2471.

8 Carp, *Holocaust in Romania*, p. 49.

9 *Final Report of the International Commission on the Holocaust in Romania*, p. 48.

10 B. Zabarko, *Holocaust in the Ukraine* (London, 2005), pp. 152–3.

11 W. Rosenzweig, 'Retelling the Jewish Slave Labor Experience in Romania', in *Forced and Slave Labor in Nazi-Dominated Europe*, ed. Center for Advanced Holocaust Studies (Washington, DC, 2004), pp. 81–2.

12 A. Angrick, 'The Escalation of German-Rumanian Anti-Jewish Policy and the Attack on the Soviet Union, June 22, 1941', at www1.yadvashem.org, accessed 15 February 2009, pp. 31–2.

13 Andrew L. Simon, in preface to the English edition of Carp, *Holocaust in Romania*, p. 1.

14 *Final Report of the International Commission on the Holocaust in Romania*, p. 83.

15 *Ethnographische Landkarte der Bukowina*, Scale 1:350,000, Goebl-Rasidescu, (Bucharest, 1910).

16 M. Bohm-Duchen, *Daghani* (London, 1987), p. 11.

17 Reproduced in I. Trunk, *Jewish Responses to Nazi Persecution: Collective and Individual Behaviour in Extremis* (New York, 1982), p. 144.

18 Perla Mark, testimony, transcripts of the trial of Adolf Eichmann, session 48, part 1, 23 May 1961.

19 D. Pohl and A. Angrick, 'Einsatzgruppen C and D in the Invasion of the Soviet Union', *Holocaust Educational Trust Research Papers* (1999–2000), vol. 1 / 4, p. 19.

20 Final Report of the International Commission on the Holocaust in Romania, p. 28.
21 Carp, *Holocaust in Romania*, p. 17.
22 Perla Mark was one of those fortunate enough to be given leave to remain. See Perla Mark, testimony, transcripts of the trial of Adolf Eichmann, session 48, part 2, 23 May 1961.
23 Bohm-Duchen, *Daghani*, p. 15.
24 *Final Report of the International Commission on the Holocaust in Romania*, p. 52.
25 Nathan Segall, unpublished personal memoir, 21 October 1943, information from private source.
26 A. Daghani, 'The Grave is in the Cherry Orchard', *Adam International Review*, nos. 291–3 (1961), p. 37, diary entry, 25 October 1942.
27 Ibid., p. 57.
28 Ibid., p. 29, diary entry, 28 September 1942.
29 Ibid., p. 42, diary entry, 15 November 1942.
30 Ibid., p. 61, diary entry, 26 April 1943.
31 Zabarko, *Holocaust in the Ukraine*, p. 263.
32 Ibid., pp. 15–16.
33 Ibid., p. 218.

9 THE END OF THE ROAD

1 Notes on Police Decodes 1943, TNA: HW16 / 68.
2 Ibid.
3 Notes on Police Decodes 1943, TNA: HW16 / 27.
4 Notes on Police Decodes 1943, TNA: HW16 / 68.
5 Ibid.
6 Order of Battle Reports, TNA: HW16 / 89.
7 Notes on Police Decodes 1943, TNA: HW16 / 68.
8 Ibid.
9 Order of Battle Reports, TNA: HW16 / 90.
10 Order of Battle Reports, TNA: HW16 / 89.
11 'Investigations versus Friese and others for Murder', Lubeck Public Prosecutors Report, 3 Js 1428 / 65 StA Itzhoe (FM268), unpublished MSS, Sussex University Library: Arnold Daghani Collection, Testimony of Hermann Hildebrand (trans.), p. 393.
12 Ibid., Testimony of Hermann Kaiser (trans.), pp. 393–4.
13 Ibid., Testimony of Werner Bergmann (trans.), pp. 398–400.
14 Ibid., Testimony of Friedrich Muehl (trans.), pp. 389–90.
15 Ibid., pp. 388–9.
16 B. Zabarko, *Holocaust in the Ukraine* (London, 2005), pp. 192–3.
17 W. Rosenzweig, 'Retelling the Jewish Slave Labor Experience in Romania',

in *Forced and Slave Labor in Nazi-Dominated Europe*, ed. Center for Advanced Holocaust Studies (Washington, DC, 2004), pp. 81–2.

18 V. Grossman, *The Years of War* (Moscow, 1946), p. 338.

19 A. Clark, *Barbarossa: The Russian-German Conflict, 1941–1945* (London, 1994), p. 366.

20 *Final Report of the International Commission on the Holocaust in Romania*, presented to the Romanian President Ion Iliescu (Bucharest, 2004), p. 102, at www.ushmm.org, accessed 20 December 2010.

21 A. Angrick, 'Forced Labor along the "Strasse der SS"', in *Forced and Slave Labor in Nazi Dominated Europe*, ed. Center for Advanced Holocaust Studies, p. 84.

22 J. M. Potter, 'Cracking the Crimea', *Military Affairs*, IX / 2 (1945), pp. 151–5.

10 THE CRY FOR JUSTICE

1 In 1944 the BBC was flooded with complaints at the broadcasting of Noël Coward's satirical revue number 'Don't Lets be Beastly to the Germans', because of its apparent call for moderation in dealing with Germany after the war, see D. C. Watt, *Britain Looks to Germany* (London, 1965), p. 117.

2 H. Friedlander, 'The Judiciary and Nazi Crimes in Postwar Germany', *Simon Wiesenthal Center Annual*, vol. 1, ch. 2, from http://motic.wiesenthal.com, accessed 10 October 2009.

3 Office of Military Government, Civil Administration Division (Denazification, Cumulative Review), Report 1, 1 April 1947–30 April 1948, Military Government Ordinance applicable to the whole of the British Zone (effective 31 December 1946), at http://digital.library.wisc.edu, accessed 28 September 2009.

4 Ibid. See also TNA: FO371 / 64647 (Control Commission for Germany, Hannover Summary, October-November 1947); FO938 / 62 (Hannover Police); FO1005 / 1658–62 (Hildesheim); FO1010 / 77 (Police Matters: British and German 1946–9); and FO1010 / 155 (Unreliability of German police 1950).

5 See T. Bower, *Blind Eye to Murder: Britain, America and the Purging of Nazi Germany – A Pledge Betrayed* (London, 1997), p. 195.

6 Ibid., pp. 197ff.

7 Edward Timms, *Memories of Mikhailowka: Labour Camp Testimonies in the Arnold Daghani Archive*, Centre for German-Jewish Studies, Research Paper No. 4 (2000), pp. 12–13.

8 Ibid., p. 23.

9 Record of Interrogation, Walter Gieseke, 11 January 1960, Bundesarchiv, Aussenstelle der Landjustizverwaltungen, Ludwigsburg, B162 / 1813 (BL. 3–4).

10 Record of Interrogation, Walter Gieseke, 2 June 1960, Bundesarchiv,

Aussenstelle der Landjustizverwaltungen, Ludwigsburg, B162 / 6150 (Bl. 17–20).

11 C. Hamilton, *Leaders and Personalities of the Third Reich* (San Jose, CA, 1996), vol. II, pp. 173–6.

12 Record of Interrogation, Walter Gieseke, 10 September 1968, Bundesarchiv, Aussenstelle Ludwigsburg, B162 / 6165 (Bl. 2554–2556).

13 'Investigations versus Friese and others for Murder', Lubeck Public Prosecutors Report, 3 Js 1428 / 65 StA Itzhoe (FM268), unpublished MS, Sussex University Library, Arnold Daghani Collection, p. 606.

14 Ibid., p. 612.

15 Ibid., pp. 603–5.

16 Ibid.

17 Timms, *Memories of Mikhailowka*, p. 27.

18 'Investigations versus Friese and others'.

19 *Jewish Chronicle*, 7 April 1967, p. 3.

20 M. Bohm-Duchen, *Arnold Daghani* (London, 1987), p. 43.

21 Timms, *Memories of Mikhailowka*, p. 27.

22 O. Bartov, 'Guilt and Accountability in the Postwar Courtroom: The Holocaust in Czortków and Buczacz, East Galicia, as Seen in West German Legal Discourse', at www.yale.edu, accessed 10 March 2009.

23 'War Crimes Unforgotten', *Time* magazine, 9 November 1962.

24 D. De Mildt, *In the Name of the People: Perpetrators of Genocide in the Reflection of their Post-war Prosecution in West Germany* (Leiden, 1996), p. 21.

25 Ibid., p. 28.

26 D. Schultz, 'The Possibilities of Pictorial Narrative: Word – Image – History in the Work of Arnold Daghani', in H. Salmi, *History in Words and Images*, www.hum.utu.fi, accessed 27 December 2010, ebook, p. 151.

27 Bohm-Duchen, *Daghani*, p. iii.

28 M. Fitzpatrick, *Kamierz Moczarski: Conversations with an Executioner* (Englewood Cliffs, NJ, 1977), p. 100.

29 Ibid., p. 103.

30 R. Stackelberg and S. Winkle, *The Nazi Germany Sourcebook: An Anthology of Texts* (London, 2002), pp. 363–4, anonymous letter.

31 I. Trunk, *Jewish Responses to Nazi Persecution: Collective and Individual Behaviour in Extremis* (New York, 1982), pp. 206–7.

32 C. F. Rüter and D. W. de Mildt, eds, *Justiz und NS-Verbrechen: The German Judgements on Capital Nazi Crimes 1945–1999*, vol. XXIV (1998), LG Stuttgart 660715, BGH 680507, Case 634, available at www1.jur.uva.nl, accessed 2 February 2009.

33 Ibid., vol. XXVII (2003), LG Stuttgart 680429, BGH 710518 Case 671.

11 BEYOND EARTHLY JUSTICE

1 *Handbook of the Organization Todt, March 1945,* c. 14, TNA, WO208 / 3018.
2 Report on requirements for the Kerch bridge, 30 March 1943, Bundesarchiv Berlin (Lichterfelde) (subsequently BA Berlin), R501 / 119.
3 Bridge plan, 9 July 1943, BA Berlin, R501 / 126.
4 Hitler-Speer conference, 11 April 1943, TNA, FO1078 / 71.
5 F. Spotts, *Hitler and the Power of Aesthetics* (London, 2003), p. 312.
6 Ibid., p. 329.
7 Dr Ertl to Transport Section, Organization Todt (Berlin), 9 August 1943, BA Berlin R501 / 107.
8 Dr Ertl to Organization Todt Offices (Dnjeperpetrovsk), 31 May 1943, BA Berlin R501 / 107.
9 Wood Requirements, 1943, BA Berlin, R501 / 110. See also Note by Major Brunner on tree-felling Kommando, 30 June 1943, BA Berlin, R501 / 107.
10 List of vessels at Kerch, or on their way to Kerch, 21 July 1943, BA Berlin, R501 / 110.
11 Note on requisition, 11 August 1943, BA Berlin, R501 / 111.
12 Hitler-Speer conference, 1 June 1943, TNA, FO1078 / 71.
13 Hitler-Speer conference, 28 June 1943, with Adam, Schieber and Erdmann in attendance, TNA, FO1078 / 71.
14 Dr Ertl to Walter Brugmann, 24 June 1943, BA Berlin, R501 / 109.
15 Note by Ernest Amtmann, 8 July 1943, BA Berlin, R501 / 110.
16 Hitler-Speer conference, 10 July 1943, with Dorsch, Sauckel and Brugmann in attendance, TNA, FO1078 / 71.
17 A. Speer, *Inside the Third Reich* (London, 1995), pp. 371–2.
18 Hitler-Speer conference, 19–22 August 1943, with Dorsch, Dethleffsen and Brugmann in attendance, TNA, FO1078 / 71.
19 Einsatzbefehl Number 242, 14 September 1943, BA Berlin, R501 / 110.
20 M. Domarus, *Hitler: Speeches and Proclamations 1932–1945* (London, 2004), vols I–IV, p. 2812.
21 Naval Headlines: Ultra Decrypts, 23 April 1944, TNA, HW1 / 2210.
22 H. Heiber and D. M. Glantz, Midday situation report 6 April 1944, in *Hitler and His Generals, Military Conferences, 1942–1945* (New York, 2004), pp. 419–20.
23 S. M. Shtemenko, 'Kak planirovalas' posledniaia kampaniia po razgromu gitlerovskoi Germanii', *Voenno-istoricheskii zhurnal,* 5 (1965), pp. 56–64, reproduced in S. Bialer, *Stalin and His Generals: Soviet Military Memoirs of World War II* (New York, 1969), p. 474.
24 W. S. Churchill Jnr, *Defending the West* (London, 1981), p. 19.

Epilogue

1 M. Maschmann, *Account Rendered: A Dossier on my Former Self* (New York, 1965), p. 220.
2 Ibid.
3 B. Kiekenap, *SS-Junkerschule: SA und SS in Braunschweig* (Brunswick, 2008), pp. 7–13.
4 D. Botting, *In the Ruins of the Reich* (London, 1985), p. 95.
5 W. Sohn, *Im Spiegel der Nachkriegprozesse: Der Errichtung der NS-Herrschaft in Freistaat Braunschweig* (Brunswick, 2003), pp. 155–78.
6 Ibid., p. 73.

SOURCES AND BIBLIOGRAPHY

UNPUBLISHED PRIMARY SOURCES

Germany: Archiv Polizeiakademie Niedersachsen
  Reichsrangliste (RRL) Der Offiziere der Ordnungspolizei, 2 Teil,
    Oberstleutnant, stand vom 1 October 1943
Germany: Aussenstelle der Landjustizverwaltungen Ludwigsburg
  B162 / 1813 (BL.3–4), B162 / 6150 (BL.14–19), B162 / 6165 (BL.2554–6)
Germany: Bundesarchiv Berlin Document Centre
  Monnier Personnel File
  Reichsfachschaft film file for Holz
Germany: Bundesarchiv Berlin (Lichterfelde)
  Organization Todt Files R501 / 107–128
Germany: Wannsee
  House of the Wannsee Conference Memorial: papers relating to the
  conference
Ukraine: Archives and Museums
  Kerch (Eltigen assault): Records relating to the crossing of the Kerch Strait
    by Soviet Forces 1943
  Kerch Museum: City History
  Simferopol Archives: Records relating to German occupation of the Crimea
  State Archives of Ukraine (Kiev): Wartime Soviet visual sources and papers
    relating to Reichskommissariat Ukraine
  Vinnytsia [Vinnitsa] Archives: Local wartime publications
Ukraine: Oral History
  Fayngold, Mania Mordkovna: Uman ghetto and work camps along DGIV
  Hucal, Ivan Stepanovych: Mikhailowka
  Kotliar, Esfir' Abramovna: Uman ghetto and work camps along DGIV
  Stepanovych, Mykola: Mikhailowka
  Umanec, Vasyl Ivanovych: Mikhailowka
United Kingdom: Sussex University Library: Arnold Daghani Collection
  'Investigations versus Friese and others for Murder', Lubeck Public
    Prosecutor's Report, 3 Js 1428 / 65 StA Itzhoe (FM268), unpublished MS
United Kingdom: The National Archives (TNA)

FO371 / 64647 Control Commission for Germany (Hannover Summary, October–November 1947)
FO938 / 62 Hannover Police
FO1005 / 1658-1662 Hildesheim
FO1010 / 77 Police Matters: British and German 1946-1949
FO1010 / 155 Unreliability of German Police 1950
FO1078 / 71 Hitler-Speer Conferences
HW1 / 135 German Police (Assorted Special Messages)
HW1 / 2210, Naval Headlines: Ultra Decrypts, 23 April 1944
HW14 / 11 Government Code and Cypher School
HW14 / 54 Government Code and Cypher School
HW16 / 6 Reports on Activities of the German Police, 1 November–1 December 1943
HW16 / 27 Notes on German Police Decodes, 1943
HW16 / 32 Government Code and Cypher School
HW16 / 68 Notes on German Police Decodes 1943
HW16 / 89 Notes on German Police Decodes
HW16 / 90 Reports on German Police Order of Battle
WO218 / 3108 *Handbook of Organization Todt*, March 1945
United States of America, National Archives II, Washington, DC
A3343 Series SSO, Microfilm Publication, SS Officer Personnel Files
Microfilm T349, Gruppe Geheime Feldpolizei 708 Arbeitsbericht, August 1942, and Gruppe Geheime Feldpolizei 721 Arbeitsbericht, July–August 1942
RG 242, Arc Identifier 44307, Local Identifier 242-MID-6039u, 'Ukraine 1943' 16 reels of film
RG 263, Entry Z217, Box 4, Seventh Army Interrogation of Heinz Guderian, 28 May 1945
RG 457, Entry HCC, Box 202, Study of German Police Communications
RG 457, Entry HCC, Box 13, German Police and SS Traffic, 86
United States of America: Holocaust Memorial Museum, Washington, DC
Central Archives of the Federal Security Services (former KGB) of the Russian Federation: Records relating to War Crimes Trials in the Soviet Union, 1939–92, RG-06.025, Box 40
Deutsche Polizeieinrichtungen in den okkupierten Gebieten (Osobyi Archive), Reels 80–83
Reichskommissariat fur die Ukraine and Einsatzstab Rosenberg Records from the Ukraine Central State Archive, RG-31.002M, Reels 1–7, 13

Internet Archives

http://adolfeichmanntrial.com/
http://digital.library.wisc.edu/1711.dl/History Office of Military

Government, Civil Administration Division (Denazification, Cumulative
    Review), Report 1, 1 April 1947-30 April 1948, Military Government
    Ordinance applicable to the whole of the British Zone (effective 31 December
    1946)
www.holocaust-history.org/
www.jewishvirtuallibrary.org
www1.jur.uva.nl/junsv/brd/htm
www.museumoftolerance.com
www.nizkor.org
http://avalon.law.yale.edu
http://ushmm.org/museum
www.yadvashem.org/

BIBLIOGRAPHY: PRIMARY SOURCES

Adenauer, K., *Memoirs, 1945–1953* (London, 1966)

Arad, Y., S. Krakowski, and S. Spector, *The Einsatzgruppen Reports: Selections
    from the Dispatches of the Nazi Death Squads' Campaign Against the Jews,
    July 1941–January 1943* (New York, 1989)

Bialer, S., *Stalin and His Generals: Soviet Military Memoirs of World War II*
    (New York, 1969)

Boeslager, P. von, *Valkyrie* (London, 2000)

Carp, M., *Holocaust in Romania: Facts and Documents on the Annihilation of
    Romania's Jews, 1940–1944* (Safety Harbor, FL, 2000)

Citrine, Sir Walter, *I Search for Truth in Russia* (London, 1938)

Daghani, A., 'The Grave is in the Cherry Orchard', *Adam International
    Review*, nos. 291–3 (1961)

Desbois, Father P., *The Holocaust by Bullets: A Priest's Journey to Uncover the
    Truth Behind the Murder of 1.5 Million Jews* (New York, 2008)

Domarus, M., *Hitler: Speeches and Proclamations, 1932–1945*, vols I–IV
    (London, 2004)

Ehrenburg, I., and V. Grossman, eds, *The Black Book: The Ruthless Murder of
    Jews by German-Fascist Invaders Throughout the Temporarily-Occupied
    Regions of the Soviet Union and in the Death Camps of Poland During the War
    of 1941–1945* (New York, 1981)

Ensor, R.C.K., *Mein Kampf* (Oxford, 1939)

Fitzpatrick, M., *Kamierz Moczarski: Conversations with an Executioner*
    (Englewood Cliffs, NJ, 1977)

Friedlander, H., and S. Milton, eds, *Archives of the Holocaust: An International
    Collection of Selected Documents* (New York, 1989–93)

Gellately, R., ed., *The Nuremberg Interviews: Conversations with Defendants and
    Witnesses* (London, 2007)

Genoud, F., ed., *The Testament of Adolf Hitler: The Hitler-Bormann Documents,*

February–April 1945 (London, 1960)

German Government, *Dienstaltersliste der Schutzstaffel der NSDAP, April 1942* (Berlin 1942)

Grossman, V., *The Years of War* (Moscow, 1946)

Hadamovsky, Eugen, *Propaganda Und Nationale Macht* (Oldenberg, 1933)

—, *Dein Rundfunk: Das Rundfunkbuch für alle Volksgenossen* (Munich, 1934)

—, *Blitzmarsch nach Warschau: Frontberichte eines politischen Soldaten* (Munich, 1940)

—, *Hilfsarbeiter Nr. 50000* (Munich, 1940)

—, *Hitler kämpft um den Frieden Europas. Ein Tagebuch von Adolf Hitlers Deutschlandfahrt* (Munich, 1940)

Heiber, H., and D. M. Glantz, *Hitler and His Generals, Military Conferences, 1942–1945* (New York, 2004)

Heiden, K., *Der Fuehrer* (London, 1967)

[Himmler, Heinrich], *Der Dienstkalender Heinrich Himmlers 1941/42* (Hamburg, 1999)

Hitler, Adolf, *Mein Kampf* (London, 1939)

Jewish Chronicle (April 1967)

[Katzmann] Final Report on the solution of the Jewish problem in Galicia by Katzmann, Commander of the SS and Police in the District Of Galicia, at www1.yadvashem.org, accessed 12 October 2007

Kruszewski, C., 'International Affairs: Germany's Lebensraum', *The American Political Science Review*, XXXIV / 5 (1940), pp. 964-75

Lochner, Louis P., *The Goebbels Diaries* (London, 1948)

Maschmann, M., *Account Rendered: A Dossier on my Former Self* (New York, 1965)

Mendelssohn, P. de, *The Nuremberg Documents: Some Aspects of German War Policy* (London, 1946)

Nazi Conspiracy and Aggression (Washington, DC, 1946), vols III, IV, VIII

Rüter, C. F., and D. W. de Mildt, *Justiz und NS-Verbrechen: The German Judgements on Capital Nazi Crimes, 1945–1999*, vol. XXIV (1998), LG Stuttgart 660715, BGH 680507, Case 634, available at www1.jur.uva.nl, accessed 2 February 2009

Shtemenko, S. M., 'Kak planirovalas' posledniaia kampaniia po razgromu gitlerovskoi Germanii', *Voenno-istoricheskii zhurnal*, 5 (1965), pp. 56–64, reproduced in Bialer, *Stalin and His Generals*, p. 474

Speer, A., *The Slave State: Heinrich Himmler's Masterplan for SS Supremacy* (London, 1981)

—, *Inside the Third Reich* (London, 1995)

Stackelberg, R., and S. Winkle, *The Nazi Germany Sourcebook: An Anthology of Texts* (London, 2002)

Taylor, F., trans. and ed., *The Goebbels Diaries 1939–41: The Historic Journal of a Nazi War Leader* (London, 1983)

The German Police: Report by Supreme Headquarters Allied Expeditionary Force Evaluation and Dissemination Section (Eastbourne, 1945)

The Times (London) (1930–65)

Time magazine (1962)

Trials of War Criminals before the Nuremberg Military Tribunals (Washington, DC, 1947), vols XI, XIII

Von Lang, J., ed., *Eichmann Interrogated: Transcripts from the Archives of the Israeli Police* (New York, 1982)

Wagner, L. A., *Hitler, Man of Strife* (New York, 1942)

Warlimont, W., *Inside Hitler's Headquarters* (New York, 1962)

SECONDARY SOURCES

Abbott, P., and E. Pinak, *Ukrainian Armies, 1914–55* (Oxford, 2004)

Adair, P., *Hitler's Greatest Defeat: The Collapse of Army Group Centre, June 1944* (London, 2000)

Adorno, T. W., *Can One Live After Auschwitz: A Philosophical Reader* (Stanford, CA, 2003)

Altman, L. J., *Adolf Hitler: Evil Mastermind of the Holocaust* (Berkley Heights, NJ, 2005)

—, *Hitler's Rise to Power and the Holocaust* (Berkley Heights, NJ, 2003)

Aly, G., and S. Heim, *Architects of Annihilation: Auschwitz and the Logic of Destruction* (Princeton, NJ, 2002)

Angolia, J. R., *Uniforms, Organization and History of the German Police* (San Jose, CA, 2004), vol. I

Angrick, A., 'Annihilation and Labor: Jews and Thoroughfare IV in Central Ukraine', in *The Shoah in the Ukraine: History, Testimony, Memorialization*, ed. Brandon and Lower

—, 'Forced Labor along the "Strasse der SS"', in *Forced and Slave Labor in Nazi-Dominated Europe* (Washington, DC, 2004)

—, 'The Escalation of German-Rumanian Anti-Jewish Policy and the Attack on the Soviet Union, June 22, 1941', at www1.yadvashem.org, accessed 15 February 2009

Aronson, S., *Hitler, the Allies, and the Jews* (New York, 2004)

Bartov, O., 'Guilt and Accountability in the Postwar Courtroom: The Holocaust in Czortków and Buczacz, East Galicia, As Seen in West German Legal Discourse', at www.yale.edu, accessed 10 March 2009

Bauer, Y., *Rethinking the Holocaust* (London, 2001)

Bauman, Z., *Modernity and the Holocaust* (Ithaca, NY, 1989)

Beevor, A., *Stalingrad* (London, 1999)

Bennett, G. H., 'Exploring the World of the Second and Third Tier Men in the Holocaust: The Interrogation of Friedrich Jeckeln – Engineer and Executioner', *Liverpool Law Review*, XXXII/1 (2011), pp. 1–18

Berenbaum, M., ed., *A Mosaic of Victims: Non-Jews Persecuted and Murdered by the Nazis* (New York, 1990)

Berkhoff, K., *Harvest of Despair: Life and Death in the Ukraine under Nazi Rule* (Cambridge, MA, 2004)

Bingel, E., 'The Destruction of Two Ukrainian Jewish Communities: Testimonies of a German Army Officer', in *Yad Vashem Studies on the European Jewish Catastrophe and Resistance*, III, ed. S. Esh (1959), pp. 303–20

Birn, R. B., *Die Sicherheitspolizei in Estland, 1941–1944* (Paderborn, 2006)

Blackburn, G. W., *Education in the Third Reich: A Study of Race and History in Nazi Textbooks* (Albany, NY, 1985)

Blanke, R., Book Review in *Slavic Review*, LIII / 3 (1994), pp. 954–5

Bloxham, D., *'Extermination through Work': Jewish Slave Labour under the Third Reich* (London, 1999–2000)

Bohm-Duchen, M., *Daghani* (London, 1987)

Boshyk, Y., ed., *Ukraine during World War II: History and its Aftermath – A Symposium* (Edmonton, 1986)

Botting, D., *In the Ruins of the Reich* (London, 1985)

Bower, T., *Blind Eye to Murder: Britain, America and the Purging of Nazi Germany – A Pledge Betrayed* (London, 1997)

Bracher, K. D., *The German Dictatorship; The Origins, Structure, and Effects of National Socialism* (New York, 1970)

Brandon, R. and Lower, W., eds, *The Shoah in the Ukraine: History, Testimony, Memorialization* (Bloomington, IN, 2008)

Breitman, R., *The Architect of Genocide: Himmler and the Final Solution* (London, 1991)

—, 'Friedrich Jackeln' in *Die SS: Elite unter dem Totenkopf*, ed. Smelser and Syring

—, 'Himmler and the "Terrible Secret" among the Executioners', *Journal of Contemporary History*, XXVI / 3–4 (1991), pp. 431–51

—, 'Himmler's Police Auxiliaries in the Occupied Soviet Territories', *Simon Wiesenthal Center Annual*, VII / 2 from http://motic.wiesenthal.com, accessed 10 October 2009

Broszat, M., *German National Socialism, 1919–1945* (Santa Barbara, CA, 1966)

—, *The Hitler State: The Foundation and Development of the Internal Structure of the Third Reich* (London, 1981)

Browning, C., *Fateful Months: Essays on the Emergence of the Final Solution, 1941–42* (New York, 1985)

—, 'La décision concernant la solution finale', in *Colloque de l'Ecole des Hautes Etudes en sciences sociales, L'Allemagne nazie et le génocide juif* (Paris, 1985)

—, *The Path to Genocide: Essays on Launching the Final Solution* (Cambridge, 1992)

—, *Nazi Policy, Jewish Workers, German Killers* (Cambridge, 2000)

—, *The Origins of the Final Solution: The Evolution of Nazi Jewish Policy,*

September 1939–March 1942 (Lincoln, NE, 2004)

—, *The Origins of the Final Solution: The Evolution of Nazi Jewish Policy, September 1939–March 1942* (London, 2005)

Burleigh, M., *The Third Reich: A New History* (New York, 2000)

Burleigh, M., and W. Wippermann, *The Racial State: Germany 1933–1945* (Cambridge, 1991)

Burrin, P., *Hitler and the Jews: The Genesis of the Holocaust* (New York, 1994)

Butsko, A., *This Can't Be Forgiven* (Kiev, 1988)

Campbell, S., *Police Battalions of the Third Reich* (Atglen, PA, 2007)

Carr, W., *Hitler: A Study in Personality and Politics* (London, 1978)

Center for Advanced Holocaust Studies, *Forced and Slave Labor in Nazi-Dominated Europe* (Washington, DC, 2004)

Ceserani, D., *Justice Delayed* (London, 1992)

—, *The Final Solution: Origins and Implementation* (London, 1994)

Chant, C., *Warfare and the Third Reich: The Rise and Fall of Hitler's Armed Forces* (New York, 1996)

Churchill, W. S., Jr, *Defending the West* (London, 1981)

Clark, A., *Barbarossa: The Russian-German Conflict, 1941–1945* (London, 1994)

Cobler, S., *Law, Order and Politics in West Germany* (London, 1978)

Cole, T., *Selling the Holocaust* (New York, 2000)

Conot, R. E., *Justice at Nuremburg* (New York, 1999)

Corni, G., *Hitler and the Peasants: Agrarian Policy of the Third Reich, 1930–1939* (New York, 1990)

Crankshaw, E., *Gestapo: Instrument of Tyranny* (New York, 1956)

Dallin, A., *German Rule in Russia, 1941–1945* (New York, 1957)

Davidson, E., *The Making of Adolf Hitler* (New York, 1977)

Dawidowicz, L., *The War against the Jews, 1933–1945* (New York, 1975)

Dean, M., 'The German Gendarmerie, the Ukrainian Schutzmannschaft and the "Second Wave" of Jewish Killings in Occupied Ukraine: German Policing at the Local Level in the Zhitomir Region, 1941–1944', *German History*, XIV / 2, pp. 168–92

De Mildt, D., *In the Name of the People: Perpetrators of Genocide in the Reflection of their Post-war Prosecution in West Germany* (Leiden, 1996)

Dimsdale, J. E., ed., *Survivors, Victims and Perpetrators: Essays on the Nazi Holocaust* (Washington, DC, 1980)

Donat, A., ed., *The Death Camp Treblinka: A Documentary* (New York, 1979)

Donnison, F.S.V., *Civil Affairs and Military Government: Central Organisation and Planning* (London, 1966)

Erhardt, F., *Lebenswege unter Zwangsherrschaft: Beträge zur Geschichte Braunschweigs im Nationalsocialismus* (Braunschweig, 2007)

Evans, R. J., *In Defense of History* (New York, 1999)

—, *The Coming of the Third Reich* (London, 2003)

Ezergailis, A., *The Holocaust in Latvia, 1941–1944* (Riga, 1996)

Feingold, H. L., *The Politics of Rescue: The Roosevelt Administration and the Holocaust, 1938–1945* (New Brunswick, NJ, 1970)

Fest, J. C., *The Face of the Third Reich* (New York, 1970)

—, *Hitler* (New York, 1974)

Final Report of the International Commission on the Holocaust in Romania, presented to the Romanian President Ion Iliescu (Bucharest, 2004)

Finklestein, N. G., and R. B. Birn, *A Nation on Trial: The Goldhagen Thesis and Historical Truth* (New York, 1998)

Fischer, K. P., *Nazi Germany: A New History* (New York, 1995)

Fitzgibbon, C., *Denazification* (London, 1969)

Fleming, G., *Hitler and the Final Solution* (Berkeley, CA, 1984)

Flood, C. B., *Hitler: The Path to Power* (Boston, MA, 1989)

Forced and Slave Labor in Nazi-Dominated Europe (Washington, DC, 2004)

France 1940: Blitzkrieg in the West (Oxford, 2002)

Frank, H., *German S-Boats in Action in the Second World War* (Barnsley, 2007)

Friedlander, H., *The Origins of Nazi Genocide: From Euthanasia to the Final Solution* (Chapel Hill, NC, 1995)

—, 'The Judiciary and Nazi Crimes in Postwar Germany', *Simon Wiesenthal Center Annual*, 1/2 at http://motic.wiesenthal.com, accessed 10 October 2009

Frischauer, W., *Himmler: The Evil Genius of the Third Reich* (London, 1953)

Furet, F., ed., *Unanswered Questions: Nazi Germany and the Genocide of the Jews* (New York, 1989)

Garrard, J., and C. Garrard, *The Bones of Berdichev: The Life and Fate of Vasily Grossman* (New York, 1996)

Gerlach, C., 'The Wannsee Conference, the Fate of German Jews, and Hitler's Decision in Principle to Exterminate All European Jews', *Journal of Modern History*, LXX / 4 (1998), pp. 759–812

—, *Kalkulierte Morde* (Hamburg, 1999)

Gilbert, M., *Auschwitz and the Allies* (London, 1981)

Giles, G. J., *Students and National Socialism in Germany* (Princeton, NJ, 1985)

Glantz, D., 'Soviet Military Strategy during the Second Period of War (November 1942–December 1943): A Reappraisal', *Journal of Military History*, LX/1 (1996), pp. 115–50

Goldhagen, D., *Hitler's Willing Executioners: Ordinary Germans and the Holocaust* (London, 1996)

Gray, C., *The Irving Judgment* (London, 2000)

Grunberger, R. A., *A Social History of the Third Reich* (London, 1974)

Guttenplan, D. D., *The Holocaust on Trial* (New York, 2002)

Hamilton, C., *Leaders and Personalities of the Third Reich* (San Jose, CA, 1996), 2 vols

Hearndon, A., ed., *The British in Germany* (London, 1978)

Hildebrand, K., *Das Dritte Reich* (Munich, 1980)

Hoffmann, H., *The Triumph of Propaganda: Film and National Socialism* (Frankfurt am Main, 1996)

Höhne, H., *The Order of the Death's Head: The Story of Hitler's SS* (London, 2000)

Holmes, R., *The World at War* (London, 2007)

Hosking, G., and S. Schöpflin, eds, *Myths and Nationhood* (London, 1997)

Jäckel, E., *Hitler in History* (Hanover, NH, 1984)

Kaienburg, H., 'Jüdische Arbeitslager an der "Strasse der SS"', in *Zeitschrift für Sozialgeschichte des 20 und 21 Jahrhunderts*, XI / 1 (1996)

Karpov, V., *Russia at War, 1941–45* (New York, 1987)

Kershaw, I., *Hitler, 1889–1936: Hubris* (New York 1998)

—, *Hitler, 1936–45: Nemesis* (New York 2000)

—, *The Nazi Dictatorship: Problems and Perspectives of Interpretation* (New York, 2000)

Kersten, F., *The Kersten Memoirs* (New York, 1957), in H. Pringle, *The Master Plan: Himmler's Scholars and the Holocaust* (London, 2006), pp. 230–31

Kiekenap, B., *SS-Junkerschule: SA und SS in Braunschweig* (Brunswick, 2008)

Koch, H. W., *The Hitler Youth: Origins and Development, 1922–1945* (New York, 1975)

Kreuger, H., *A Crack in the Wall: Growing Up Under Hitler* (New York, 1982)

Kuznetsov, A., *Babi Yar: A Document in the Form of a Novel* (New York, 1970)

Lacquer, W., *Young Germany: A History of the German Youth Movement* (New York, 1984)

Larionov, V., N. Yeronin, B. Solovyov and V. Timokhovich, *World War II: Decisive Battles of the Soviet Army* (Moscow, 1984)

Laska, V., *Women in the Resistance and in the Holocaust: The Voices of Eyewitnesses* (Westport, CT, 1983)

Leapman, M., *Master Race: The Lebensborn Experiment in Nazi Germany* (London, 1995)

Lichtenberger, H., *The Third Reich* (Freeport, NY, 1969)

Lower, W., *Nazi Empire Building and the Holocaust in the Ukraine* (Chapel Hill, NC, 2005)

—, 'From Berlin to Babi Yar: The Nazi War against the Jews, 1941–44', *Journal of Religion and Society*, IX (2007)

Merkl, P. H., *The Making of a Stormtrooper* (Princeton, NJ, 1980)

Miller, W., *A New History of the United States* (London, 1970)

Mommsen, H., *From Weimar to Auschwitz* (Princeton, NJ, 1991)

Munoz, A. J., *Hitler's Eastern Legions* (Bayside, NY, 1998), vol. I

Newton, S. H., *Panzer Operations: The Eastern Front Memoir of General Raus, 1941–1945* (Cambridge, MA, 2003)

Olick, J. K., *In the House of the Hangman: The Agonies of German Defeat, 1943–1949* (Chicago, IL, 2005)

Owings, A., *Frauen: German Women Recall the Third Reich* (London, 1993)

Padfield, P., *Himmler: Reichsführer-SS* (London, 2001)

Petersen, E. N., *The Limits of Hitler's Power* (Princeton, NJ, 1969)

Pohl, D., and A. Angrick, 'Einsatzgruppen C and D in the Invasion of the Soviet Union', *Holocaust Educational Trust Research Papers*, 1/4 (1999–2000)

Poliakov, L., *The Aryan Myth: A History of Racist and Nationalist Ideas in Europe* (London, 1974)

Pringle, H., *The Master Plan: Himmler's Scholars and the Holocaust* (New York, 2006)

Prusin, A. V., '"Fascist Criminals to the Gallows!": The Holocaust and Soviet War Crimes Trials, December 1945–February 1946', *Holocaust and Genocide Studies*, XVII (2003), pp. 1–30

Rempel, G., *Hitler's Children: The Hitler Youth and the SS* (Chapel Hill, NC, 1989)

Rhodes, R., *Masters of Death: The SS-Einsatzgruppen and the Invention of the Holocaust* (New York, 2003)

Rich, N., *Hitler's War Aims: Ideology, the Nazi State, and the Course of Expansion* (London, 1973)

Ripley, T., *Wehrmacht: The German Army in World War II, 1939–1945* (London, 2003)

Rosenzweig, W., 'Retelling the Jewish Slave Labor Experience in Romania', in *Forced and Slave Labor in Nazi-Dominated Europe*, ed. Center for Advanced Holocaust Studies (Washington, DC, 2004)

Schultz, D., 'The Possibilities of Pictorial Narrative: Word – Image – History in the Work of Arnold Daghani', in H. Salmi, *History in Words and Images*, ebook, at http://www.hum.utu.fi, accessed 27 December 2010, pp. 149–56

Schulz, A., G. Wegmann, and D. Zinke, *Die Generale der Waffen-SS und der Polizei* (Bissendorf, 2003–5), 2 vols

Sereny, G., *Albert Speer: His Battle with Truth* (London, 1995)

Sharp, T., *The Wartime Allince and the Zonal Division of Germany* (Oxford, 1975)

Shirer, W. L., *The Rise and Fall of the Third Reich* (New York, 1959)

—, *The Rise and Fall of the Third Reich: A History of Nazi Germany* (London, 1987)

Smelser, R., and E. J. Davies II, *The Myth of the Eastern Front: The Nazi-Soviet War in American Popular Culture* (Cambridge, 2008)

—, and E. Syring, *Die SS: Elite unter dem Totenkopf* (Paderborn, 2003)

Smith, A., 'The "Golden Age" and National Renewal', in *Myths and Nationhood*, ed. G. Hosking and G. Schöpflin (London, 1997)

Sohn, W., *Im Spiegel der Nachkriegsprozesse: Der Errichtung der NS-Herrschaft in Freistaat Braunschweig* (Braunschweig, 2003)

Spielvogel, J., and D. Redles, 'Hitler's Racial Ideology: Content and Occult

Sources', *Simon Wiesenthal Center Annual*, III/9 from http://motic.wiesen-
thal.com, accessed 10 October 2009

Spotts, F., *Hitler and the Power of Aesthetics* (London, 2003)

Stackelberg, R., *Hitler's Germany: Origins, Interpretations, Legacies* (London,
1999)

Streim, A., 'The Tasks of the Einsatzgruppen', *Simon Wiesenthal Center
Annual*, IV/9, from http://motic.wiesenthal.com, accessed 10 October 2009

Sydnor, C. W., 'On the Historiography of the SS', *Simon Wiesenthal Center
Annual*, VI / 10, from http://motic.wiesenthal.com, accessed 10 October
2009

Taylor, B., *Barbarossa to Berlin: A Chronology of the Campaigns on the Eastern
Front, 1941–1945* (Staplehurst, 2004), 2 vols

Timms, Edward, *Memories of Mikhailowka: Labour Camp Testimonies in the
Arnold Daghani Archive*, Centre for German–Jewish Studies Research Paper
IV (2000)

Toland, J., *Adolf Hitler* (New York, 1976)

—, *The Last 100 Days* (New York, 1965)

Trunk, I., *Jewish Responses to Nazi Persecution: Collective and Individual
Behaviour in Extremis* (New York, 1982)

Wasserstein, B., *Britain and the Jews of Europe, 1939–1945* (Clarendon, 1979)

Watt, D. C., *Britain Looks to Germany* (London, 1965)

Weber, R.G.S., *The German Student Corps in the Third Reich* (New York, 1986)

Westermann, E. B., *Hitler's Police Battalions: Enforcing Racial War in the East*
(Lawrence, KS, 2005)

Yerger, M. C., *Waffen-SS Commanders: The Army, Corps and Divisional Leaders
of a Legend* (Atglen, PA, 1997–9), 2 vols

Zabarko, B., *Holocaust in the Ukraine* (London, 2005)

Ziemke, Earl F., *Stalingrad to Berlin: The German Defeat in the East*
(Washington, DC, 1968)

ACKNOWLEDGEMENTS

Research for this book has taken me to several different countries spread across two continents. I have depended heavily on generous hospitality and innumerable favours from many individuals and organizations. These acknowledgements are an altogether inadequate way of expressing the gratitude I feel for their kindness, co-operation, encouragement and friendship.

In Germany my research was assisted by Gerhard Haase (Polizeiakademie Niedersachsen, Polizeigeschichtliche Sammlung), Dr Mariana Hausleitner (Deutsche Hochschule der Polizei Berlin, and Project Director 'Die Polizei im ns-Staat'), Deborah Schultz, Edward Timms, and the archivists at the Bundesarchiv in Berlin.

My visit to Ukraine would have been less interesting and less instructive without the help of such experts as Yuri Wiktorovych and Faina Abramovna Vinokurova (Vinnytsia Archive), Natalya Valentinovna (Kerch Archive/ Museum), Bran'ko Yaroslaw Andriyovych (Historian, Hitler Bunker, Vinnytsia), Lubov Aleksandrovna Lysykh (Eltingen Descent Museum, Kerch), Vira Ivanivna Snizhko (Halbstadt), Victor S. Havrylenko (Askania Nova Reserve), Natalya Ivanovna Yasincekaja (Askania Nova Reserve), Ivan Mikhajlovich Elinov (Director of University Museum, Dnipropetrovs'k), Taras Schumenko (Kiev) and Grigoriy Iosifovich Kojsman (President of the Jewish organisation of prisoners). My meetings with Esfir' Abramovna Kotliar and Mania Mordkovna Fayngold (Uman), the Viktorovych family (Pechora), and Mykola Stepanovych, Vasyl Ivanovyvh Umanec', and Ivan Stepanovych Hucal (Mikhailowka) were all fascinating and deeply moving, both in the historical detail they could provide and in the quiet dignity of people who had endured much.

In the United States the National Archives II (Washington, DC) and the Holocaust Memorial Library provided excellent facilities and a truly impressive variety of archival material. The staffs of these two institutions were unfailingly helpful. I was particularly fortunate in the assistance and expert advice so kindly offered by Professor Richard Breitman.

In the United Kingdom staff at the National Archives (Kew) provided the knowledgeable and efficient service for which they are renowned, and which historians should never just take for granted.

My research in the Arnold Daghani Collection received invaluable guidance from the University of Sussex Centre for German Jewish Studies and the staff at the Special Collections Department of the University of Sussex Library. Quotations from the Daghani Collection appear by kind permission of the University of Sussex Library.

I am indebted to many colleagues and associates at the University of Plymouth who have not only given me help and encouragement but have also been extremely tolerant of my fixation with one short, black-and-white film. I would especially like to pay tribute to Dr Sandra Barkhof, whoe generously translated material from German into English. The staff at the University of Plymouth Library have, as always, provided an excellent service.

For arousing my initial curiosity in an old reel of film and for all their subsequent friendly help I owe a debt of gratitude to Elayne, Mike, Graham, Jennie, Bob and Carolyn at the South West Film and Television Archive (SWFTA). I am particularly grateful to David Stone, a noted expert on the German army, for sharing his thoughts on identifying the German military units featured in the Cullompton film. I only wish that his report to SWFTA on the units depicted had been available to me at the outset of the research.

My heartfelt thanks also go to Simon Mansfield, Claire Byrne and Val Mai (Cardiff), Ian McGinty (London), Jeremy Black (University of Exeter); the staff at the Exeter University Library, Gary Tregidga (Institute of Cornish Studies); Kevin Wheatcroft (Wheatcroft & Son); Neil Leavesley (Project Coordinator, s-130 Restoration Project), and to John, Terry, Ben, Robert, Ak and the crew at Southdown.

Nearer home, my father Roy Bennett (Ashbourne), has always shown an informed interest as the book has taken shape, and so have my sons Edward (who coined the nickname 'The Fat Man') and George (who is a far better writer than his father if only he would realize it).

The staff and members of the Axis history forum were unfailingly helpful and knowledgeable. I would like to pay special tribute to Andrey, who provided conclusive evidence that the 'old man' in the film is Generalmajor Günther Meinhold, Camp Commandant in Dnepropetrovsk between May 1942 and January 1944.

It has not been possible to identify and locate copyright holders for some of the material in this book, but if such holders should contact me I will gladly see that they are identified in any future editions of this book.

Finally, thanks are due to the guiding angel, Lady Luck (call her what you will) who must have been there at my shoulder at every stage of the research – from the Baptist church at Cullompton, via the windy shores of the Black Sea and the mountains of documents in various archives, to the silent grave sites of Ukraine and Germany.

PHOTO ACKNOWLEDGEMENTS

INDEX